Impartiality
in Context

*Grounding Justice
in a
Pluralist World*

Shane O'Neill

State University of New York Press

Published by
State University of New York Press, Albany

© 1997 State University of New York

For information, address State University of New York Press,
State University Plaza, Albany, NY 12246

Production by David Ford
Marketing by Nancy Farrell

Library of Congress Cataloging-in-Publication Data

O'Neill, Shane, 1965–
    Impartiality in context : grounding justice in a pluralist world /
Shane O'Neill.
        p.   cm. — (SUNY series in social and political thought)
    Includes bibliographical references and index.
    ISBN 0-7914-3387-0 (hc : acid free). — ISBN 0-7914-3388-9 (pb :
acid free)
    1. Justice. 2. Fairness. 3. Pluralism (Social sciences)
4. Situation ethics. I. Title. II. Series.
JC578.O55 1997
320'.01'1—dc20   96-34723
                                                                CIP

10 9 8 7 6 5 4 3 2 1

For my mother
and to the memory of my father

CONTENTS

ACKNOWLEDGMENTS

This book developed out of my doctoral dissertation. I am grateful to Glasgow University for the postgraduate scholarship that helped me to survive three wet but happy Scottish winters. During my graduate work at Glasgow I was fortunate enough to enjoy the excellent supervision of Michael Lessnoff. The arguments I present here have undoubtedly benefited greatly from being subjected to the carefully penetrating criticism that he was always ready and willing to offer. Both Steven Lukes and Christopher Berry were generous, encouraging and critically astute as examiners.

I received critical feedback from a number of sources on various drafts of this work. Nick Smith read much of the contents with a critical eye at an early stage and has continued to encourage the development of the argument. Iain MacKenzie read over the entire manuscript with a keen eye for detail at a late stage. In between the comments of William Rehg and two anonymous readers were also very much appreciated. Some sections were read as seminar or conference papers and I am grateful to all who offered constructive criticism by engaging with the relevant issues. Others, too many to list, responded to the earlier versions of sections that appeared in print before. Each response has played some role in urging me to reflect further on the implications of the theoretical claims I have been seeking to support.

Thanks are due to editors and publishers for permission to use revised versions of the following material: "Morality, Ethical Life and the Persistence of Universalism," *Theory, Culture and Society* 11.2 (May 1994); "Pluralist Justice and its Limits: the Case of Northern Ireland," *Political Studies* 42.3 (September 1994); and "Tensions in Rawls's Liberal Holism," *Philosophy and Social Criticism* 22.1 (January 1996).

The patience and support of Ken Baynes, Clay Morgan, and all at SUNY Press has been most welcome, especially toward the end as I juggled with a number of other tasks in my efforts, finally, to deliver the manuscript.

Critical discussion over a number of years with friends, teachers, colleagues, and students has almost always provided me with the desire to sharpen my thinking on the questions I grapple with here. A debt of gratitude is owed to all who have helped to contribute to my enjoyment of philosophical argument about politics. This includes those who first introduced me to the subject at the Politics Department of University College, Dublin; John Baker, Maeve Cooke, Attracta Ingram, Fergal O'Connor, and Jennifer Todd; fellow classmates and those I taught in Dublin and Glasgow; former colleagues and students at the Department of Government, Manchester University, especially Norman Geras, Geraint Parry, Maurizio Passerin d'Entrèves, Ursula Vogel, and Ricardo Blaug. I am also indebted to my present colleagues and students at the Department of Politics, Queen's University, Belfast, for providing me with a suitably stimulating environment for the completion of this work.

There are also, of course, some more personal debts. I have drawn repeatedly on the unstinting support of my sisters, Thérèse, Sheila, and Mary. The loving companionship of Grace McCarthy has, since a number of years before I began this work, been my most treasured source of consolation and encouragement. But I have learned most things of value, not least about justice, from my parents. This work is dedicated to my mother and to the memory of my father.

INTRODUCTION

To demand justice or to claim that an injustice has been suffered is to engage in the practice of social criticism. In this book I wish to examine certain important features of the idea of justice as a tool of social criticism in a modern context. Social criticism in any society depends on a descriptive understanding of how the institutions and practices of that society came to be as they are. This involves an analysis of the struggles of the society's history, its achievements, and its failures. It is to the work of historians, social scientists, and legal scholars that we should look for the resources necessary to inform this descriptive understanding.

But criticism also depends on a normative understanding of the society. This normative understanding can be thought of as a substantive account of justice. Such an account provides a test for historical achievements. It articulates the standards or principles by which the institutions and practices of that society are called to account. A social critic will argue that some aspect of society fails this test of justice. The critic is expressing a tension between the descriptive and the normative understandings of the people to whom the criticism is addressed. This tension should be a matter of public concern, the subject of an informed and inclusive discussion.

My chief concern is to inquire as to how a substantive account of justice is to be grounded and justified in any modern political society that is situated in a pluralist world.[1] The modern world is a pluralist world in at least two significant respects. First, there is a plurality of conceptions of the good that different individuals endorse in modern societies. Second, there is a plurality of differently constituted modern political societies, or states. Each modern state is more or less pluralist with respect to individual conceptions of the good. But each modern state is also unique in that it is embedded in a specific, historically constituted, political culture.

How are we to conceive of the demands of justice in a world that is characterized by pluralism in both of these senses? First, since people do not share a comprehensive conception of what constitutes a good life for human beings, there is no one general worldview that is shared universally

1

by all the people of any particular modern society. Furthermore, people can have very good reasons for not coming to an agreement about crucially important questions as to what might constitute a good human life. It would appear therefore that no one worldview can ground, by itself, an account of justice that all people in a modern society would have good reason to affirm. There is a more or less wide-ranging plurality of worldviews within each modern society, and there is always a potential for conflict when these worldviews clash on matters of political significance. It is this potential for conflict that typically has exercised the minds of liberal political theorists in recent debates about normative justification. Most notable among these theorists is John Rawls, who has propounded what has become the most influential theory of justice in the twentieth century.[2]

Given the many divergent beliefs about how a human life should be led, and the corresponding variety of lifestyles that are represented in modern societies, it is apparently no easy task to say what it is to ground an account of justice. It does seem to be the case, however, that the notion of impartiality, the idea that no one person or group is arbitrarily favored by any account of justice that could claim to be valid, must be central to our concerns here. Under modern conditions, justice must be grounded, not in one comprehensive worldview, but within some framework that treats people who do not share worldviews in a fair and impartial manner. This is the focus not only of Rawls's work but of all deontological theories of justice that follow Kant in maintaining that the right has priority over the good.[3] I agree with this emphasis on the notion of impartiality as the key to taking pluralism in this first sense adequately into account in a theory of justice.

But pluralism in the second sense must also be taken seriously. Here liberals have been far more cautious and wary. Inspired by the Enlightenment's aspiration to a universalist, rational account of impartial justice, liberals have tended to emphasize that which modern societies have in common. The corollary of this is that they have tended to disregard that which makes each modern society unique, its embeddedness in a particular, historically constituted, political culture. What matters most to people who argue about, or struggle, for justice is first and foremost a burning desire to make their own society a just one. Theories that disregard the uniqueness of each modern political society can appear to be irrelevantly abstract or excessively general to those who are most strongly motivated to achieve justice in practice. It is not that they will be indifferent to the justness of other states, but rather that the more immediate concern for them is to work out what justice demands of them in their own context, given the history of their political society and the urgency of the challenges it now faces.

While taking pluralism in the first sense seriously, liberals have often been hostile to the attempt to take pluralism in the second sense into account at all in a theory of justice.[4] This has been one of the concerns of the communitarian critique of liberalism, particularly as it is expressed in the work of Michael Walzer.[5] Walzer seeks to show that a substantive account of justice must be embedded in the shared understandings of a particular political community. The emphasis of his theoretical work on justice has been less on that which modern societies have in common but rather on the ways in which the demands of justice will differ from one political community to the next.

I want to argue in this book that if we are to work toward an adequate theory of justice for a pluralist, modern world, then there is something fundamentally right about both Rawls's emphasis on impartiality and Walzer's emphasis on contextualism. The impartialism of Rawls's theory of justice takes the first sense of pluralism seriously, that is, the plurality of conceptions of the good within each modern society. The contextualism of Walzer's theory takes pluralism in the second sense seriously, that is, the plurality of unique, historically constituted, political communities in the modern world. Neither, however, takes both senses of pluralism sufficiently seriously to offer a compelling theory of justice. I want to do justice to pluralism in both of these senses. We need to take on board both the distinctively liberal concern with impartialism and the distinctively communitarian concern with the particular contexts of justice. We need, in other words, a contextual impartialism. If an adequate theoretical grounding for justice in the pluralist world we inhabit is to be provided, then we will need to know how impartiality can be rooted in historical context.

The basic framework for such an approach is, I will suggest, made available in Jürgen Habermas's discourse ethics.[6] Habermas's work, to this extent at least, can be thought to have transcended the debate between liberals and communitarians. It has a concern with impartialism at its heart, yet it has the potential to be sensitive to the differences between the variety of cultural contexts in which the plurality of political communities are situated in the modern world. This potential is perhaps not fully realised in Habermas's own work, which has tended, all the more recently, to adopt a friendly stance towards contemporary liberalism, while becoming increasingly critical of communitarianism.[7] There is, however, no doubting the aspiration in his work to offer an account of impartiality that is sensitive to context.[8] I will be highlighting the ways in which discourse ethics can and should be developed so as adequately to do justice to pluralism in both of the senses I have been considering here.

It is worth pointing out at this stage some of the very basic features of the approach that I will take, following Habermas's lead, in seeking to ground justice under conditions of pluralism. We might first wonder who is qualified to work out and to justify a substantive account of justice that is to act as a normative guide to criticism in a modern society. No one philosopher, political theorist, or indeed anybody else, is qualified to provide a justification for such an account of the substance of justice. To claim to do so is to overestimate the extent to which any one citizen could adopt an objective and impartial standpoint where the various perspectives of all citizens are equally represented. Philosophers are no more or less qualified than other citizens in this regard. Any citizen, who claims to be able to overcome the difficulties involved here, fails to take sufficiently seriously the very real possibility of disagreements, differences, and tensions surfacing between the plurality of worldviews and the social groups they represent in modern societies. A substantive account of justice can only be produced in an ongoing manner, as the outcome of democratic deliberation where this plurality of perspectives is adequately represented. This could only happen if exhaustive measures were taken to ensure that, in so far as it is practically possible, each and every social group can speak and act on its own behalf.

For this reason the attempt to derive philosophically a definitively justified substantive account of justice for a living political community would appear to be an unproductive one. To pursue that task would be to deny the historical nature of a community's normative self-understanding by closing off any future discussion or revision. This would involve the assumption that the community's history had reached its end, that public debate about justice could with good reason be closed off since things were not going to change in any significant way in the future. This assumption, that history has no future, has a particularly poor track record. Substantive accounts of justice must be justified dialogically, as the temporary and provisional outcome of ongoing democratic deliberation.[9]

We might also wonder under what conditions a substantive account of justice that is valid could be produced. Even though philosophers are not themselves qualified to justify as valid a substantive account of justice, I want to argue that they can attempt to provide a philosophical justification for a procedure that would serve as a test of validity for substantive principles of justice in any modern society. The point of advocating such a procedure is to clarify the criteria according to which a political community could judge fairly between competing claims about justice under particular circumstances. According to Habermas, philosophers can, and should, refrain from claiming any special qualification to give a substantive account of justice. They can however, simultaneously, defend a discursive procedure of justification that places certain normatively justified constraints on the ongoing democratic deliberation that aims to yield principles of justice for particular political communities.

The discussion is divided into four parts. Three of them will examine critically the important and influential theoretical contributions to recent debates about justice of our three principals. In the two chapters of the first part I will assess critically the concern for impartialism as it is articulated in John Rawls's work. The second part will consist of two chapters on the contextualist concerns of Walzer's work. In the third part I will use Habermas's work as a springboard that will allow me to outline what I take to be a more adequate theoretical approach to justice in modern societies. The fourth and final part seeks to develop this approach further, first, by countering certain influential criticisms of Habermas's work and, second, by applying the theory to the pressing demand for political justice in Northern Ireland.

As I have already suggested, certain important features of the theories of both Rawls and Walzer will feed into the approach I advocate. I do not, however, want to suggest that a compelling theory of justice could be developed simply by using a combination of Rawls's impartialism and Walzer's contextualism. Rawls's theory has significant limitations as an account of impartiality. Similarly, Walzer's theory encounters serious theoretical difficulties as a contextualist account of justice. I will argue that these two sets of problems, internal to the two contrasting approaches, can both be overcome in the appropriately revised account of discourse ethics developed in the third and fourth parts.

Rawls presents a procedural device of representation that is intended to specify the conditions of an impartial point of view. He also derives from that procedure two substantive principles of justice that are to regulate the basic structure of a modern democratic society.[10] In the first part of the book I will assess Rawls's proceduralism as a philosophical articulation of impartial conditions for the choice of substantive principles of justice. The discussion offers a critique of Rawls's account of impartiality by reconstructing arguments that could be made from the theoretical perspectives of communitarianism and feminism. I will develop arguments from a communitarian perspective in chapter 1 and from a feminist perspective in chapter 2. My suggestion is that Rawls's conception of impartiality relies on an unconvincingly restricted account of political discourse.

Rawls attempts, in his recent work, to clear the ground for an over-lapping consensus that could provide general support in a modern society for his conception of justice and the conditions of impartiality that it outlines. He does so by isolating political aspects of citizens' morality from other more comprehensive aspects of their moral views. Having discussed these recent developments in Rawls's theory in relation to certain communitarian criticisms of his work, I will argue, in chapter 1, that this recent strategy that seeks to isolate the political is seriously misguided. First, it overestimates the extent to which any modern liberal state can be neutral between competing conceptions of the good. This is connected to Rawls's failure to take sufficiently seriously the plurality of unique, historically constituted, modern, political societies.[11] Second, this strategy underestimates the extent to which the notion of a vibrant public sphere must be placed right at the heart of a theoretical account of impartial justice.

These criticisms of Rawls's liberal approach to questions of justice will be reiterated from a somewhat different angle in the second chapter when I explore certain objections to his work that have been raised by feminist political theorists. I will argue that the question of justice in the family highlights the most fundamental problem with Rawls's attempt to isolate political morality. This attempt falls prey to the convincing feminist assault on a distinctively liberal separation of public and private that fails to deal in a sufficiently rigorous manner with the injustices of patriarchy.

Furthermore, the work of feminist critics can be drawn on to show how the restricted notion of political discourse that is an integral part of Rawls's conception of impartiality is ill-equipped for one task that is vital for any theory of justice that can ground valid normative standards for a modern society. This is the task of maintaining a critically sensitive perspective on the possibility that the political concerns of some social groups, particularly oppressed groups, remain at the margins of a specific political culture. The democratic need to allow for the political articulation of different perspectives on matters of basic justice calls for a more interactive, discursive conception of impartiality than that which is found in Rawls's account.

Before moving on to present the more adequate alternative conception of impartiality that is to be found in Habermas's work, I will consider, in the second part, Michael Walzer's theoretical approach to questions of justice. Walzer rejects entirely the claim that philosophy can defend an impartial procedure that tests the validity of substantive accounts of justice. Proceduralism is rejected for the sake of democratic pluralism. Walzer believes that no philosophically articulated procedure of impartiality can reflect adequately the real differences of context for the plurality of modern democracies. He does not therefore seek an alternative procedure to that advocated by Rawls but rather he rejects the procedural project altogether. Walzer advocates instead a hermeneutic, or interpretive, approach to justice and social criticism where substantive principles of justice are thought to be embedded in the shared understandings of particular communities. He shifts the focus of a theory of justice away from impartial procedures of rational justification toward the articulation, through democratic dialogue, of the substance of justice in particular contexts.

I will begin, in chapter 3, with a brief discussion of the merits of Walzer's account of complex equality over the two substantive principles of justice that are defended by Rawls. My purpose here is initially to add some weight to Walzer's claim that any theory of justice that stresses procedures of impartiality is necessarily insensitive to particular contexts. I will suggest that Walzer's account of complex equality does have important advantages over Rawls's two principles because it facilitates a detailed elaboration of the substantive demands of justice in a way that is highly sensitive to cultural particularity. Of course, the fact that Walzer's indeterminate notion of complex equality has significant advantages over Rawls's principles as an account of the substance of justice does not in itself justify his rejection of proceduralism. In fact, it merely underlines the fact that a substantive account of justice that proposes particular, determinate principles should not be presented as an integral part of a philosophical theory of justice. The democratic task of articulating a substantive account of justice must be thought of as being strictly separate from the philosophical task of clarifying an impartial point of view.

In the remainder of this chapter I will explore at greater depth the implications of Walzer's contextualist approach to justice. This will involve outlining certain important points of contrast between this version of what we might refer to as a hermeneutics of justice, and that which is adopted in Rawls's political constructivism. Having outlined the manner in which Walzer highlights the need to take the plurality of modern societies into account in a theory of justice, I will suggest that, despite the views of many critics, his contextualist, interpretive approach need not defend tradition in a conservative way. On the contrary, it brings to light some of the most important features of justice as a tool of social criticism in modern contexts.

In chapter 4 we will examine the other side of the coin. While his hermeneutics of justice can facilitate an important form of social criticism,

I will argue in this chapter that his failure to treat the justification of procedures of impartiality as a key component of a theory of justice makes
Walzer's work one-sided and dangerously inadequate. Without giving
proper emphasis to conditions of impartiality, Walzer fails to do justice to
the plurality of conceptions of the good in every modern society. In this
way, his theory is flawed even as a contextualist account of justice that is
to address the needs of modern societies. This can be demonstrated by
exposing the extent to which Walzer lacks a sufficiently critical perspective on the operation of power among social groups. Furthermore, I will
argue that, without some philosophically grounded conception of impartiality, Walzer cannot justify the minimal universalist moral code that has
become more significant in his recent work.[12] This discussion will point us
once more in the direction of an account of impartiality that is more thoroughly discursive than we found Rawls's to be.

The third part seeks to outline an alternative approach to questions
of justice in modern societies. This is to be found in Habermas's discourse theories of morality and ethics. In my view Habermas's work represents the best guide available to us in addressing questions as to how
we can test the validity, or rational acceptability, of substantive principles of justice in the public life of a modern society. It has the potential
to take seriously both the plurality of conceptions of the good and the
plurality of political societies. This is because it presents a contextualist
version of impartialism. It is not however to be favored as a theoretical
approach to justice simply because of its capacity to take both senses of
pluralism into account. Its discursive proceduralism has important
advantages over Rawls's procedure as an account of impartiality. Furthermore, its sensitivity to the operation of power in modern societies
make it a more useful tool for contextualist criticism than Walzer's
hermeneutics of justice.

The discursive procedure that Habermas defends is grounded in certain pragmatic presuppositions of everyday communication that are
both necessary and unavoidable. I will first of all explain, in chapter 5,
the nature of the philosophical argument that Habermas claims to make
in justifying this procedure. The way in which his moral theory is, like
his critical social theory, built on the notion of communicative action
will be explained. By presenting a moral theory in terms of a theory of
communication, Habermas can conceive of an impartial point of view in
a way that is necessarily dialogical and thoroughly discursive. This is
because communicative action always takes place within the context of
an intersubjective encounter that can never be reduced to the reflections
of one isolated individual.

After giving a detailed reconstruction of Habermas's justification of discourse ethics I will argue, in chapter 6, that the dialogical view of impartiality that this represents is sufficiently sensitive to differences between social groups as to avoid successfully the weaknesses exposed in the earlier critique of Rawls's attempt to isolate political morality. Habermas's more thoroughly discursive procedural test of the rational acceptability of substantive principles of justice proves to be sensitive to the concerns of both communitarians and feminists in ways that Rawls's recent work is not. At the same time he avoids the dangers of contextualist hermeneutics by retaining the notion of impartiality as the core of justice in any modern society. Furthermore, by justifying his impartial procedure of justification in terms of the pragmatic presuppositions of communicative action, Habermas gives his moral theory a strong universalist grounding. This universalist thrust establishes a critical foothold that is more adequate to the task of challenging the effects of power in contemporary societies than anything that is available to a hermeneutic conception of justice and social criticism.

In the final part I will seek to develop and then to apply Habermas's discourse ethics. Chapter 7 offers an argument that stresses the potential for context sensitivity in Habermas's discursive approach to matters of justice. A suitably revised account of discourse ethics can be defended from the contextualist criticisms of those who are sceptical of its universalist grounding. I will be suggesting that a heavier emphasis must be placed on the role of ethical discourses in disputes about justice.[13] This will highlight the ways in which pluralism in our second sense can more adequately be taken into account.

Finally, in chapter 8, this last claim will be supported by a detailed analysis of the demands of justice in one modern society where disputes about justice have been especially intractable. I will be assessing the implications of my argument for the politics of Northern Ireland, a society where problems of pluralism in our first sense are also exceptionally acute. I will give evidence there in support of the claim that discourse ethics succeeds much better than Walzer's contextualist approach in clarifying the demands of justice in that particular context.

Habermas's discursive approach to normative justification can be thought of as an account of impartiality in context. As a theoretical guide to matters of justice, it can accommodate the importance of both impartialism and contextualism. In contrast, both Rawls's liberal theory of justice and Walzer's communitarian theory tend to emphasize one at the expense of the other. In this way, discourse ethics can take pluralism seriously both in relation to the plurality of conceptions of the good in each modern society and the plurality of historically situated modern societies. Furthermore, discourse ethics gives both a more critically sensitive account of impartiality than Rawls, and a more critically sensitive account of contextualist criticism than Walzer. What I am suggesting here is that in so far as Habermas's work enlightens us in relation to theorizing justice, then it can be presented as a synthesis of the approaches of Rawls and Walzer. It preserves what is of greatest significance in both while also overcoming their differing weaknesses.

My argument overall suggests that, in a modern, pluralist society, political philosophy can at best provide a procedural test of the rational acceptability of substantive claims about justice. Disputed claims can only be addressed in the actual context of particular political communities. The discussion can be thought of as a contribution to our understanding of what is at stake when we argue about justice in any modern pluralist society. My hope is to clarify how we might best support the aspiration to a more just social reality as it is articulated in the ongoing public disputes that sustain us as living democratic communities.

I

John Rawls's Impartialism

1

The Isolation of the Political

The separation of a political domain from other aspects of social life is fundamental to liberal accounts of justice. The isolation of a political domain sets a limit to the aspects of social life that are of public concern and anything that falls outside this domain is thought to be beyond the scope of justice. It is certainly nothing new to be critical of naive attempts to isolate the political domain by limiting it to matters of formal civil and legal rights of individuals while ignoring the effects of social and economic structures on the effective exercise of those rights. In this part of the book I want to argue that even though this naiveté is not characteristic of the most highly sophisticated theory of justice yet presented within the liberal tradition, that of John Rawls, his approach to questions of justice remains crucially flawed in this regard.

SOCIAL JUSTICE AND IMPARTIALITY

Rawls takes the primary subject of justice to be the basic structure of society. Each of us is born into a particular position in relation to the political system and the major economic and social institutions of our culture. Our starting position has profound effects on our life prospects and it is clear that some people are privileged over others in this regard. Rawls wants to defend principles of justice that test the acceptability of such deep inequalities by allowing us to "regulate the choice of a political constitution and the main elements of the economic and social system."[1] These main elements of the basic structure of society certainly include aspects of life that would be taken by earlier liberals to be beyond the scope of public concern. They incorporate economic institutions such as the competitive market and private property in the means of production as well as social institutions such as the monogamous family.

Many critics have failed to note the extent to which Rawls shares with socialists many serious and compelling objections to rampant free market capitalism. This becomes very clear if Rawls's egalitarian liberalism is contrasted with the influential libertarianism of Robert Nozick.[2]

While Nozick simply disregards structural constraints on individual autonomy, Rawls is concerned that the cumulative effect over time of isolated, historical, and supposedly free transactions between individuals, can lead to intolerable structural limitations on the possibility of autonomous living for some citizens. This indicates that for Rawls, as for Marx, formal freedom is of questionable worth if it is not supported by effective means for each individual to live a dignified, creative, and autonomous life. Rawls is therefore keenly aware of the fact that in a well-ordered society the basic structure of society must consciously be controlled to the extent that nobody can be denied the chance to live autonomously because of bad fortune with regard to social circumstances or the distribution of natural talent. It is for this reason that the basic structure is the primary subject of justice.

So Rawls's theory provides critical standards for a public evaluation of the basic structure of society understood in an impressively broad sense. In spite of this, however, Rawls's defense of his account of justice as fairness depends, in his later work at least, on an implausible attempt to separate the political from the nonpolitical by dealing with questions of political morality in isolation from the comprehensive moral views of citizens. One implication of this that I hope to clarify here is that Rawls's procedural test of moral justification is not sufficiently rigorous to ground effectively principles of justice appropriate to a modern democratic society. I will suggest that the attempt to isolate the political involves an unnecessarily restrictive conception of moral reasoning about justice, one that is insufficiently sensitive to the differing perspectives among the diversity of social groups that will be present in any modern society.

The intention here is to offer a critique of the procedural test of justification that Rawls defends in his theory rather than a detailed critical assessment of the two substantive principles that Rawls believes to be justified according to that procedural test.[3] The critique will focus on the consequences of Rawls's attempt to isolate the political. I argue that the boundary between the political and the nonpolitical, that sets a limit to the scope of justice, can never be assumed in any convincing procedure of justification. Rather it must always be treated as an on-going matter of public debate and democratic contestation. Rawls's procedure is not adequate to our democratic needs as an account of relevant conditions of fairness, or an impartial point of view.[4] Furthermore, by ruling out the explicit articulation of different perspectives in the choice of substantive principles of justice, Rawls runs the risk of failing to take account of the particular concerns of marginal social groups.

The main thrust of my argument against Rawls is that his conception of an impartial point of view does not have a central enough role for political discourse. It presents an account of public reflection on the justification of principles of justice in a rather static and restrictive manner. If the always present potential for unjustifiable political bias against marginal groups in a democratic society is to be tested with the required rigor, then we will need a more dynamic and interactive conception of what it means to adopt an impartial point of view in our considerations about the demands of justice. In other words we will need an account of impartiality that is more adequately discursive.

Liberalism has often been accused of failing to overcome certain biases in its understanding of justice. Marxism has presented a powerful challenge to liberalism by highlighting the potential danger of bias involved for any theorist who seeks to construct theoretically an account of justice that claims to be acceptable to all.[5] Marxism concerns itself with the potential danger of a class bias being built into such a construction. This bias may, of course, be rooted in certain assumptions that the theorist brings unwittingly to the task. Such a bias would render the account of justice an ideological, and therefore partial, account, in spite of the theorist's best attempts to remain impartial. In this respect at least, Marxism can be thought of as a precursor of the two perspectives that I will consider as significant challenges to Rawls's conception of an impartial point of view. In political theoretical debates of recent years, communitarianism and feminism have eclipsed Marxism as the most influential critical perspectives on liberalism.

Communitarian and feminist critics concern themselves in different ways with potential biases in Rawls's account of justice. Both claim to represent distinctive, and often marginal, voices in public debates about justice in the context of a modern society. I will consider the possible objections that could be raised from these perspectives in relation to certain key features of Rawls's theory. In this chapter I will assess the impact of communitarian objections to the way that Rawls defends the Kantian claim that the right is prior to the good. The next chapter is concerned with feminist objections to Rawls's neglect of issues of justice within the family and also with the relation between justice and solidarity.

My own strategy in both of these chapters will be to assess the extent to which the criticisms that I reconstruct can be sustained against Rawls. While I seek to underline the importance of the procedural task that Rawls has set for himself, that of offering a philosophical justification of an impartial point of view that can test the acceptability of substantive principles of justice, I reject the procedure that he himself proposes. The most damaging criticisms of Rawls's procedure that can be reconstructed from both communitarian and feminist perspectives converge in highlighting the theoretical difficulties involved in the attempt to isolate the political.

The main problem for Rawls is that this strategy of isolating the political relies on an unhelpful and restrictive notion of political discourse. Differences in perspective must be overcome, in his account, prior to the choice of principles of justice. This means that the procedure itself is static, whereas what democratic legitimation would seem to require is a dynamic, interactive procedure of justification. Furthermore, the basic theoretical assumptions that Rawls builds into his construction are not self-evidently open to question within the framework of the procedure of choice itself. In later chapters I hope to show that a procedure of justification that is adequate to the critical task required of it in a modern society must incorporate, more successfully than Rawls does, the concerns of the communitarian and feminist critics whose work I examine in this part. Before we assess the challenge of feminism in the next chapter, let us turn to the concerns of communitarian critics of Rawls's political liberalism. In order to put these concerns in perspective we will first need to say something about the general character of Rawls's theoretical approach to questions of justice.

POLITICAL CONSTRUCTIVISM AND THE IDEA OF AN OVERLAPPING CONSENSUS

The Kantian claim that the right is prior to the good is one of the striking characteristics of Rawls's theory. In contrast with teleological theories, such as utilitarianism and various forms of perfectionism, in Rawls's account of justice as fairness there is no reason to suppose that the right will maximize the good. The right, as represented by principles of justice, is not dependent on any one particular conception of the good. In fact it imposes "restrictions on what are reasonable conceptions of one's good."[6] Justice defines the scope within which we can choose a reasonable plan of life and it limits us to a conception of the good that will not violate the principles of right.

It follows from this that while a well-ordered society depends on its citizens reaching some agreement about justice, those citizens do not have to share a full conception of the good.[7] Neither do they all have to affirm the same comprehensive religious, philosophical, or moral doctrine in order to reach an agreement about justice. Agreement on comprehensive doctrines is an unreasonable expectation under modern democratic conditions. Within free democratic institutions such a comprehensive moral consensus is not only impossible but it is also both unnecessary and undesirable. This is because of what Rawls refers to as the fact of reasonable pluralism.[8] A plurality of reasonable comprehensive moral doctrines is the inevitable result of the workings of practical reason through free political institutions under modern conditions. While this fact of reasonable pluralism is not to be considered as an unfortunate and regrettable condition of modern life, it does imply that an agreement on principles of justice could not be derived from a comprehensive moral doctrine but it must rather be affirmed by a plurality of reasonable comprehensive doctrines in an overlapping consensus.[9] This affirms the priority of right since it indicates that in a well-ordered society it is the principles of justice, and not a full conception of the good or a comprehensive moral doctrine, that form a basis of social unity.

As I have already indicated, the particular way that Rawls seeks to separate issues of justice, about which we must agree, from moral questions that are not susceptible to agreement, reflects an attempt to isolate political aspects of morality from other comprehensive aspects of morality. Matters of justice fall within the domain of the political in Rawls's sense to the extent that we can make legitimate claims on each other, and on our public institutions, if we believe that some principle of justice has been violated. On the other hand, there are many questions about which we cannot in principle agree, due to the fact of reasonable pluralism. These must be considered to be outside the political domain and, so long as they do not violate the principles of justice, they can be treated as matters for individuals to decide on for themselves.

The aim of this present chapter is to assess critically Rawls's strategy of defending the priority of right by attempting to treat matters of political morality in isolation from other aspects of citizens' comprehensive moral views. Some communitarians have questioned Rawls's assertion of the priority of right and have accused him of supporting that priority on the basis of an untenable atomistic ontology.[10] I want to defend Rawls from this charge by arguing that his work is best understood as a version of what I will call liberal holism. Nonetheless, the discussion leads to the suggestion that a liberal holist defence of the priority of right is undermined by Rawls's attempt, in his recent work, to isolate political aspects of morality.

The initial communitarian challenge to Rawls's work was based on the claim that the priority of right, as expressed through the original position, produces an account of justice that is arbitrarily biased toward certain conceptions of the good.[11] Rawls excludes from the original position information about the particular conceptions of the good that each party is to have.[12] He argues that, given the fact that there is a plurality of reasonable conceptions of the good, such a restriction is necessary if unanimous agreement is to be secured. Rawls also maintains that the parties are to be thought of as being mutually disinterested.[13] These conditions of choice are said to favor liberal conceptions of the good that are content with the loose social bonds characteristic of highly individualistic cultures over conceptions that depend on a stronger basis of social unity. Indeed the implication is that this restriction could only be justified with reference to some such liberal conception of the good.

Furthermore, Rawls's account of primary goods is also said to constitute an arbitrary bias toward individualistic conceptions, as it is blind to the significance of irreducibly common goods, such as solidarity. The primary goods can, it is argued, be thought of as being of greater value to those individuals for whom such common goods do not matter greatly. The outline of the original position presupposes highly fragmented social conditions and the individualistic bias in the account of the primary goods undermines whatever bonds of social solidarity actually do exist.

Rawls has responded to these criticisms by stressing the central role that the Kantian conception of moral personality plays in providing a normative justification for both the outline of the original position and the account of the primary goods.[14] According to this conception we view each person as

> a moral person moved by two highest-order interests, namely, the interests to realise and to exercise the two powers of moral personality. These two powers are the capacity for a sense of right and justice (the capacity to honour fair terms of cooperation), and the capacity to decide upon, to revise and rationally to pursue a conception of the good.[15]

Rawls accepts that this is an historically specific conception of the person. It is a conception that he believes to be embedded in the institutions and practices of modern liberal democratic societies. The constructivist method that Rawls adopts sets itself the practical task of securing agreement on the first principles of justice that are to specify fair terms of social cooperation.[16] It is intended to reveal how a workable conception of justice can be supported with moral reasons that can be affirmed by all those who hold reasonable comprehensive moral views. In this way justice as fairness is itself grounded in the public political culture of modern democratic societies. Rawls assumes that there are embedded in this public culture certain political beliefs that all reasonable citizens can share.[17]

The elaboration of this constructivist method allows Rawls to respond to the criticism that the original position is arbitrarily biased toward individualistic conceptions of the good. Since we are to assume the conditions of modern pluralist democracies, justice as fairness is not defended as a true conception of justice but rather as one that is reasonable. Political constructivism does not employ the notion of truth but rather leaves the "concept of a true moral judgment to comprehensive doctrines."[18] In summing up the advantages of such an approach Rawls points out that

> there can be but one true comprehensive doctrine, though as we have seen, many reasonable ones. Once we accept the fact that reasonable pluralism is a permanent condition of public culture under free institutions, the idea of the reasonable is more suitable as part of the basis of public justification for a constitutional regime than the idea of moral truth. Holding a political conception as true, and for that reason alone the one suitable basis of public reason, is exclusive, even sectarian, and so likely to foster political division.[19]

The implication here is that grounding our principles of justice on any one comprehensive moral doctrine that claims to be true, or indeed one conception of the good, would lead to intolerable coercion by the state of those who hold reasonable yet different comprehensive moral views.[20]

We might note at this point that while Rawls's political constructivism draws on ideas he believes to be embedded in the public culture of democratic societies, his position should not to be thought of as a contextualist one.[21] This is because the political conception of justice is constructed not out of one particular democratic tradition but rather from ideas of practical reason. It develops, in other words, out of ideas that can be shared by citizens of any and every democratic society "by using the principles of their common practical reason."[22] Furthermore, political constructivism aspires to present, in the outline of the original position, an objective point of view.[23] Rawls's political conception of justice could, he suggests, satisfy the requirements of objectivity if it can be defended with reasons "sufficient to convince all reasonable persons that it is reasonable."[24]

But what of the communitarian objection that Rawls's procedure is biased toward individualistic conceptions of the good? It is now clear that the original position is to be thought of as a device of representation that "serves as a means of public reflection and self-clarification."[25] It models our two moral powers in a way that prioritizes the reasonable, our capacity to act according to general principles of justice, over the rational, our capacity to pursue a conception of the good.[26] The reasonable is prioritized by the requirement, introduced by the veil of ignorance, that in choosing principles of justice that are fair, we must adopt the perspective of every citizen.

Since the thrust of the original position is to guarantee an agreement about justice that is acceptable to all, it is not intended to favor any particular conception of the good. The assumption that the parties are mutually disinterested is to be thought of in the context of Rawls's claim that in a pluralist society principles of justice cannot reasonably be based on one particular conception of the good or on one comprehensive moral doctrine. Two persons with opposing religious beliefs can be mutually disinterested once they can agree on a framework of justice based on a shared notion of moral personality. It does not follow that they are self-interested nor can we assume that they pursue individualistic ends.[27]

It is clear that what motivates the parties in the original position to choose the primary goods are in fact the two highest-order interests. Rawls wants to rule out any interpretation of the parties as merely egoistic rational consumers of goods who are motivated to accept the principles of justice solely in response to external constraints.[28] The primary goods are to be understood as the necessary conditions for realizing the powers of moral personality and as all-purpose means for a wide range of final ends.[29] This is the practical nature of the primary goods. They cohere with the conception of the person to provide a framework of social cooperation that is both workable and stable as a basis of social unity in spite of the wide range of reasonable conceptions of the good. This is, according to Rawls, the most reasonable manner of proceeding in the practical task of securing fair terms of cooperation and so it cannot be charged with being arbitrarily biased in favor of individualistic conceptions of the good.

JUSTICE AS POLITICAL AND THE CHARGE OF ATOMISM

While this emphasis on the two powers of moral personality does seem to allow Rawls to deflect the charge of arbitrary individualistic bias,

some ambiguities remain. The constructivist approach has been interpreted as a shift toward a form of perfectionism where this ideal of
moral personality is held up as a moral goal that is actively to be pursued. The institutions of the basic structure are judged according to the
extent to which they facilitate our highest-order interests in exercising
our two moral powers. The basic structure is to express our nature as
free and equal rational beings.[30] Rawls does not want to accept such a
perfectionist interpretation, as it is based on a comprehensive moral
view involving controversial personal ideals that are not likely to be
shared by all reasonable citizens. On the other hand, Rawls insists that
justice as fairness is not to be interpreted as a modus vivendi, a conception based merely on a convergence of interests. That approach would
seem to presuppose some form of moral scepticism since such a basis for
agreement is prudential rather than moral.[31] Rawls's constructivism
seeks to steer a course between perfectionism and scepticism.

Rawls maintains that justice as fairness is to be thought of as a political and not a metaphysical conception.[32] Although, as I have already
pointed out, Rawls argues that justice as fairness is not dependent on
any one comprehensive moral view, he is keen to stress the fact that it is
a moral conception both in its aim and on the grounds that support it.[33]
A political conception of justice for the basic structure of society is itself
a freestanding moral conception.[34] Furthermore, justice as fairness is
affirmed as an overlapping consensus in that all citizens who affirm it do
so on the basis of their own reasonable comprehensive moral views.
Their comprehensive moral views coincide in the moral conception of
the citizen as free and equal and the notion of a well-ordered society as
a fair system of cooperation that is characterized by the principles of justice and by political virtues such as tolerance and reasonableness.[35] Justice as fairness is affirmed for its own sake and so it is more stable than
a modus vivendi that is always vulnerable to a shift in the balance of
power between different social groups.

In his writings since the publication of *A Theory of Justice*, Rawls
has used an impressive range of arguments to defend the priority of right
as one of the essential elements of the account of justice as fairness that
he now presents as a conception of political liberalism.[36] At the same
time he has, with some sophistication, managed to use a number of ideas
of the good in the construction of his theory that serve to reveal that he
understands the right and the good to be complementary.[37] However, his
recent defense of the priority of right is deeply flawed in one crucial
respect. It depends on the implausible attempt to treat questions of political morality in isolation from the rest of our comprehensive moral

views. From Rawls's point of view, it would appear that for each of us morality has a political aspect that relates to questions regarding the regulation of the basic structure of society, and a nonpolitical aspect that relates to other dimensions of our lives. [38] This key element in Rawls's recent strategy leaves him vulnerable to a number of arguments that can be supported by the work of his communitarian critics. These arguments undermine Rawls's attempt to isolate the political in his efforts to ground the priority of right.

Perhaps the most celebrated critique of Rawls from a communitarian perspective was put forward by Michael Sandel. [39] According to Sandel, the Kantian conception of the person, on which Rawls's account of justice is constructed, presupposes an idea of an unencumbered self that is prior to and independent of its purposes and ends. The values and ends espoused by the individual are thought to be chosen voluntarily and are never constitutive of the identity of the self. It is the capacity for choice rather than the ends that are chosen that is of importance in Sandel's reconstruction of this Kantian conception of free and equal moral personality. Furthermore, it is assumed that any attributes I have, my talents, my physical appearance, or any of my idiosyncratic psychological dispositions, are accidental and contingent to my identity. For Sandel this conception of the person lacks any depth of moral character. Our character comes from our being situated historically within a particular network of social ties. Each of us interprets our individual identity in a context that we did not choose and under circumstances that we cannot fully control. The issue here is an ontological one between atomistic and holistic conceptions of the self. [40]

An atomistic conception of the self, such as the unencumbered self Sandel describes, is indeed quite untenable. Holists are right in so far as it is impossible to imagine a recognizably human being whose identity could be said to be prior to and independent of all constitutive ends. Each person's values and ends, and therefore the person's identity, are conditioned and shaped, to a greater or lesser extent, by attributes that are not chosen (family, nationality, sex, race, natural talents, and limitations). The person's identity is formed, in many ways, independently of the will. An identity is never chosen by a free-floating individual but rather it emerges through a dialogical encounter of recognition with others. Self-understanding always depends to some degree on the recognition of people who matter: parents, friends, lovers, a community of scholars, or even perhaps, for believers, God. [41]

The formation of an identity involves some degree of acceptance of the recognition we receive as well as a certain degree of struggle. If we struggle against the recognition, of our parents for example, we will want to move away, to draw on encounters with new significant others who can help us to become human beings that we could not have been had we not engaged in that struggle. We are never simply encumbered with whatever values and ends our communities of origin happen to espouse. But nor are we ever unencumbered. We never change our ends or alter our identity without some struggle with or acceptance of the recognition of significant others.

The citizens of a liberal democracy are, in most circumstances, members of a particular political community that few have chosen voluntarily. Many citizens do come to identify with the other members of their political community of origin. They will accept the recognition of their compatriots as constitutive of their identity. The fact that they are British, Irish, French, or Portuguese becomes for each of them a part of their answer to the question "Who am I?" The good of their political community is in part constitutive of their own conception of the good. This is usually true even of those citizens who consider themselves to be entirely apolitical.

However, in an extreme case, even if I were to leave my nation of origin, because I do not identify with its ends even to a minimal degree, I would want to find some new significant others on whom I could draw in the formation of a new political aspect to my identity. This might involve immigration or naturalization and this process is obviously more common in a predominantly immigrant society like the United States. Yet even in such cases, for those who come to identify with their new political community, the community's good will in part constitute their own personal good. So it would seem reasonable to assume that the personal identity of each individual citizen depends, to a greater or lesser degree, on the common good of the political community. If, for example, a political community were to be invaded by an aggressive foreign power, the personal identity of each individual citizen, as well as the political identity of the community, would be under some threat.

Of course, ruling out atomism does not rule out liberalism. It would rule Rawls's theory of justice out if Sandel were right, that it depends on a conception of an unencumbered self.[42] In fact, Rawls's position would best be described as that of a liberal holist. There are two main reasons for interpreting Rawls in this way.

First, he can allow for the fact that individual identities are in part constituted by moral ties, such as ties, within the family and various associations, that are not chosen voluntarily. By locating such associations beyond the scope of justice, Rawls assumes that he can disregard them in developing a political conception of justice.[43]

Second, and more importantly here, Rawls points out that the establishment and successful maintenance of just democratic institutions is itself a common good. Rawls insists that the citizens of a well-ordered society do have final ends in common.

> While it is true that they do not affirm the same comprehensive doctrine, they do affirm the same political conception of justice; and this means that they share one very basic political end, and one that has high priority: namely the end of supporting just institutions and of giving one another justice accordingly.[44]

The extent to which we realize and exercise our two moral powers depends, at least in part, on the achievement of this common good. The good of political society also guarantees for each citizen the satisfaction of fundamental needs in that it secures for them justice and the social bases of self-respect. This good is also fundamentally a social good in that it is achieved and realized "through citizens' joint activity in mutual dependence on the appropriate actions being taken by others."[45] Democratic institutions are quite appropriately a source of pride and a cause for celebration among the peoples who enjoy them.

It would appear therefore that the common achievement of just institutions is a necessary constituent of the identity of each of the citizens of a well-ordered society. In this sense Rawls is clearly a holist. He is a distinctively liberal holist to the extent that he continues to assert the priority of right by defending his conception of justice as a political conception that is not dependent on any one comprehensive moral view.[46] This reading of Rawls obviously contradicts the communitarian claim that the outline of the original position depends on an atomistic conception of the self. But it also contradicts Rawls's own view that the original position has "no specific metaphysical implications concerning the nature of the self."[47] Rawls's defense of political liberalism is incompatible with an atomistic ontology. The holistic ontology that underlies his work has itself certain implications that undermine the attempt to isolate political aspects of morality. I will consider two of these here.

NEUTRALITY AND ITS LIMITS

As we have already seen, communitarians have been critical of the liberal view that the state can, and should, be neutral with regard to the plurality of competing conceptions of the good in a modern society. This is taken to be one implication of the assertion of the priority of right. Rawls is, with good reason, exceptionally careful about the use of the term "neutrality."[48] He maintains that his conception of justice as fairness is not neutral in a strictly procedural sense. This is because the principles of justice it defends, as well as its political conceptions of the person and of society, involve substantive commitments to particular values.[49] Nor is it neutral in attempting to ensure that all citizens are free to pursue any conception of the good. Only some conceptions of the good, those that are reasonable to the extent that they can affirm the principles of justice, are permissible in Rawls's well-ordered society of political liberalism. Nor again is justice as fairness neutral in effect since Rawls believes that the basic structure of a just constitutional regime will "inevitably encourage some ways of life and discourage others."[50] What the "neutrality" of justice as fairness does require is that the state refrain from acting in any way that intentionally favors one comprehensive moral doctrine or one particular conception of the good. It seems to me however, that within the context of any one state, even this ideal of neutrality has its limits.

First, a particular liberal democratic state is not neutral, for example, between on the one hand, those patriotic citizens who count as a constitutive aspect of their own good the justness of that state's institutions, as they have been shaped historically in a distinctive cultural context, and on the other hand, antipatriotic citizens who, for whatever reason, have come to despise those same institutions and who long for their destruction. These need not be actively involved in attacking the institutions of the state, whether by violent or other means. They may be relatively passive and simply resigned to the fact that they have been unfortunate enough to live in a political community for which they feel much resentment but no loyalty. For personal or historical reasons their identity precludes that loyalty.

Every democratic state has a particular history and lays claim to a certain territory. It is not unusual to have some citizens within that territory who do not identify with the political community in which procedural justice for them is to be embodied historically. These antipatriots may not despise liberal democracy or principles of justice as such but only liberal democracy and justice under the British state or the Spanish state or whatever.[51] In other words, it might be the case that they can embrace the ideals of political liberalism but not the historical embodiment of those ideals in their own context.

Citizens typically, even constitutional liberals, are loyal not to an abstract form of political justice as such but to a distinct cultural and historical embodiment of the principles of justice. They identify with the historical reality of a particular democratic community and that identification is, at least in part, the source of their allegiance to the state and their acceptance of its claim to legitimacy. The state cannot but favor patriotic citizens over its antipatriots. In any society divided in this way, the state can never be neutral between the conceptions of the good of those who identify themselves with its historical constitution and those who do not.[52]

This does not mean that the state should discriminate against minority cultures. On the one hand, the state cannot but promote one particular conception of the good, a conception that celebrates the historical achievements of its people. It would appear therefore that state institutions embody principles of justice in ways that will inevitably express the cultural distinctiveness of a particular democratic community. On the other hand, the real challenge facing culturally divided societies is not simply to guarantee rights for their minorities but rather to create an inclusive political culture with which all citizens can identify.[53] If this were achieved, then there would be no reason to fear that the historical constitution of the state could generate antipatriotic feelings among certain groups of its citizens. We will leave aside for now an examination of the implications of this point so that we can turn to the other reasons that can be offered in support of the view that Rawls overestimates the extent to which a liberal state can be neutral.

Rawls accepts that the assertion of the priority of right means that only some conceptions of the good are permissible in a well-ordered society. It is enough that the overlapping consensus be supported by a substantial majority of its politically active citizens.[54] We recall that to support the overlapping consensus one need not endorse liberalism as a comprehensive moral view, by affirming the doctrines of say Kant or Mill, but only as a political morality. The question that this claim raises however is whether or not political liberalism could be compatible with comprehensive moral views that are not themselves comprehensively liberal.

Rawls admits that justice as fairness does affirm a particular set of virtues, the liberal political virtues of tolerance, reasonableness, and fairness.[55] He maintains that what is required of citizens who hold comprehensive moral views that are not themselves comprehensively liberal, is that they recognize the great significance of these liberal virtues to the extent, for example, that they accept that they will be promoted in the education of their children.[56] While there may be other virtues, such as religious ones, that are encouraged at home, it is the political virtues that prepare the young for citizenship in a well-ordered society.

But surely this is so demanding that the variety of comprehensive moral views that could accept it is quite limited. There will arguably be many citizens of modern democratic societies who would find this unreasonable in so far as it clashes too sharply with certain important aspects of their comprehensive moral views. Take, for example, anybody who adheres to a religious conception of the good of all humanity in a fundamentalistic way. For them to accept that the promotion of the liberal virtues as a central aspect of the education of their children is to ask them to risk something that may matter to them a great deal, that the religious upbringing they give to their children will be undermined at school.[57] The comprehensive moral views that could affirm an overlapping consensus begin to look pretty comprehensively liberal. Not only does this reflect quite dimly the diversity of moral views that are actually held in modern societies but, more importantly, it leaves a great number of people outside of the overlapping consensus. They will be expected to accept the political morality of Rawls's constitutional state not as a matter of conviction but rather merely as a modus vivendi.[58]

The problem here can be illustrated somewhat differently with reference to divisive moral issues that are part of the political agenda in contemporary democratic societies. These include abortion, euthanasia, animal rights, and questions such as the criminalization of sado-masochistic sex or the right to freedom of expression in the light of the Salman Rushdie affair. Take abortion, for example. Every modern state has to take some political position on this question and it must reach some conclusion about what rights are involved. Could the state do this by avoiding controversial comprehensive moral claims? If the state were to reach its conclusion by affirming only the liberal virtues of tolerance, reasonableness, and fairness, what are we to make of its expectation that these considerations should override the comprehensive moral views of dissenting citizens?

Rawls suggests that with regard to the question of abortion, a reasonable balance of the relevant political values "will give a woman a duly qualified right to decide whether or not to end her pregnancy during the first trimester."[59] At an early stage of pregnancy, the political value of the equality of women as citizens overrides other values, such as due respect for human life, and the ordered reproduction of political society over time. Any other conclusion would be unreasonable and it might also be "cruel and oppressive." This is hardly a convincing response as it merely asserts the reasonableness of one position in this controversy.[60] It favors certain comprehensive moral doctrines over others and these others might well be considered not to be unreasonable.

It seems clear that there is no way that convinced pro-life campaigners could accept that a distinctively liberal virtue such as tolerance should override their conviction that a mother and her unborn fetus are of equal moral value from the moment of conception, without radically changing their most fundamental moral beliefs. In other words, if they were to be able to digest political liberalism to the extent that they could accept that it would be unreasonable for the state to ban abortion, then they would already have swallowed a fairly large dose of comprehensive liberalism. Accepting that legal abortion is reasonable is incompatible with the comprehensive moral view that abortion is murder.[61] Political liberalism is only compatible with comprehensive moral views that are themselves thoroughly liberal.

Nor could Rawls dissolve this difficulty by claiming that the question of the liberal state failing to be neutral, even in his favored sense, is not at issue in the dispute about abortion, since this is a matter of political right and not a question of morality in a more comprehensive sense. The problem with a moral issue such as abortion is that we do not agree on a conception of the right. There is no consensus on who has rights nor on the matter of which rights have priority. But the disagreements involved will always be premised on and informed by disagreements between competing comprehensive moral claims.[62] For one party, perhaps the fetus has equal rights with the mother because it is loved equally in the eyes of God. For another party, the fetus may have a right to life in a qualified sense but this right can be trumped by the rights of the mother, depending on her circumstances. For a third, the woman's right to choose always takes priority over other considerations. Even among those who hold this position there is a no agreement on the time scale involved. The reasons given in support of these various positions as to what is right with regard to abortion will depend on the range of moral resources that could be drawn from the comprehensive moral commitments of the participants. An appeal to a conception of rights does nothing to avoid the moral controversy involved.

A state that permits abortion cannot but favor conceptions of the good that are comprehensively liberal. The attempt to avoid comprehensive moral commitments in political discussion runs the risk of allowing for the imposition, without any attempted public justification, of a particular comprehensive morality. It fails to facilitate a critical public assessment of constitutional essentials or matters of basic justice.[63] Such a critical public assessment cannot mark out in advance the issues that must be avoided for the sake of affirming an overlapping consensus. It must allow the relationship between the politically right and the comprehensively moral to be the subject of deliberation in an open democratic encounter. Controversial moral views, even those on abortion on which agreement seems to be most unlikely, must not be excluded from the political agenda, but rather they must be worked through politically.[64] However, while there can be no shirking away from difficult moral issues, these matters must not be decided simply on the crude basis of majority rule. Given the fact of reasonable pluralism, we must continue to defend the priority of right. This is not best achieved by the attempt to avoid moral controversy and the assertion of a rigid isolation of the political domain. We need rather to defend procedures of justification that can facilitate more easily an open and critical assessment of the ways in which the politically right and the comprehensively moral relate to one another.

This brief analysis of one divisive moral issue should make it clear that it is not as easy as Rawls seems to think to isolate a political morality from other comprehensive moral views. It is never obvious which aspects of our morality are political and which are not. Only comprehensive liberals could accept that their moral views on abortion should be trumped by the claims of political liberalism. The limits of a state's neutrality between conceptions of the good can once more easily be underestimated. Not only must the conception of a patriot be privileged over that of an antipatriot, but a politically liberal state must, by promoting the virtues of tolerance, reasonableness, and fairness, also privilege comprehensively liberal moral views over comprehensive moralities that are not themselves thoroughly liberal.

CITIZENSHIP AND THE PUBLIC SPHERE

A second implication of liberal holism, which is related to the first, is the need to stress the centrality of democratic will-formation as the only guarantee of securing the basic liberties that justice as fairness defends. Some of Rawls's communitarian critics emphasize the bonds of solidarity among citizens that are essential to the flourishing of the common good of just institutions. The political rights provided by those institutions could only prove to be of fair value to all citizens, as Rawls suggests they should be, if they can be exercised within the context of a vibrant and vigilant public sphere where open and unrestricted discussion can take place about questions of the common good. Rawls's attempt to isolate the political domain does not lend itself very easily to such a conception of democratic politics. This is connected to Rawls's

understanding of individual rights as a means of removing certain controversial issues from the political agenda. In seeking to balance individual rights to privacy with the political rights associated with democratic will-formation, Rawls continues to give undue weight to the former
at the expense of the latter.

Communitarians who are concerned to revivify modern democratic
life tend to stress the need for structures of power that encourage citizens
to participate actively in the public sphere.[65] The idea is that all citizens,
or at least their genuine representatives, can actively inform and shape
political decisions on matters of common concern. This participatory
model of citizenship with its complementary notion of a vibrant public
sphere can be contrasted with the strong emphasis on individual rights
within certain strands of the liberal tradition.[66] The communitarian
model of citizenship is based on the republican ideal of citizen self-rule.
In contrast, the individualistic, liberal model of citizenship is based on the
power of the individual to assert rights that are intended to protect an
area of private interest from the possible encroachment of an intrusive
political domain. These rights delimit the scope of public concern and
they are retrieved by the individual through the judicial process.[67]
Crudely put, communitarians are primarily, but not exclusively, concerned with political rights of participation, while liberals are primarily,
but not exclusively, concerned with individual rights to privacy.

It is apparent that both of these sets of citizenship rights, private and
political, are equally central to any theory of justice that is presented in
liberal holist terms.[68] Political rights are presupposed by any defense of
private individual rights since these latter rights can only be securely
guaranteed within the context of a self-ruling democratic community. At
the same time, private rights are presupposed by any defense of political
rights of participation since no community could be genuinely democratic if it did not respect the dignity and the personal autonomy of each
individual citizen. I have suggested that a liberal holist approach to justice involves the claim that the identity of each citizen is constituted in
part by the achievement of the common good of just institutions. This is
necessarily an achievement of democratic citizen self-rule. If the notion
of democratic citizen self-rule and the liberal commitment to individual
rights are thought of as two sides of the one coin, then it would not be
possible to give an account of political justice either solely in terms of
the private rights of isolated individuals nor solely in terms of the democratic will of a political community. While the former depends on an
untenable atomistic ontology, the latter cannot adequately facilitate the
views of dissenting individuals. A liberal holist theory of justice must

instead be presented as a normatively justified procedure that is grounded in intersubjectivist terms. Neither private nor political rights can be given priority over the other.

Although I have suggested that Rawls is a liberal holist, he does tend to stress an individualistic model of citizenship, one that is given in terms of private rights that set limits to the scope of political discussion. This leads to a conception of democratic self-rule that is inadequately vigilant in seeking to secure fair value of the political rights of each citizen.[69] I think that the following passage makes it clear that Rawls does give priority to private individual rights. He maintains that

> liberal principles meet the urgent political requirement to fix, once and for all, the content of certain political basic rights and liberties, and to assign them special priority. Doing this takes those guarantees off the political agenda and puts them beyond the calculus of social interests, thereby establishing clearly and firmly the rules of political contest. To regard that calculus as relevant in these matters leaves the status and content of those rights and liberties still unsettled; it subjects them to the shifting circumstances of time and place, and by greatly raising the stakes of political controversy, dangerously increases the insecurity and hostility of public life.[70]

There are obvious attractions in what Rawls is seeking to do here but there are also reasons to worry about this approach to the defense of individual private rights.

Again the attempt to isolate political aspects of morality from other comprehensive moral views is crucial here. This sets a limit, once and for all, to the scope of open political discussion by excluding issues about which it is presumed that we will not agree. I have already suggested that this method of avoidance that Rawls has adopted, fails to isolate political morality as neatly as he seems to imply. Furthermore, the method does not do justice to the diversity of conceptions of the good that could be represented in the public domain since, as we saw in the discussion about neutrality, it marginalizes conceptions that are not comprehensively liberal.

In a holist account of liberalism the common achievement of just institutions is thought of as a necessary constituent of the identity of each citizen. But this achievement is an ongoing historical project that must not be confused with some particular agreement at any one time that seeks to exclude certain issues from the political agenda, for once and for all! By seeking to take issues of private concern off the political agenda, Rawls makes the unwarranted assumption that the line between political and nonpolitical aspects of our identities can be fixed.[71] Not only is it not fixed but, as the example of abortion illustrates, it is constantly being called into question. It is challenged and contested in every moral dispute where political claims are informed by more comprehensive moral views. It is also challenged whenever a social group that had previously been marginalized begins to articulate its own needs and interests. The scope of the political domain must be left as an open question so as to leave room for the potential voices of social groups who have not yet articulated their own needs and interests.[72]

Rawls's emphasis on the liberal political morality that forms the basis of the overlapping consensus does not reflect very satisfactorily the kind of differences that characterize a vigilant public sphere in a modern society. The equal opportunity of all social groups to participate in public discourse must be incorporated into any procedural account of justice that is to be adequate as a test of the legitimacy of substantive principles that are to regulate the basic structure of a modern society. Rawls's procedure, by limiting political discussion, does not give the central role to the notion of a vigilant public sphere that an adequate version of liberal holism would require. Basic principles are after all, on Rawls's account, agreed upon before any real public discussion even begins to take place.[73] This causes a further problem, as to how the procedure that Rawls defends is itself to be assessed critically and legitimated.[74]

The importance of the communitarian model of citizenship that stresses political rights and active self-rule should not be overlooked. Within the framework of liberal holism, citizens are committed to the common good of their shared achievement of just institutions and the vigilant maintenance of those institutions over time. Only this will secure their individual rights and the effective value of the liberties they guarantee.[75] From this perspective all of our moral claims must be open to question since there is no reasonable way to decide in advance which claims are matters of political morality and which are not. The boundary between the political and the nonpolitical is constantly under negotiation in the ongoing democratic debates that are informed by our moralities. It seems to me that this is unavoidable as our comprehensive moralities, and therefore our conceptions of the good, always underpin our political moralities.

If we wish to question and to assess critically the presuppositions of those political moralities, then we are inevitably drawn into democratic deliberation about morally controversial issues. Given the plurality of reasonable conceptions of the good, it does not of course follow that a shared comprehensive morality should be the aim of our deliberation. There is no viable alternative to theorizing justice in a modern societies but to start by defending the priority of right. In this respect, I fully endorse Rawls's crucially important project. What I have argued here is that Rawls himself has not provided us with a convincing defense of that priority. In the third part of the book, I will argue that Habermas provides us with the basis for constructing a more convincing alternative.

A rejection of the method of avoiding public discussion over comprehensive moral views is necessary if we want to ensure that our democratic practices can be engaged in a self-critical assessment of their most fundamental moral presuppositions.[76] Rawls's recent strategy of avoidance gives sufficient evidence to suggest that he has not yet abandoned the unhelpful isolation of the political domain that dominates liberal thinking about justice. The most persuasive communitarian criticisms of liberalism can be used to highlight the inadequacy of that aspect of his procedural account of justice. I have argued in this chapter that if a convincing defence of liberal holism is to be mounted, then Rawls's attempt to isolate the political must be abandoned. In the next chapter I hope to strengthen this claim by assessing the work of some of Rawls's feminist critics.

2

The Feminist Challenge

The notion of an original position is to be thought of as an impartial procedure of justification for substantive principles of justice. Rawls introduces this particular procedure because he conceives of principles of justice as the fundamental terms of association that free and equal moral persons would agree to in an initial situation of fairness. These principles would then be accepted as the standards according to which all features of the basic structure of society are to be regulated.[1] In this chapter I want to draw on recent feminist political theory to argue that the original position represents an unjustifiably restrictive conception of political reasoning. By building on the assumed possibility of an isolated political morality, a possibility that I have already denied in the last chapter, Rawls's account of an impartial point of view is insufficiently sensitive to the pervasiveness of patriarchal injustice. If we are concerned to ensure that all political voices, particularly those at the margins of our political culture, are to be heard in our deliberations about justice, then the original position is seriously limited as a procedure of justification.

THE ORIGINAL POSITION AND THE DANGER OF MARGINALIZATION

The original position represents conditions of fairness that specify an impartial point of view. Rawls seeks to justify his two substantive principles of justice by arguing that they are the ones that would be chosen in the original position. If the conditions of agreement are fair, then the object of the agreement will also be fair and so the principles chosen provide us with a reasonable and stable basis for social unity. Obviously the outline of the original position is itself in need of some justification. Why should we think of it as specifying the conditions of an impartial point of view?

The idea that is central to Rawls's procedure is that all morally arbitrary aspects of our personality should be excluded from our considerations about justice. The feature of the original position that achieves this is the veil of ignorance. According to this notion, we must assume that in the original position none of the parties know their place in society, their class, their social status, their natural abilities such as intelligence, good looks, strength, their particular psychological propensities such as a tendency toward optimism, risk-taking, or envy.[2] We have already discussed communitarian objections to the fact that we are also to assume that in the original position none of the parties know their conception of the good. The idea of the veil of ignorance is to ensure that

> no one is advantaged or disadvantaged in the choice of principles by the outcome of natural chance or the contingency of social circumstances. Since all are similarly situated and no one is able to design principles to favor his particular condition, the principles of justice are the result of a fair agreement or bargain.[3]

All of the personal attributes that are excluded are to be thought of as morally arbitrary, as the contingent results of our good or bad fortune. Such matters should be considered irrelevant to the concerns of justice. Rawls supports this by pointing out that it is one of our considered convictions that the fact that I have a particular natural asset (say physical strength) or that I occupy a certain social position (say I'm a lawyer) is not a good reason for me to accept a conception of justice that favors people like me. I clearly have no good reason to expect others to accept such a conception either.[4] No person should be disadvantaged simply because they are not physically strong or because they are not lawyers. If they were to be so disadvantaged, that would be unjust. The argument is that the conditions of the original position provide the best available match for our considered moral judgments in reflective equilibrium.[5] They are, in other words, according to Rawls the conditions that we, here and now, actually do regard as fair.[6]

Rawls wants the parties to the contract not to be prejudiced or biased by knowledge of their particular natural assets or social circumstances for at least two reasons.[7] First, allowing such knowledge of contingencies would in practice make any agreement unlikely as different parties would be biased in different ways depending on their own good fortune. It would be impossible for us to say anything definite about justice at all. Second, the moral basis of the agreement would be undermined as the encounter in the original position would be informed by factors that do not reflect the highest-order interests of the parties. If we were not to exclude such knowledge, then any contract would almost certainly be partial toward those in a more powerful bargaining position. The less powerful would accept it for prudential, and not for moral, reasons.

Free and equal moral persons are to be motivated by their interests in choosing and revising a conception of the good and in exercising their sense of justice. This is why the conditions of the original position must be reasonable and fair, independent of chance and contingency, and grounded in the concern for rational autonomy that characterizes our moral personality. In the original position our interests are to be reconciled in a reasonable and impartial way.[8]

Rawls's use of the veil of ignorance reflects the isolation of the political by excluding from the original position all aspects of our moral personality that are not relevant to our public life as citizens of a democratic community. Our public identity as citizens does not include certain convictions and attachments that may be constitutive of our moral or "noninstitutional" identities.[9] While I might be disoriented, or even thrown into a crisis of personal identity, were I to think of myself as no longer committed to certain religious or moral convictions, these same convictions are not a part of my public, or political, identity as a citizen.

Thus, for example, Rawls would maintain that if it is my firm belief that Jesus is my Lord and Savior then that is undeniably fundamental to my self-understanding, but it is irrelevant to my public identity. For that, it is enough that I view myself as having the moral power to form and to revise some conception of the good, as a self-originating source of valid claims and as a being capable of taking responsibility for my own ends. In this way each of us is a politically free citizen. Since we all share this public identity, we are not only free but also equal as citizens. This concentration on our public identity as citizens is part of the method of avoidance that Rawls has espoused in his later writings. He wants to stay "on the surface, philosophically speaking" and to construct a workable conception of justice while avoiding controversies about religious, moral, and philosophical doctrine related to metaphysical questions of the truth or the nature of the self.[10]

We have already discovered, in assessing the import of some communitarian criticisms of Rawls's work, that the attempt to isolate the political leads him, first, to overestimate the extent to which the state can be neutral between conceptions of the good and, second, to underestimate the extent to which a procedural account of justice must reflect active participation by citizens in defense of the shared good of just institutions. The attempt to isolate the political will also ring alarm bells for feminists who will be suspicious of the possibility that patriarchal power is driving this attempted isolation. While Rawls feels the need to isolate the political for the sake of providing some moral basis of social unity, many feminists will suspect that the conception of the political involved may marginalize the concerns of women, and of certain excluded minorities, in its terms of reference.[11] It will repress difference for the sake of unity. It will exclude the concerns of some "other."[12]

Who are the "others" of Rawls's theory? If any social groups are likely to be excluded by his approach then it would probably be those who have been marginalized in the political culture of modern democratic societies. A nonexhaustive list of such groups might include women, nonwhites, non-Christians, lesbians and gays, children, future generations, those with special physical needs, those categorized as insane. Does the outline of the original position exclude these "others"? Does it in some way devalue them or marginalize their concerns? Does it, in other words, build certain hierarchical assumptions into its procedure of justification?

The parties to the original position are representative persons who hold the various social positions that are established by the basic structure of society.[13] Since all persons are to be represented, then at first glance it seems unlikely that Rawls can reasonably be accused of excluding from his framework some social groups. All features of people's lives that are the result of natural fortune or social circumstance are hidden behind the veil of ignorance so as not to disadvantage anyone for such arbitrary reasons in the choice of principles of justice. Although Rawls may not always be fully explicit about all of these features, the parties would have to be deprived of knowledge of their sex, their race, their social status, the generation to which they belong as well as their conception of the good, which presumably could include their religion, their ethnicity, and their sexual orientation and preference.

The strategy Rawls adopts in trying to ensure that no human actors are excluded in the original position, is to think of the parties in such a way that they are all identical to each other. All aspects of their lives that make them different from each other are shrouded in the veil of ignorance. The veil excludes all human features other than those features of our public identity as free and equal citizens. For Rawls, this exclusion is necessary in order to avoid the only exclusion that we should worry about in terms of a theory of justice between persons, that of other human actors. Only by eliminating from the original position whatever differentiates us from one another can we have any guarantee of impartiality, social unity, and justice for all citizens.

Feminists will be concerned that the conception of the citizen involved here may obliterate differences that are important in terms of the way that power operates. The use of the veil of ignorance amounts to an assumption that what is relevant for our public identity and what is not is uncontroversial and already fixed before we even come to assess possible principles of justice. Since the contract is hypothetical Rawls must presume that every reasonable person would and should agree to the conditions of the original position. The outline of the original position is built on the unwarranted assumption that we can isolate the political in our moral deliberations. To make this assumption is to overlook the fact that power, particularly patriarchal power, is not confined to the basic structure of society which is, for Rawls, the subject of justice.[14] Power does not respect a nonpublic sphere of autonomy for each individual but rather it can pervade all domains of modern society. It is for this reason that feminists are sceptical of a liberalism that typically concerns itself with rights and legislative practices while ignoring power in the form of "invisible societal constraints that defy such practices while continuing to influence them."[15]

Rawls's theory offers no clear way of testing whether or not marginalized groups within his own society have good reasons to accept the particular characterization of the political domain that the veil of ignorance represents. There is no account taken of the possibility that his understanding of the political will fail to match the considered moral judgments, on due reflection, of members of such groups. He runs the risk, therefore, of building his own biases into the outline of a supposedly impartial procedure from which a substantive account of justice is to be constructed. Rawls's conception of citizenship may actually draw on a particular view that reflects the self-image of a dominant social group. The only adequate test for this would be to conceive of an impartial point of view not as a hypothetical contract but rather as an open public debate where the participants could raise any matter as a potential subject of justice and where the constraints on the debate are not fixed once and for all before substantive issues can be considered.[16]

The public political culture from which Rawls begins to construct his political conception of justice, including the account of the original position and its veil of ignorance, has been shaped, in part at least, by the operation of power.[17] This means that there are potentially biased assumptions built into his conception of impartiality. What we need is an account of a public discourse where this account could rigorously be tested for potential bias. It would be a necessary feature of such a test that all those affected by its outcome could make a contribution in deciding what is and what is not politically relevant and what the most appropriate conditions of political justification would be. The potential bias of the ideas that Rawls takes to be implicit in our public political culture are, of course, not effectively tested within the original position itself. In that setting all parties are identical and so what takes place is not a dialogue but a monologue. The only real participant is Rawls himself as the constructivist theorist who provides us with a "philosophical soliloquy."[18]

What is most disturbing here is the danger of generating principles of justice that reflect, to some degree, the biases of dominant social groups within our public political culture. If the more subtle forms of social domination are adequately to be confronted in our procedure of justification for substantive principles of justice, then we will need an account of how such potential bias is to be detected and criticized. Feminists remind us to be suspicious of any account of impartiality that obscures difference for the sake of unity. In order to examine more carefully the defects of Rawls's conception of impartiality in this regard we should now look in more detail at the feminist charge that Rawls's theory has a male bias because he fails to comprehend the effects of power, and the need for justice, within the family.

JUSTICE IN THE FAMILY

There is some ambiguity in *A Theory of Justice* regarding the status of the family as a subject of justice. When Rawls gives examples of the major social institutions that are to be included as features of the basic structure of society, and therefore as parts of the primary subject of justice, he includes the "monogamous family." Since the basic structure is basic precisely because "its effects are so profound and present from the start" there was no option for Rawls but to include the family as one institution within that structure. The family is arguably the institution that most profoundly influences the life-prospects of individuals, "what they expect to be and how well they can hope to do."[19] Some starting places in life are favored over others due to the family circumstances into which an individual is born and in which nurturance and growth of that individual occurs.

It is clear that from Rawls's point of view the very deep inequalities involved here could not be said to be merited or deserved by those who have had the good fortune to benefit from them. Family circumstances determine to a very significant degree the expectations (the index of social primary goods; liberties and opportunities, income and wealth, and, most significantly, the bases of self-respect) that any representative individual could reasonably look forward to.[20] This is surely one of the most urgent problems that must be addressed if we are to try to regulate the major institutions of society according to the principles of justice that Rawls constructs from the procedure of the original position. We would have to ensure that any unequal distribution of primary goods is to the advantage of the least favored.[21] The fleeting reference to the monogamous family as part of the basic structure does not make it at all clear how the principles of justice are to apply to that institution.

It seems plausible that what Rawls meant by including the family as part of the basic structure was to indicate that it is a matter of justice whether or not some such public commitment between consenting individuals is legally protected. Marriage, for example, is a social institution that provides an important publicly supported option as to how individuals exercise their capacity to choose a long-term rational plan of life. If the existence of legal marriage, or any other legislation related to the family such as divorce or adoption law, could be shown to lead to inequalities that are not to the advantage of the least favored, then that would be unjust.

According to this interpretation, the family is a matter of justice only in this external sense in that we can and should regulate the legal constitution of the family so that the relevant options available for individuals are consistent with the principles of justice. This is quite different from the claim that the family is a matter of justice in an internal sense, that what goes on within the family can be assessed publicly in terms of justice and injustice. What this implies is a distinction between what constitutes the family externally and the order of the family internally. It seems to me that Rawls must assume some such external-internal distinction and that, furthermore, his inclusion of the family as a feature of the basic structure is only intended to allow for an assessment of the justice of the family in an external, but not in an internal, sense. If this were not the case it would be difficult to make sense of what he says, and does not say, about the family.

In *Political Liberalism*, with its attempted isolation of the political domain, this ambiguity concerning the justice of the family is all the more evident. The internal order of family life is assumed not to conflict with the demands of justice.[22] Rawls makes a clear distinction between the ideals of familial relationships and those expressed in a political conception of justice.[23] The familial is nonpolitical.[24] Although he does not do so explicitly, Rawls could perhaps discuss the external constitution of the family as a feature of the political domain. Since however the familial is nonpolitical, he could not treat the internal order of the family as a subject of justice. As we will see, the question of justice in the family highlights once again the overwhelming problems associated with Rawls's attempt to isolate the political. We must first consider why the family should be thought of as just or unjust internally as well as externally.

Feminists have argued that the internal structure of the traditional, monogamous, heterosexual family does raise questions of justice. The gender structure of modern societies, that is the social construction and institutionalization of sexual difference, particularly with regard to the division of labor within the traditional family, has led to serious injustice against women in terms of political and economic powers, opportunities and responsibilities.[25] To assume that the family is beyond the scope of a theory of justice is to deny that the traditional division of labor within the family is unjust. It is to deny that the public sphere of political and economic life is inextricably intertwined with the private domestic sphere of family life. We have already noted however that it is highly implausible to maintain that there are aspects of our private lives that are immune from the effects of power. This is what feminists mean by asserting that the personal is political. They mean that any attempt to exclude the general structure of personal, even intimate, relations from public reflection serves to conceal and protect the more subtle effects of power on the lives of women. Substantive political and economic equality between the sexes is now widely accepted, in public at least, to be a reasonable norm. Yet any genuine aspiration to make this substantive equality a reality demands a radical reconsideration of the ways in which the public and private spheres of life are intertwined.

In the first place it is impossible for the state not to have some effect on the domestic sphere. While much of the most obvious sex-based discrimination in family law has been removed, some laws, divorce laws for example, continue to privilege men in Western societies.[26] This creates a power imbalance both in marriage and in relationships where marriage, or its dissolution, is under consideration by one, or both, of the parties. There is a clear connection here between the external legal constitution of marriage and the internal order of family life. In any society that is rigidly gender-structured, the legal constitution of the family will affect women and men in different ways. What goes on within the family, the internal, is always being shaped and determined in part by legislation on the family, the external. If the family is part of the basic structure of society externally, then it is difficult to see how it could be argued that it is beyond justice internally.

It is not only direct legislation on the family that causes the internal order of the family to be intertwined with the basic structure. We have to take seriously the related facts that men continue to dominate in the public workplace while women continue to perform far more unpaid labor in the domestic sphere, most notably in the reproduction of life and the care of children. These facts combine to lead both to a serious underrepresentation of women in the public sphere and to the maintenance of significant obstacles to the achievement of equal respect for women in the workplace. Furthermore the continuing imbalance of work in and out of the home for women and men leads, through its effects on children, to the perpetuation of a patriarchal gender structure.

It appears to be the case therefore that the feminist deconstruction of any straightforward dichotomy between public and private supports the objections I raised in the last chapter to Rawls's attempt to isolate the political domain. It also seems clear that Rawls's failure to consider the internal order of the family to be a subject of justice highlights the danger of undetected and arbitrary bias infecting his conception of impartiality. This danger is connected to Rawls's restrictive conception of political reasoning. We can begin to analyze this in greater detail by assessing Susan Moller Okin's argument that Rawls's work is blind to the injustice of gender as embodied in the internal structure of the traditional family.[27]

GENDER BLINDNESS IN RAWLS'S THEORY

Given the sexism of the tradition in which Rawls writes, we might, with good reason, have expected that it would be made very explicit at every relevant point that the theory applies to women as well as to men.[28] In his initial account of the original position he does not mention that the parties should be deprived of knowledge of their sex.[29] Perhaps Rawls implicitly considered sex to be, from a moral point of view, an irrelevant category, but the fact that he neglects to mention it specifically may indicate an oversight on his part in failing to recognize the highly contentious issues surrounding the past exclusion of women from the scope of theories of justice as well as the continuing injustices of the gender structure.[30]

I have already suggested that we should think of Rawls's initial inclusion of the family as part of the basic structure to have been intended in an external sense only. This seems plausible because certain other features of his theory seem to require him to assume that the family is internally just. He never discusses the institutions of the family directly when he comes to assess how the principles of justice he derives from the original position apply to the institutions of the basic structure, such as the political constitution, property relations, and economic arrangements. This might lead to some doubts as to whether or not he intended to include the family as a subject of justice even in an external sense.[31] It is not clear why he ignores family law as an institution of the basic structure of a well-ordered society except perhaps that he realized that it would be impossible to discuss the question of the external justice of the family's legal constitution without also treating the internal order of the family as a matter of justice. There are reasons why he would want to avoid this.

Rawls suggests that we think of the parties in the original position as heads of families.[32] This allows us to think of them as being motivated to care for some members of the next generation and so ensures that the interests of the latter are taken into account, something that is particularly important in relation to the question of justice between generations and the savings principle.[33] Although Rawls adheres to traditional assumptions by using examples of fathers and sons in the discussion of this problem, it could fairly readily be claimed that the head of the family need not be the father.[34] However, what cannot be denied is that by suggesting that we think of the parties to the original position as representatives of families he does assume that the family itself is internally just. As Okin puts it

> he is thereby effectively trapped into the public/domestic dichotomy and, with it, the conventional mode of thinking that life within the family and relations between the sexes are not properly regarded as part of the subject matter of a theory of social justice.[35]

This of course means that the claims of less advantaged members of a family, usually women and children, are not adequately taken into account in the original position. Even though Rawls challenges discrimination against women in the public sphere, it is his inability to theorize adequately the relationship between the political and the nonpolitical, the external constitution and the internal order of the family that leaves him vulnerable to this charge.[36] He simply does not dig deep enough into the gender structure to identify effectively the roots of discrimination based on sexual difference.

Further evidence that Rawls assumes an internally just family can be offered by considering his comments on how the family sets a limit to the operation of fair equality of opportunity.[37] Families within one social sector may differ in the way in which the aspirations of the children are shaped. For this reason Rawls considers whether or not the family should be abolished. But he feels that the difference principle and the principles of "fraternity" and redress, all of which are designed to ensure that any social inequalities are to the benefit of the worst-off, make any disadvantages in this regard easier to bear. At no stage does Rawls question whether the traditional division of labor within the family should be confronted and challenged as a matter of justice. This seems to indicate that he is blind to the importantly different ways in which the aspirations of girls and boys are shaped in the context of the traditional family. He is also blind to the fact that this difference contributes to the perpetuation of the present gender structure.

Finally, Rawls assumes that the family is internally just in his discussion of the central role it plays in the development of the individual's sense of justice.[38] Children's moral development depends crucially on the internal order of the family and the way in which the parents exemplify their own morality. Throughout his account Rawls fails to consider how the division of labor within the family might involve an injustice to one of the parents. This is a serious flaw in the theory since it depends so heavily on our moral capacity to have a sense of justice. If our sense of justice is distorted from the start because of the structure of the traditional family then it seems likely that the subsequent moral development of the individual will be shot through with assumptions about gender.[39]

It seems that Rawls never satisfactorily deals with the family as a subject of justice.[40] He includes it in the list of institutions of the basic structure because it would be absurd not to do so given the profound effects of family circumstances on the individual's chances in life. Yet he omits to question whether or not the family is itself internally just. I have argued here that this omission was unavoidable for him since he needs to assume an internally just family for the sake of some other central features of the theory. This is why he only included the family as part of the basic structure in an external sense. We might note however that that the question of external justice is itself never adequately dealt with in Rawls's very detailed analysis of the institutions of a well-ordered society. Surely, family law relating to marriage, divorce, and adoption, as well as questions related to claims of rights for gay and lesbian marriages, and issues such as polygamous or arranged marriages merited some discussion in this broad analysis of the basic structure.[41] It would appear that Rawls is unwilling to consider seriously justice in the family in any sense.

Perhaps this is so because he wants to avoid the communitarian criticism, that he presupposes in his account of the original position a metaphysical conception of an atomistic, unencumbered, disembodied human self. As we have already seen, Rawls has responded by arguing that the original position, as a device of representation, relies only on a political conception of the person as a free and equal citizen and not on any metaphysical view of the person. This political conception simply avoids any aspects of our comprehensive moral views that are not relevant politically. At the same time, these views may reflect private ties of affection, devotion, or loyalty in the personal life of the citizen.

Now it is often within the family that such ties of affection, which constitute in part the personal identity of the citizen, will be most intensely experienced. From Rawls's point of view it is necessary to abstract from these ties of affection, to leave them behind the veil of ignorance, in order to construct a workable conception of justice. This might help to explain why he is reluctant to consider the family as a subject of political justice. But, as we have seen, the use of the veil of ignorance involves certain dangers because it tends to take for granted what is and what is not of relevance to a publicly affirmed political morality. In the last chapter I argued that the political is not so easily isolated. I think that the consideration of feminist arguments related to injustices within the family strengthens that criticism.[42]

Justice, Care, and Solidarity

There is another important issue, related to the procedure outlined in the original position, that has been put on the agenda by feminist theorists. This has to do with the charge that to consider the type of abstract reflection on justice that takes place in the original position to be representative of the highest stage of moral reasoning is to reveal a male bias. Justice emphasizes separation and autonomy, while care, which according to the empirical research of Carol Gilligan is of greater significance in the actual moral judgments of women, emphasizes connectedness and interdependence.[43] It has been argued that Rawls's concentration on justice and his abstraction from the concrete context of care for others contributes to the continued repression of the voice of women in contemporary moral theory. This argument has been made most effectively by Seyla Benhabib.[44]

Benhabib builds on Gilligan's claim that women's moral judgment is typically more immersed in the details of relationships, in the awareness of the standpoint of particular others, in feelings of empathy and sympathy for the differing needs of others whom we encounter in the context of concrete human interaction. If the findings of Gilligan's research are valid then it seems to imply that any vision of moral maturity that stresses separation and abstraction rather than connection and interaction arbitrarily undervalues care and our responsibility to concrete others. An ethic of care provides a necessary complement to an ethic of justice and a fully adequate account of morality cannot afford to divorce one from the other. They must both be placed together at the center of a moral theory's concern.[45] The important implication from our point of view here is that an adequate theory of justice must take an ethic of care into account.

It does not follow that care is essentially a matter for women or that justice is essentially a matter for men. On the contrary, this has been one of the chief ideological weapons that has helped to institutionalize the present gender structure, which deprives women of an adequate voice in public affairs. The point that Gilligan's work underlines is that if we neglect the contexts of care in our theoretical accounts of justice, then we are reinforcing patriarchal assumptions that privilege the traditionally male public concern for justice over the traditionally female private concern for care and nurturance. Our efforts to overcome gender-based oppression will be better supported by developing perspectives on justice that draw on, rather than exclude, the moral role that care plays in the everyday relationships that women and men have with particular others.

Benhabib argues that Rawls eliminates from his procedure of justification any real differences between us and any connection we might have to other concrete individuals. He tries to theorize justice without taking any account of an ethic of care. He deals only with the need for public justice among autonomous individuals. Of course, there is still a very important distinction between justice and care, but Rawls makes too sharp a division between them and so fails to pay sufficient attention to the role that care for the concrete other has to play in theorizing justice.

In the original position the other is a generalized other, not a concrete other, since all features that distinguish one party from the other are hidden. The parties do not experience any interactive encounter with concrete others. They do not hear any call for mutual recognition of the differing needs, desires, and perspectives that would be represented in such an encounter.[46] The moral dignity of each party comes from whatever they have in common, their two formal moral powers, rather than whatever particularizes them, their individuality, their distinctive needs and interests. This implies that our reflections on justice are informed by abstract reasoning alone and not by moral considerations that emerge in the light of an experience of the distinctive needs of concrete others. Much of our moral experience is thereby ignored.

Benhabib's objection to Rawls's procedure indicates that in order to make any moral decisions about justice we need to draw on our knowledge of the particular needs of concrete others. Without this we run the risk of assuming that care for one another, and for the intersubjective bonds that bind each of us to some significant others, has no role to play in the justification of a public conception of justice. These moral concerns are relegated to the private sphere of the family and other intimate relationships. Benhabib's accusation is that Rawls's procedure marginalizes these concerns in a way that distorts our thinking about justice.[47]

This does not mean that the generalized other, the stress on the formal moral powers that we all share, has no role to play in characterizing an impartial point of view. According to Benhabib

> the recognition of the dignity and worthiness of the generalized other is a necessary, albeit not sufficient, condition to define the moral standpoint in modern societies. In this sense the concrete other is a critical concept that designates the ideological limits of universalistic discourse. It signifies the unthought, the unseen, and the unheard in such theories.[48]

What is important is that we come to recognize the dignity and the rights of the generalized other through an acknowledgment of real concrete others. This can only take place in a process of political engagement and dialogue and not through abstraction from everything that differentiates individuals, or social groups, from one another.

Now it may be argued that an ethic of care simply involves an inappropriately strong commitment among citizens who seek justice but not any ties of sentiment or affection. Certainly an intimate concern for the needs of each individual is not a realistic requirement for all participants seeking fair terms of cooperation in a political context. But the demand to incorporate the standpoint of the concrete other in our reflections on justice need not be interpreted as requiring such care for all concrete individual others. Rather we could shift the emphasis, as Nancy Fraser suggests, from the standpoint of an individualized concrete other to that of a collective concrete other.[49] Adopting the standpoint of the collective concrete other still involves real interactive encounters and so rules out any attempt to hide particular needs, desires, and feelings behind a veil of ignorance. We encounter the others, however, not so much as individuals for whom we have feelings of care but rather as members of social groups with distinctive identities, needs, and forms of life. Such a shift leads us to think of the bonds of solidarity that are to sustain collective concrete others as a necessary component of our thinking on justice. We cannot concern ourselves with the rights of concrete others without also taking into account the bonds of solidarity on which the formation of their particular identity depends.[50]

The controversy about justice and care invites a reconsideration of the type of reasoning that is required of each of us if we are to consider matters of justice from an impartial point of view. Once behind the veil of ignorance, the parties to the contract cannot be sensitive to the actual experience of the least advantaged groups in society, the worst-off collective concrete others. This is because none of the parties, who are of course identical to one another, can speak from that particular perspective. Yet how are we to convince ourselves that the original position does in fact represent conditions of fairness? Surely, we would not accept the idea that we should reason about justice behind a veil of ignorance if we were not already sensitive to the plight of actual groups that are least advantaged in our own society? But this sensitivity could only develop through reflection on the ways in which the needs of some collective concrete others, particularly the least advantaged, are different from our own. Yet such reflection on differing needs is excluded from Rawls's procedure of justifying principles of justice.

If all participants reflecting on the demands of justice were to adopt the standpoint of the collective concrete other, then each of them would be enabled "to speak and be heard, to tell one's own life-story, to press one's claims and point of view in one's own voice."[51] This would be an important feature of a procedure of impartiality that, in contrast to Rawls's original position, would reflect differences in an effective way. Each social group that is suffering some form of injustice at present could articulate publicly its own needs. This articulation generates solidarity among those who come to recognize the particular injustice for what it is. The necessity of bringing this generation of solidarity into the heart of a theory of justice owes much to recent feminist theory. But there is nothing essentially feminine about the recognition of collective concrete others. The insights involved correct a distortion in the thinking of men and women who seek to eliminate all particularity from impartial procedures that are to test principles of justice.

IMPARTIALITY AND DIFFERENCE

The extent to which Rawls's approach could be revised in ways that would allow him to evade the sting of these criticisms has been a matter of some dispute among feminist theorists. Okin believes that Rawls's work represents a potentially rich source for a critique of the gender structure of contemporary societies.[52] This would, of course, require certain modifications in order to overcome all aspects of gender blindness in the theory. For example, it should be made very clear that the parties to the original position must not only be deprived of knowledge of their sex, but they must also be thought of as representing individuals rather than heads of families. This would remove one obstacle to a consideration of the internal order of the family as a subject of justice. We might then be able to confront the question of fair equality of opportunity between the sexes and the tendency for gendered assumptions to infect the moral development of children at an early stage of development. We might also suggest that the parties be deprived of knowledge as to whether they are to be parents or not, thus providing some guarantee that the interests of the next generation are taken into account, without assuming a just family.

While there seems to be some potential here for a cogent critique of certain aspects of the gender structure, there remain more fundamental flaws in Rawls's conception of impartiality that undermine its potential usefulness as a tool of feminist criticism. We must recall the fact that while Rawls himself remains reluctant to allow the family to be considered as a subject of justice in an internal sense, his theory will, according to Okin, contain "an internal paradox."[53] On the one hand, the theory depends on an understanding of moral development where our capacity to have a sense of justice must be nurtured in the context of a loving and just family. On the other hand, however, Rawls does not himself apply the principles of justice to the realm of the family. But we have seen that he cannot afford to do so while continuing to advocate the strategy of avoidance that is involved in his attempt to isolate the political.

Furthermore, Rawls is not sufficiently aware of the fact that within a gender-structured society it seems likely that there will be a difference of emphasis in the ways in which men and women reason morally. It is for this reason that it is absolutely imperative, from a feminist perspective, that solidarity be considered to be a core concern of any adequate theory of justice. Under gendered conditions the structure of the society in general, and of the family in particular, leads to the fact that women are more likely to be involved in nurturing activities and hence they are more likely to stress solidarity in their moral reasoning, while men, for whom separation appears to be more important, will stress justice in terms of abstract individual rights. In a society where gender-based oppression had been overcome one might expect all members of both sexes to have integrated successfully solidarity and justice in their capacity for moral reasoning.

Now this relates to the way in which impartiality is conceptualized in the account of the original position. The conditions of choice that the original position represents may not be equally acceptable to all. Those conditions require us to abstract in our reflections on justice from concrete experiences in which solidarity is generated. Unanimity, if it is to be possible at all regarding principles of justice, can only be the result of open common deliberation where all participants reach the same conclusion having argued through their differences. It could not be reached by abstracting from those differences. Only in an open public encounter could the effects of the gender structure on the differing stresses in people's moral reasoning be identified and challenged. Ironically, our conclusion must be that rather than enabling us to overcome gender structuring, the original position must presuppose that this has already been achieved if it is to fulfil its task as a critical tool that could ground an agreement on principles of justice.[54]

While Okin is aware of the fact that contemporary gendered conditions place the coherence of the original position in doubt, she defends its usefulness against the criticisms of theorists who, like Benhabib and Fraser, maintain that the original position is fundamentally flawed in that it allows no role at all for a sense of solidarity with collective concrete others.[55] For these critics, the original position abstracts from all particularity and represents a monological procedure that obscures, represses, and denies difference. In response, Okin recalls the fact that the combination of mutual disinterest and the veil of ignorance in the original position "achieves the same purpose as benevolence"[56] without requiring Rawls to make strong assumptions about the motivation of the parties. But rather than endorse a rational choice interpretation of the argument, Okin maintains that moral feelings are crucial to the derivation of the principles of justice.[57] Since the parties do not know which position they are going to have in society, they would have to consider the interests of people in all possible positions. They cannot think from the position of nobody, but rather they must think from the position of everybody.

It follows that for us to enter the original position, to adopt it as a morally impartial point of view according to Okin's interpretation of it, we would have to be motivated by empathy and strongly committed to benevolence. These are hardly weak assumptions. This is because we have to consider the goals and aims of all others, no matter how different they are from us, to be of equal concern in our reflections in the original position. Indeed, this would involve our "caring about each and every other as much as about ourselves."[58] Far from abstracting from all particularity, this implies that the original position indicates a deep concern for all human difference. An ethic of care is, on this reading, indistinguishable from an ethic of justice. We must be capable of recognizing differences between ourselves and "concrete others," of being empathetic with them and of caring for them if we are to formulate principles of justice that could be acceptable to all.

Okin's stress on care here again seems rather inappropriate. It is a feeling of solidarity with all social groups who suffer injustice, rather than a intimate feeling of care for all individual others that is relevant in our reflections about justice. Not only is such care too demanding in this context, it is also, unlike solidarity, a feeling that can easily allow for overprotective, patronizing attitudes toward marginalized groups. Emphasizing care also tends to obscure the important distinction between those significant others with whom our personal identity is inextricably entwined and our fellow citizens with whom we share little else but a commitment to just political institutions.

Solidarity better embodies the type of respect for collective concrete others that supports all who suffer injustice and drives each of us to choose principles and to design institutions so as to put that injustice right. As I already outlined, it is solidarity for the collective concrete other rather than care, that must be integrated with the generalized other's claim to justice. The integration of solidarity into the core of a theory of justice does not involve the incorporation of inappropriate affective elements into the choice of principles of justice. It merely affirms the fact that one cannot respect the rights of individuals without also protecting and generating the intersubjective bonds of solidarity on which the particular identities of those individuals depend.

Benhabib agrees with Okin to the extent that she recognizes the need for a universalist moral theory that defines an impartial point of view, where the needs and interests of all concerned must be taken into consideration. The crucial question here is how we, as citizens, are best enabled to adopt this point of view, where we can acknowledge the rights of others through a recognition of their concrete otherness. The issue brings into opposition what Benhabib calls "substitutionalist" and "interactive" universalist moral theories.[59] While Okin undoubtedly has provided an interpretation of Rawls where an ethic of justice and an ethic of care are no longer opposed, she still defends a version of "substitutionalist" universalism that is inadequate to the task of facilitating genuine mutual understanding of otherness.

It is the restrictions on reasoning set by the veil of ignorance that make any possible reading of the role of the original position to be necessarily "substitutionalist." All we can know about the others is that they have the same very general interests as ourselves. We do not have to confront whatever it is that makes us different from the other imaginary participants, since none of the parties can speak from any particular perspective. The result is that no intersubjectively generated insight into principles of justice is possible. In imagining oneself in the original position, one does not have to listen to the particular experiences of others. This is surely inadequate as a device that is to enable us to take up the perspective of all.

It would seem much more plausible that we would come to a mutual understanding of each other's needs and interests if we were to discuss them and argue about them in the light of all the information that would open our eyes to the differences between us. Despite Okin's optimism we cannot simply trust that empathy and benevolence will guarantee that the interests of all are adequately taken into account. We need to listen and to reflect in ways that allow us to take into account what it would really be like to occupy a different position in society, to be a woman rather than a man, to be black rather than white, to be unemployed rather than a managing director of a large company.

I am suggesting that in any procedural test for substantive principles of justice, all citizens must be allowed to speak for themselves and the only way that we can hear them is if we reason without the veil of ignorance in a real dialogue where our prejudices and hostilities could be tested and worked through interactively. We cannot substitute ourselves for all others in the original position but rather we must confront each other interactively in collective moral and political deliberation. If we were to have the capacity to take the interests of all into account, we could not do it alone but only as participants in a collective venture. Once we had attempted to engage with each other in public dialogue by trying to work through our disagreements, then perhaps we might decide to test our collective views about justice in a monologically carried out thought experiment, such as that outlined in the original position. We may indeed all reach the same conclusions. If this were so then our collective deliberation would have done its work and the original position would not have been in any way necessary. If we reached different conclusions, then it would be a sign that we were still in need of more collective deliberation. Again in this case the original position would do nothing to resolve those disagreements except perhaps to confirm what should already have been obvious from the public discourse, that we were still some way short of reaching agreement on appropriate principles of justice.

In the original position all social groups are to be represented but the identity of each is to be concealed, as if their faces were blank. This does not seem nearly as effective a challenge to unreasonableness as the prospect of encountering other real participants and having to deliberate over principles of justice with them, with the full face of each in view. The prospect of reasoned agreement is best served by lifting the veil of ignorance and allowing all participants to express themselves fully, to be visible in their particularity to all the others, as they engage in the cooperative venture of determining principles of justice to fashion their political institutions in a way that does justice to them all.

In such a real dialogue there is no restriction laid down in advance as to what is a subject of justice and what is not, what is an aspect of political morality and what is not. That must be worked out by the participants themselves, and the boundary between the political and the nonpolitical is always under negotiation. In this way, we can see that communitarian and feminist critiques of Rawls coincide on this point that I have returned to throughout this discussion—that Rawls's attempt to isolate the political prior to public discussion fails. If we wish to work out adequately what the scope of justice is, then we will need a moral and political theory that can incorporate the stronger arguments of these critical perspectives. We will need a theory that does not assume a political domain that can be dealt with in isolation from the rest of the moral domain but rather one that deals with the constitution of that political domain as a matter of ongoing concern for all the citizens of a democratic community.

We can think of a number of social groups that have in the past suffered some form of arbitrary exclusion from the public arena. These groups have asserted their rights as citizens to have their perspectives represented adequately in public deliberations. Their appeal for full inclusion depends on the assertion of their difference and that appeal demands that the boundary of the political domain be renegotiated.[60] Whatever was previously considered to be a matter of no political relevance is placed in the public realm as an effect of power and a subject of justice. Examples might include the struggle for legislation to improve working conditions that followed the inclusion of working people in the public realm, the struggle against cultural stereotyping that followed the inclusion of ethnic and racial minorities, the struggle to include domestic violence as a matter of public concern that followed the inclusion of women, and the struggle against discrimination on the basis of sexual orientation that followed the open inclusion of lesbians and gays in the public arena.

These groups have resisted the power that had previously constituted them as citizens, they have refused that identity and have struggled for new forms of subjectivity that demand a renegotiation of the boundary of the political domain. It has been through public reflection on the differences between various groups of citizens, and not what they have in common, that has made possible this form of resistance to power. An adequate conception of the political can only be produced dialogically in an ongoing public struggle. The choice of substantive principles will be all the more inclusive, with less potential for bias, if every social group represents itself and is allowed to, and encouraged to, articulate its own particular needs and concerns. Of course, such a public dialogue would have to be subject to some constraints that would constitute an impartial point of view or else no agreement on principles of justice would be possible at all. We will see in the third part, however, that these constraints can be justified without restricting the content of our public dialogue about justice.

In this part of the book I have sought to highlight certain serious defects in John Rawls's procedural test for the justification of substantive principles of justice. The most serious defect is the attempt to isolate political aspects of morality from other aspects of our comprehensive moralities. This strategy for the construction of an overlapping consensus is less inclusive, and therefore a less stable basis for social unity, than Rawls must assume it to be. I have maintained that, despite certain communitarian claims, Rawls advocates a version of liberal holism. His attempt to construct an overlapping consensus is, however, undermined by the concern to avoid moral controversy in our disputes about justice. I have not questioned the claim that impartiality remains a crucial dimension of social justice in a modern society that seeks to accommodate a plurality of reasonable conceptions of the good. We will need a conception of impartiality that can make room for public articulation of the differing perspectives and comprehensive moral views that characterize modern pluralism. In other words, we need to think of impartiality more contextually, to ground our conception of an impartial point of view in our experience of diversity and public contestation.

The project then is to conceive of how we might reflect critically, and impartially, on principles of justice without abstracting from concrete needs and interests that are particular to some social group or other. The hope is that we can bring to the task of justifying principles of justice our comprehensive moralities, our conceptions of the good, our feelings of solidarity for specific collective others, our experiences of family life, our criticisms of the procedure of justification itself. How can all of these matters be raised and discussed openly without giving up on the claim that impartiality represents the core of justice in a modern context? This will only be possible if we can ground impartiality not in a hypothetical contract but rather in a conception of a reasonable yet open and unrestricted dialogue in the public domain. This is precisely the kind of conception that is presented in Habermas's discourse ethics. Before we look in detail at that alternative we should consider an influential theory of justice that is presented as an alternative to impartialism. I will turn now to Michael Walzer's contextualist account of justice, where the emphasis is on taking seriously the plurality of historically unique political societies.

II

Michael Walzer's Contextualism

3

Hermeneutics and Justice

So far we have considered one highly influential presentation of a procedural test for the justification of substantive principles of justice. The
aspiration of Rawls's project is to conceive of an impartial point of view
that could ground a normative assessment of social institutions and
practices. The hope is to do this by providing us with a standard according to which the reasonableness of competing claims about justice that
might arise in a modern society could be assessed critically. The procedure deals with the plurality of conceptions of the good in modern societies by insisting that in order to adopt an impartial point of view, we
must abstract from our comprehensive moral commitments so as to
eliminate them from our reflection about the choice of principles of justice. I have highlighted the weaknesses of Rawls's approach without,
however, endorsing a rejection of his impartialist project. In this part of
the book I will consider the views of a political theorist who urges us to
do precisely that.

COMPLEX EQUALITY

For Michael Walzer, the attempt to provide a philosophical justification for
an impartial point of view that can test the reasonableness of substantive
claims about justice should be abandoned. He maintains that justice is
always embedded in the moral world of a particular form of life and that
such abstract proceduralism therefore necessarily violates the self-understanding of particular communities.[1] For Walzer every account of justice is
a local account.[2] It must be given, not with reference to an abstract procedure that claims to represent an impartial point of view, but rather from
within the context of a particular commitment to a shared understanding
of social goods. A substantive account of justice is an interpretation of the
meaning of social goods, and more specifically the principles of distribution
that are inherent in those meanings for a particular community. The meanings that are interpreted are necessarily common social meanings to which
no one individual has privileged access. The conditions under which such

an account can be given must therefore be characterized by a public encounter where these meanings are cooperatively interpreted. The implication for theoretical reflection on justice is that the historical particularity of different political communities must be taken seriously. Walzer's main concern is to do justice to pluralism in our second sense, the plurality of differently constituted political societies. He does this by stressing the interpretive, or hermeneutic, dimension of our reflection on justice.

Walzer advocates a conception of substantive justice that he calls complex equality.[3] According to this conception, substantive principles of justice depend on the meanings that social goods have in particular societies. Principles of justice are implicit in the social meanings of particular goods, and each society will have its own distinctive account of justice. The account depends on the meanings that goods have in that particular historical and cultural context. While no bald principle of simple equality can be sensitive to cultural particularity in this way, Walzer's claim is that complex equality can prevent injustice by allowing each citizen to have their due in each of the variety of spheres of justice that are constituted by the meanings that the variety of social goods will have in any given society.

It is interesting to contrast complex equality with the two substantive principles of justice that Rawls advocates.[4] Complex equality is intended to provide the contours for a detailed, contextually sensitive account of justice for a particular society. It indicates explicitly how justice varies in its demands in different cultural contexts. The cultural creativity of particular communities must be given expression in the details of each substantive account of justice. The stress that Walzer places on context sensitivity leads him to reject the impartialist project. Principles of justice are for him necessarily a cultural product and so they cannot be derived from any abstract, moral-philosophical procedure. The substance of justice must be interpreted openly in public deliberation where all citizens are encouraged to participate.

The problem with Rawls's two substantive principles from Walzer's perspective is that they are too general to be of any use in real concrete disputes about justice. This is a consequence of their being derived through a procedure that abstracts from cultural particularity. The abstraction allows Rawls to consider only the distribution of what he calls primary goods such as "rights and liberties, opportunities and powers, income and wealth."[5] These are the goods that are supposedly wanted by all individuals whatever else they want.[6] In other words, the primary goods are not dependent on any particular conception of the good. Furthermore, the logic of distribution from the standpoint of the original position is, of course, the same with regard to all the primary goods. It is assumed that the parties "would prefer more primary goods rather than less."[7] This, then, is the only logic of distribution that enters into Rawls's consideration of the demands of justice.

Walzer rejects both the notion of a primary good, one that can be conceived of independently of a particular shared conception of the good, and also the reductive logic of distribution that such an idea entails. A primary good is necessarily too abstract to be of any use in working out particular just distributions. Even goods that are valued as necessities in almost all particular contexts have different social meanings from one culture to another.[8] Distributive principles are intrinsic to the meaning of the social goods that are to be distributed. In other words, just social arrangements demand that goods get distributed for different reasons, depending on what reasons are relevant to the social meaning of a specific good in a particular cultural context. The details of what is involved in any dispute about justice will require empirical investigation since there is "no merely intuitive or speculative procedure for seizing upon relevant reasons."[9]

The most significant feature of Walzer's approach is that it encourages us to think about substantive principles as being internal to a variety of spheres of justice. Each sphere has its own logic of distribution and each society has its own complex map of distributive spheres.[10] This enables Walzer to elaborate in detail on the requirements of equal citizenship. Walzer's conception of citizenship conceives of politics as "only one (though it is probably the most important) among many spheres of social activity."[11] This pluralist conception demands that social goods be distributed not according to one reductive logic, but for reasons internal to their social meaning.[12] Citizenship is therefore not to be conceived of as a political notion in a narrow sense but rather more broadly as membership of a community where the task of justice is to be thought of as a matter of allowing each social good to be distributed according to the logic intrinsic to its own sphere.[13]

Complex equality involves the critique of the dominance of any one social good.[14] Justice for Walzer is a matter of protecting separate spheres of social goods from the imposition of principles that are not intrinsic to the meaning of those goods. This concern leads him to formulate an open-ended distributive principle:

> No social good x should be distributed to men and women who possess some other good y merely because they possess y and without regard to the meaning of x.[15]

This principle recognizes the plurality of historically unique political communities in two ways. First, each particular community will have its own map of substantive justice that will reflect its distinctive, culturally created social meanings. Second, there will be an indeterminate number of distributive principles in any given society, each of them being appropriate to a particular sphere of justice. Each distributive norm must operate with relative autonomy within its own sphere but it should have no direct bearing on the distributions in other spheres.

Complex equality is concerned with blocking exchanges between goods if the exchanges violate the social meaning of the goods involved. Thus if I hold political office I should not be able to convert that good into better health care than that available to other citizens. That would be to violate the social meaning of health care, at least in certain Western societies. The meaning of health care in that context is that it is something which is provided to those in the community who are ill, and so its logic of distribution must be the criterion of need.[16] But this does not mean that I should not have certain political privileges. If I have been fairly elected to office then I have been entrusted with a certain amount of power because my constituents find me to be a capable representative of their political views. So while it is just for me to speak in parliament say, it is certainly not just that I receive better health care on the basis of my success at being elected for political office. It follows that while we may receive unequal shares within a particular sphere no group can convert this to their own advantage across all the spheres. The separation of spheres allows citizens to enjoy their own accomplishments without the threat of any one group constituting a ruling class.[17]

The broad conception of citizenship involved in complex equality allows us to think of citizens as ruling themselves without binding them as individuals too tightly to the community. What it requires is

> not that citizens rule and are ruled in turn, but that they rule in one sphere and are ruled in another—where "rule" means not that they exercise power but that enjoy a greater share than other people of whatever good is being distributed.[18]

Walzer can claim to be an egalitarian in so far as complex equality can "spread the satisfaction of ruling more widely," thus ensuring the "compatibility of being ruled and respecting oneself."[19] His conception of a political community therefore does not depend on the active participation of all citizens in the narrowly defined political domain. It does however depend on citizens being active in one sphere of justice or another.[20] This involves a rejection of a strongly holist, Aristotelian or Rousseauean, conception of community in favor of a more liberal holism that does not tie the citizen too closely to the narrowly defined political aspects of community life.[21] Rawls's vision of community as a social union of social unions has much in common with Walzer's view.[22] I am arguing here that complex equality facilitates a more detailed account of justice for that vision than do the principles Rawls himself defends.

Complex equality is, for example, not vulnerable to the charge that has been made against the difference principle, that in treating natural talents as common assets it undermines Rawls's commitment to the distinctness of individuals.[23] From Walzer's point of view there is no need to ensure that all inequalities are to the greatest benefit of the least advantaged in any one sphere of justice. Once the autonomy of the spheres is protected, there is good reason to believe that each citizen will be able to benefit from whatever individual talent they happen to have. If we get the map of complex equality right, then nobody will be excluded or marginalized.[24] Complexity is our best defense against tyranny.

The move away from direct state intervention as a means of achieving justice obviously sits more easily with the critics of Rawls's work who draw attention to the fact that he fails to theorize adequately the idea of a public sphere or a realm of civil society.[25] We might think of autonomous associations as groups of citizens who are actively concerned with the regulation of spheres of justice that are not political in a narrow sense. By defending the boundary of a sphere, they act as a check on the danger of state tyranny. Walzer, unlike Rawls, does not treat intermediate, voluntary associations as marginal to the subject of justice.[26] Rather than depending on the active intervention of the welfare-state into civil society, the other spheres of justice play a vital role in defending us against tyranny. Since each of us could "rule" in one sphere or another, we can all participate in the achievement of just institutions without all of us being actively involved in the more narrowly defined institutional domain of politics. A complex map of justice allows for the political domain to be differentially related to, rather than isolated from, the other spheres of social activity.[27]

Walzer's open-ended, hermeneutic approach to substantive principles of justice is therefore context-sensitive in ways that Rawls's impartialism is not. As well as taking seriously the plurality of differently constituted political societies, his understanding of social goods as being conceived of and created in particular cultural contexts brings out very clearly the significance of the notion of self-rule as an important source of the dignity of citizenship.[28] This reflects the fact that the defence of just institutions must be conceived of holistically, as a communal project. Furthermore, justice is more concerned on this account with the recognition of difference, both between and within communities, rather than building on the assumption that everybody will reason in the same way regarding the choice of principles.[29] From a feminist perspective, Walzer can, and does, include the family as a sphere of justice.[30] His particularist focus also indicates the significant role that solidarity with concrete others has to play in our reflections on justice. With all this in mind we must now turn our attention to the contextual form of justification that Walzer offers as an alternative to an impartialist grounding for substantive principles.

JUSTICE WITHOUT PROCEDURES

The recent shift toward contextualist approaches to justice reflects a general trend away from universalism in moral theory.[31] This is a trend which raises important philosophical questions, not least with regard to the inherent dangers of relativism. It might be suggested for example, that a hermeneutic approach to justice, such as that which is advanced by Walzer, must necessarily involve a relativistic endorsement of institutions and practices that characterize a particular culture. It might then be thought to be irredeemably conservative and incapable of grounding any adequate form of social criticism. The implication of this type of objection is that hermeneutically grounded accounts of justice always legitimate the dominance of one particular account of justice in a way that is entirely inappropriate in a modern pluralist society.

In the next chapter I will seek to highlight the serious limitations of a hermeneutics of justice. I will argue there that if we are to do justice to the plurality of individual conceptions of the good in each modern society, pluralism in the first sense, then we need to endorse, and not to abandon, the impartialist project. In a modern context some procedural conception of an impartial point of view is indispensable to an adequate understanding of how substantive principles of justice are to be justified. Hermeneutic criticism will be shown to be dangerously partial. In relation to the demands of justice, hermeneutics could not, for this reason, act as a substitute for a philosophical conception of an impartial point of view. While I will begin to defend this position in the next chapter, the argument will not be complete until we consider Habermas's alternative procedural conception of impartiality.

In the remainder of this chapter, however, I want to suggest that hermeneutics can defend itself, at least to some extent, from the charge of conservatism. How can principles of justice derived within one tradition be used to criticize the institutions and practices of that same tradition? In response to this critical question I want to indicate how we might understand the interpretation of substantive principles within particular traditions as an important form of social criticism. Ethical reflection on the identity of a political community can allow for self-criticism in highly significant ways. When faced with the question as to whether or not a particular community has lived up to its own ideals as to what it should be, a significant space is opened up for immanent critique. This can happen in a way that is related to the interpretation of the demands of justice in particular contexts. The communal self-clarification that this type of ethical reflection involves is also related to the idea of a holist approach to justice in that the historical embodiment of just institutions in a particular context is constitutive of the identities of the individual members of that community. In order to support this view, I will turn to the philosophical hermeneutics of Hans-Georg Gadamer.[32]

In this analysis of hermeneutics as a form of social criticism, I will first of all explain why Walzer, mistakenly as we will see later, rejects the project of philosophically justifying an impartial point of view. We will then examine his alternative notion of connected criticism. This will allow us to go on to explore the key role of interpretation in Walzer's understanding of the substance of justice by considering arguments that could be offered in defense of complex equality. Having clarified what is involved in a hermeneutic interpretation of substantive principles of justice we can then explore the similarities and differences between the work of Rawls and Walzer. Finally, we will see how Gadamer's work can underscore the critical potential of hermeneutics.

First of all then we must give a detailed account of Walzer's rejection of impartialist accounts of justice. Substantive principles of justice are the legitimate tools of social criticism. These principles do not, according to Walzer, depend for their justification on any procedural conception of an impartial point of view. In order to engage legitimately in the practice of social criticism, we must, he suggests, resist the philosophical urge to abstract from the particular commitments of the political community with which we identify. Critics do not stand outside of, but rather within, though a little to the side of the community. For Walzer, "critical distance is measured in inches."[33] The critic remains connected to the community and to the commonly created social meanings of its goods. The derivation of substantive principles is necessarily a common task. Walzer's interpretive contextualism provides a clear link here between standards of justice and the particular identity of a political community. The holist view, that the maintenance of just institutions and practices is constitutive of the identity of individual citizens, comes to the fore. Furthermore, the link between standards of justice and the shared identity of the members of a community reveals quite clearly why it is that citizens should care about the maintenance of just institutions. The extent to which our community has just institutions tells us, in one important respect, what kind of a community we are.

For some time before he had developed fully his views on complex equality, Walzer was convinced that, in working out what justice demands, any quest for objectivity will be insufficiently sensitive to cultural differences between the creations of various communities.[34] To this extent that quest has tendencies that run counter to the ideals of democracy. Justice must reflect the social meanings of the community even if this does not accord with the reflections of a philosopher who withdraws from the community, so as to be more objective. The democratic will has priority over the conclusions that a philosopher might come to with reference to a conception of an impartial point of view that is intended to inform us as to what is right.

For Walzer, justice depends not on philosophical knowledge but on political knowledge.[35] While philosophical knowledge, as Walzer characterizes it, comes from the outside as an attempt to articulate universal truth, political knowledge comes from within, from the shared historical experience of "negotiation, intrigue and struggle" that in an important sense constitutes a group of people as a political community.[36] To impose philosophical knowledge on a community's choice of substantive principles would involve a failure to respect their own shared experience and their democratic will. Democracy is therefore prior to philosophy.[37]

> Any historical community whose members shape their own institutions and laws will necessarily produce a particular and not a universal way of life. That particularity can be overcome only from the outside and only by repressing internal political processes.[38]

The philosopher attempts to see beyond the particular, to leave the cave with its shadow images of reality, so as to see in the light of the sun. This Platonist vision of philosophy involves a claim to the superior status of philosophical knowledge to the mere opinion of the citizens. If we are to respect the shared creations of political communities and the social meanings that constitute their common life then it is the opinion of the citizens and not the knowledge of the philosopher that matters.[39]

Walzer has since offered a more explicit rejection of proceduralism as idealized philosophical conversation.[40] Procedures that claim to test the validity of an account of justice are designed to represent a kind of hypothetical conversation "whose protagonists are protected against both bad agreements and bad disagreements."[41] These hypothetical conversations press the protagonists toward a "preordained harmony"[42] that has already been determined in the design of the conditions under which the imagined encounter takes place. In other words, the agreement that is generated in these conversations merely articulates the views of the philosopher who designed them. "Once one has a conversational design, it is hardly necessary to have a conversation."[43]

In contrast, Walzer suggests that critical assessments of our institutions should be based not on hypothetical conversations, but rather on what he refers to as "real talk." We can expect real talk in a modern pluralist society to reach democratic conclusions that are unpredictable and inconclusive. They will have no definitive full stop. This is because real conclusions must reflect the indeterminacy of any nonideal conversation and these conversations have no moment of special philosophical authority.[44] Real talk then is our only protection from bad agreements. It is this that forms the "conscious and critical part of the processes that generate our received ideas and reigning theories—reflection become articulate."[45] Its only constraints are those of everyday life, of time and circumstance, that demand some provisional and temporary conclusions if our institutional framework is to allow us to get on with the business of living anything close to an ordinary life in the modern world. But it has no constraints of a philosophical design.

It is clear that Walzer's rejection of the impartialist project is related to his own self-understanding as a committed democrat. This rejection is however a mistake, one that rests to a large extent on a misunderstanding of impartialist proceduralism. Before I mount my defense of Habermas's impartialism, I want to assess the merits of Walzer's alternative. We must examine in more detail how real talk relates to justice and to the practice of interpretive social criticism.

INTERPRETATION AND CONNECTED CRITICISM

We have already anticipated one obvious problem with Walzer's interpretive approach to justice. This is the danger of presenting an insufficiently critical affirmation of the beliefs and values that happen to dominate in a particular community at a given time. Is there any scope, inside the cave, for criticism of opinion as ideology? Walzer's response to this attack has been to emphasize the extent to which we, as members of one community, already inhabit a moral world that has its own critical standards.[46] We can be more or less successful in our attempts to live up to these standards. Every community inhabits its own unique moral world in which its internal critical standards are embedded. Walzer maintains that "the critical enterprise is necessarily carried on in terms of one or another thick morality."[47]

It seems that from Walzer's point of view, any philosopher who is tempted by the hope of discovering or inventing moral principles from some external perspective is in danger of making two mistakes.[48] First, this project does not adequately recognize the extent to which our morality, and our principles of justice, are constituted by the thick social meanings that reflect our self-understanding as a particular historical community. Criticism is a matter not of abstracting from this moral world but of interpreting those social meanings from within it. Second, moralities that are discovered or invented turn out to be "remarkably similar to the morality we already have."[49] In other words, this project fails to recognize the historical and cultural presuppositions that always frame its supposedly objective constructions, inventions, and discoveries.[50]

Our shared moral world is authoritative for us as the only source that can inform our substantive account of justice. In engaging in real talk we argue about the meaning of this moral world, how it is best to be interpreted. A good interpretation can affirm, but it can also challenge, the institutions and practices of our community. Just as the best interpretation of a poem is the one that "illuminates" its meaning in the most "powerful and persuasive way,"[51] so the social critic aims to articulate as authentically as possible the meaning of a shared moral world. A bad interpretation articulates poorly the critical standards that are constitutive of our moral community. These bad interpretations might actually be embodied in our current institutions and practices.

Presenting an account of justice should be thought of, according to this interpretive approach, as the articulation of a central aspect of the identity of a community.[52] For Walzer the identity of the community is constituted by its particular shared social meanings. The social meanings we share with regard to justice are important aspects of our identity. We argue about them because it matters to us in clarifying who we are as a community. It matters if we have managed to live up to our own standards of justice or not because that says something significant about the type of human community we are. The social critic challenges us to live up to our deepest shared convictions, to be true to the moral commitments embedded in our common life. Criticism then fuels the ongoing collective project of communal self-interpretation and each member of the community can take on the role of the critic.

We can see more clearly now why reflection on the substance of justice must be, for Walzer, a common task, a project for the community as a whole. Since the identity of the community itself is at stake, the lone philosopher can never be invited to take on the task of articulating for the community even very basic features of its own account of justice. Wide participation in the democratic process is central to this task and it is this that Walzer is clearly most concerned about in his suspicion of philosophy. Furthermore, the task of working out the substance of justice, since it involves a question of identity, must not be thought of in a static manner but rather as an ongoing matter of clarification and communal self-interpretation. In this sense, Walzer is right to insist that there can never be a definitive full stop at the end of such an account.[53] The substance of justice can only be interpreted in an open discursive encounter, and not in the reflections of any one citizen.[54] The social critic makes a contribution to this ongoing democratic task by attempting to convince fellow citizens of a particular interpretation of their shared social meanings that actually conflicts with current social practice.[55] This interpretation may illuminate the community's self-understanding in radically new ways that not only conflict with current practice but that also challenge and undermine certain dominant beliefs.[56]

Walzer illustrates how connected criticism operates with reference to Antonio Gramsci's critique of bourgeois morality.[57] According to Walzer's reconstruction of this critique, Gramsci offers a radical reinterpretation of values such as liberty and equality. Although these values are attached to the idea of citizenship in bourgeois conceptions of law, they are given an interpretation that serves to justify economic arrangements satisfying the interests of the bourgeoisie at the expense of the proletariat. These ideas of freedom and equality did, however, have a real attraction for the proletariat at that time since they reflected important aspects of the moral world they inhabited. They captured, for example, what was of significance in the rejection of aristocratic privilege.

What Gramsci sought to do was to argue that liberty and equality ought to be embodied differently in the economic and social structure than they had been up to that point. He interpreted these values to require substantive material egalitarianism and not simply formal equality before the law. This reinterpretation justified his rejection of the market relations of a capitalist economy. On Walzer's reading we should take Gramsci's argument to imply that capitalist market relations make it impossible for the democratic community with which he identifies to live up to the most coherent account of the moral standards by which it understands itself. This critique comes from within the particular moral world of the people to whom it is addressed and not from some supposedly objective, external standpoint.[58]

For Walzer, criticism articulates a common complaint in the ordinary language of the people.[59] Abstract theoretical language tends to alienate critics from the sentiments of their fellow citizens. We must recall that according to Walzer, it is not the search for philosophical knowledge or objective truth that motivates criticism but rather the political knowledge of citizens articulated through the democratic process. It is the failure of the community to be whatever it aspires to be, its failure to live up to its deepest convictions that generates the disappointment that drives criticism. In this way the critic can never be in total opposition to the community that is criticized.[60] Loyalty, though not blind loyalty to the status quo, is the prerequisite of connected criticism.

The issue at stake might be put in the form of a question; why should people take a critic seriously if that critic is not committed in any way to the good of the criticized community's form of life? Such an external voice has no standing in the community. It is the voice of a stranger, an enemy, a colonizer. The connected critic is, in contrast, committed not primarily to a philosophical theory but rather to a shared form of life. It is the moral sensitivity and the passion of this critic that can inspire solidarity and resolve throughout the community. Connectedness allows for a sensible flexibility toward theoretical commitments that can be revised in the light of historical events. Such revision is not an occasion for despair as it can invigorate rather than undermine the potential for criticism.[61] What matters is not so much theoretical correctness but the identification with a form of life that lives up to its own moral commitments.

Walzer invokes the image of a critic holding a mirror up to fellow citizens.[62] A look in the mirror can shatter any illusions as to the success with which the community has lived up to these commitments. While these can never be fully articulated, the critic's mirror is intended to help citizens to face up to the disparity between what the community is and what it aspires to be at any given time. The tasks of the critic are "to question relentlessly the platitudes and myths of his society and to express the aspirations of his people."[63] The critic also reminds the community of the particularity of both its aspirations and its failures. Each community has its own mirror telling its own story. Each mirror tells the story of one community's moral world, not the story of the entire world or of humanity as such.[64]

Criticism facilitates the justification of our institutions and practices to each other. We engage in this critical activity as we seek recognition from each other. We understand our personal identity, at least in part, in relation to the political community with which we identify. In this sense it matters to each of us whether or not we can be whatever we aspire to be together. Our aspirations give us direction and a standard by which we can assess critically the historical reality of our common life. Walzer's work on connected criticism is intended to support the argument he makes in favor of complex equality. Our disputes about substantive justice are to be thought of as an aspect of the common task of articulating as fully as possible the social meanings that constitute us as a community.

RIVAL INTERPRETATIONS

We noted earlier that one of the strengths of Walzer's account of complex equality is its capacity to recognize difference. Each modern society will have a different map of justice, reflecting a number of different spheres each with its own different logic of distribution. Walzer recognizes the culturally particular social meanings of goods and at the same time he defends heterogeneity and the plurality of narratives of substantive justice from the repression of a forced metanarrative unity.[65] He reminds us that we must respect both the boundaries that separate the spheres of justice within our own community and also the boundaries that separate our community from communities of others.

But if we are concerned about the recognition of difference, we might worry about the fact that Walzer also tends to assume too much unity. While he may be sensitive to differences between communities, perhaps he forces a unity of interpretation on to the citizens of one community. In other words, while the external other is recognized there may be a blindness to the internal other.[66] Many liberals argue that Walzer's assumption that justice must be based on shared understandings is simply inappropriate in the context of a modern democratic society.[67] The reality of pluralism seems to suggest that we simply do not share understandings of the meanings of social goods. For a liberal, we are not a moral community in the way that Walzer presupposes in his approach to substantive accounts of justice and in his understanding of social criticism.

Does Walzer's moral community dissolve if it is fractured by dissensus over shared meanings?[68] As we saw in the discussion of Rawls, procedural liberalism is a response to the fact that in Western democratic societies we do not share comprehensive conceptions of the good. It is for this reason that we must settle for an agreement on some procedural framework of justice.[69] We are not one moral community but rather a fractured, multicultural, political community that needs justice in order to regulate fair terms of cooperation for mutual advantage. This view stresses plurality and difference within rather than between communities.[70] While Walzer's critique of procedural liberalism is driven by his concern to take seriously pluralism in our second sense, the variety of differently constituted political communities in the modern world, his liberal critics charge him with a failure to take sufficiently seriously pluralism in our first sense, the variety of individual conceptions of the good within each modern society.

Ronald Dworkin argues that the notion that justice is based on shared understandings represents a serious flaw in Walzer's defense of complex equality.[71] Let us take, for example, his interpretation of the meaning of health care in Western culture. Walzer argues that health and longevity are socially recognized needs and that in order to meet those needs we have provided a public health care system. Communal provision for needs in part constitutes and also sustains communities. The social meaning of health care then is that it is a good that should be distributed according to need. We should each receive it as citizens in proportion to our ill-health. The crucial claim of an account of complex equality is that this good should therefore not be distributed according to wealth, occupation, education, or any other criterion that is unrelated to the social meaning of health care as a need.[72]

Of course, this interpretation of health care does conflict with current practice in most Western democracies. Wealth is, in fact, often a criterion that can determine the quality of health care that is provided. Presumably some people are willing to argue in defense of this situation and so it would appear that Dworkin is right about the fact that not everyone is in agreement with Walzer about the social meaning of health care. Does this mean that we lack the shared meanings that are constitutive of a moral community? A liberal conclusion might be that we simply cannot find internal solutions to our disagreements about justice and we must therefore appeal to some general moral principle. But as our discussion of Rawls's work should confirm, the problems involved in justifying such general substantive principles of justice are indeed onerous. Rather than abstracting from the particularity of social meanings, hermeneutics seeks to avoid these problems by digging more deeply into those meanings.[73]

Walzer could be defended from Dworkin's critique if we bear in mind the fact that we could not even have a disagreement unless we shared common terms of reference, a common vocabulary.[74] The sharing is at a deeper level than the conflicting opinions about specific disputes about justice. In a moral disagreement about the merits of private medicine, we must draw on the resources made available to us in our shared moral vocabulary. We will use concepts such as needs, rights, welfare, and so on that are for us shared meanings. While we may not be able to reach an explicit agreement, we must assume that we all know what we are talking about or else the debate would be pointless. But these moral concepts do not just facilitate understanding between us. They are concepts that themselves express the shared moral commitments that are constitutive of our common way of life. These terms of reference that make up this common vocabulary are not primarily derived from explicit agreements among individuals. They are part of our tradition and they reflect moral assumptions that underlie our social practices and the language we use about them.

For example, the existence of a National Health Service of some description does in itself indicate a certain shared meaning of health care, no matter how much we might disagree about how it should be organized. This shared meaning involves a moral commitment. Even those who are completely opposed to the idea of such a service, seeing it as an unjustifiable waste of resources, cannot but debate within the context of a form of life where health care is now understood as a need for which communal provision has been made. The language used in current debates about health care, terms such as "neglect," "understaffing," "unacceptably long-waiting lists," reflect deep common assumptions that direct the dispute in a particular way. Shared understandings are contextualized within a tradition and they certainly do not preclude intense disagreement among individuals. Social meaning is not "a matter of individual opinion but of the nexus of social values, norms and practices about which individuals have opinions."[75] Despite the views of some of Walzer's critics, a debate such as that about just health care will not be resolved by appealing externally to a general substantive principle of justice, but rather with reference to the moral resources that are constitutive of the community's shared way of life.

What Walzer does in *Spheres of Justice* is to present, as a connected critic, his interpretation of our shared understandings in relation to the various spheres of justice. He believes that we can mark off "deep and inclusive accounts of our social life from shallow and partisan accounts."[76] The deeper accounts give a fuller and richer interpretation of the standards to which we aspire as a community. Walzer is not, unlike those in search of general principles, claiming to offer the one and only objectively right account of justice for us. If we understand his work in this way, then we can see that the fact of moral disagreement does not imply that his emphasis on shared meaning is misguided. We can evaluate his interpretations of the social meaning of justice and test them against other interpretations. It is the attempt to offer the interpretation that best illuminates the moral commitments we already share that engages the connected critic.

We can, I hope, see more clearly both the similarities and the remaining important differences between Walzer's contextualism and Rawls's political constructivism. Rawls's proceduralism is not driven by a philosophical urge for truth but rather by the practical purpose of constructing a workable conception of political justice. The content of justice as fairness

> is expressed in terms of certain fundamental ideas seen as implicit in the public political culture of a democratic society. This public culture comprises the political institutions of a constitutional democratic regime and the public traditions of their interpretation.[77]

Furthermore, the original position itself is intended as a model for

> what we regard—*here and now*—as fair conditions under which the representatives of free and equal citizens are to specify the terms of social cooperation in the case of the basic structure of society.[78]

The principles he believes the parties would adopt identify "the conception we regard—*here and now*—as fair and supported by the best reasons."[79] It would appear that Rawls too is seeking in some sense to provide a "deep and inclusive" account of justice that best illuminates the moral commitments that we can share, at least from a political point of view. But this does not dissolve the significant differences between the two accounts. Rawls complements his political conception of justice with the idea of an overlapping consensus of reasonable comprehensive doctrines because the fact of pluralism implies for him that we do not actually have very much shared meaning to work with.[80] We need philosophical abstraction when our disagreements are deep, when "our shared understandings, as Walzer might say, break down."[81] This explains a number of features of Rawls's constructivism; first, the centrality of the notion of impartiality; second, the need to introduce the abstraction of the original position as a device of representation; and third, the generality of the principles that are derived there.

All of these features also underline the fact that what Rawls is seeking to outline is a procedure of construction that "embodies all the relevant requirements of practical reason and [that] shows how the principles of justice follow from the principles of practical reason."[82] Rawls believes that his political conception of justice could be the focus for an overlapping consensus because he seeks to develop his principles from certain fundamental ideas that all citizens could, "by using the principles of their common practical reason," come to share.[83] Rawls's political conception of justice is therefore not to be thought of as being particular to one democratic society. It seeks rather to capture the ideas that are fundamental to any political culture that could claim to be democratic.

Walzer, in contrast, outlines a much more detailed account of the substantive principles that he identifies in a wide variety of spheres of justice. He rejects the centrality of a conception of impartiality because he is so concerned to resist abstraction. Our disagreements will be resolved only if we can give a deeper and more inclusive interpretive account of the specific meanings that are shared by citizens in a particular cultural context. It is our attention to the detail of the contextual meanings that are contested in actual disputes about justice that drives Walzer's hermeneutics. His concern is not so much with ideas of practical reason that are embedded in any and every democratic culture but rather with the thick cultural meanings that constitute a particular community's shared way of life. Again we can see that Rawls's work is generated primarily by a concern for the plurality of individual conceptions of the good, Walzer's by a concern for the plurality of differently constituted political communities.

The question that must still be addressed however is how a hermeneutic approach can deal adequately with rival interpretations of shared meaning. This is a matter of seeing how each interpretation coheres with a community's values, its self-understanding and its aspirations. Substantive justice in any society is always the subject of an ongoing public debate. Such debate does strive to reach some conclusions, bearing in mind that these will be temporary and provisional, without any definitive full stop. In order to see how a hermeneutic approach might help to reveal how these debates could be brought to a temporary but legitimate conclusion, I will follow the lead of Georgia Warnke by turning to the philosophical work of Hans-Georg Gadamer.[84]

THE DIALOGUE OF JUSTICE

Hermeneutics developed as a method for interpreting the meaning of authoritative texts, so as to apply that meaning in a new context.[85] It is not surprising that this field of study emerged in the context of theological and legal controversies about how to interpret texts correctly, to draw the proper normative conclusions for effective adherence to the authority of the text. If we want to understand a particular passage from the Bible, or an aspect of the law, then we have to begin with an initial projection of its meaning that we derive from our interpretation of the whole of the scripture or our overall understanding of the law. Interpreting the part in question will require that we alter and revise in turn our understanding of the whole. Early hermeneutical theorists were concerned with the objective interpretation of meaning.[86] They thought of hermeneutics as a method or a skilful technique whereby the interplay within the hermeneutical circle between part and whole, could allow the interpreter eventually to master the meaning of the text by arriving at an objective and definitive interpretation of its meaning.

Gadamer argues that the idea of an objectivist hermeneutics is fundamentally misconceived.[87] We can never give an objective interpretation of any text, or any account of the substance of justice, because we always remain in a particular context of interpretation. This context is limited and constrained by the historically situated perspective that we might consider, following Gadamer, as the interpreter's horizon of understanding.[88] There is no method that could possibly take us beyond the limited horizon of our own historicity. In this way the meaning of a text can never be tied to the notion of authorial intention. In the light of new circumstances and from the vantage point of a future reader who can interpret it in a wider perspective, the text may come to mean something that the author never intended.[89] Similarly there is no definitive and fixed meaning of substantive justice since we are always moving within a limited horizon of understanding.

The quest for objectivity places the interpreter in the role of an observer who claims to understand the moral commitments of a community from a neutral standpoint. Gadamer insists that understanding is not a matter of neutral observation but rather one of participative interpretation. We always understand from the perspective of a tradition. I suggested earlier that even if we disagree about what just health care requires of us as a community, we already presuppose a deep common commitment to a particular form of life. This common commitment to that form of life is an aspect of the forestructure of our understanding, something presupposed by the very disagreement. It is what Gadamer refers to as a prejudice.

> Prejudices are not necessarily unjustified or erroneous, so that they inevitably distort the truth. In fact the historicity of our existence

entails that prejudices, in the literal sense of the word, constitute the initial directedness of our whole ability to experience. Prejudices are biases of our openness to the world. They are simply conditions whereby we experience something—whereby what we encounter says something to us.[90]

In the context of a disagreement about substantive principles of justice within modern democratic societies, we can think of these prejudices as the weight of our tradition. This is a particular tradition that has, through the struggles of its history, come to place values like equality, liberty, and citizenship at the center of its deliberations about justice. These prejudices give us an initial direction in our attempts to work out what justice demands of us here and now.

Our awareness of the prejudices of our own tradition constitutes our historically effected consciousness.[91] This concept allows us to understand more clearly why the project of objectivist hermeneutics is misconceived. Take for example the way in which the law is applied by the Supreme Court in the United States. The judges interpret the Constitution with the historically effected consciousness of precedent.[92] The history of previous interpretations of the Constitution as it was applied in various cases is the history of the Constitution itself. The requirements of the law in a new case cannot be tied to the original intention of the Founding Fathers but nor can they be understood as merely subjective interpretations on the part of the judges. What is expected of the judges is that they engage in a dialogical encounter whereby they can incorporate the context of the new case into their understanding of the law. They carry forward the tradition by testing its prejudices in new historical circumstances.

Georgia Warnke suggests that we understand the differences between the substantive accounts of justice offered by Rawls and Walzer as two interpretive accounts of our political tradition.[93] Neither of them can capture fully the meaning of that tradition and each of them stresses different aspects of it, but we can take both to be making significant contributions to a public understanding of what justice requires of us. In so far as it seems clear that there are disagreements about the substance of justice, we must engage in a dialogical encounter whereby we test the various prejudices of our tradition in our attempts to come to terms with new circumstances.[94] This can take the form of a hermeneutic dialogue where each of us can test our differing interpretations of justice in an encounter where we seek to deepen our views by learning from one another. We are seeking a fusion of horizons with each other as partners in dialogue.[95]

In this interpretive dialogue our prejudices are tested by the encounter with the other. If the partners to this dialogue really listen to each other then they will not simply remain entrenched in the position they were in before the dialogue took place at all. A public dialogue about justice that is genuinely open will involve a process of self-transformation for each of the participants and also for the identity of the community as a whole. If we have listened, then we will have taken the differences between us into account, and while it is possible that none of us will change our minds to a significant degree, all of us will have benefited in terms of a deeper understanding of our own views on justice and a more adequately articulated account of the issues of justice that matter to us communally.[96]

The accounts of substantive justice offered by theorists such as Walzer and Rawls draw very heavily on traditions that could be thought of as the dominant strands of modern Western political culture. These are the traditions of liberalism, socialism, and republicanism. But there are other traditions within modern democratic societies that are rooted in minority cultures, such as immigrant cultures or perhaps new cultures that have developed through the progress of social movements, such as that of the gay and lesbian community. We have already considered, in our discussion of feminism, how certain cultures are in danger of being marginalized in our deliberations about justice. On this dialogical account, these cultures must be included in these interpretive encounters that seek to carry forward the political tradition as a whole. The onus is on those who draw most heavily on dominant traditions to listen to the voices of these other cultures.[97] As members of our democratic community they can make important contributions to our self-understanding. The horizon of a minority culture is not simply incorporated into that of a dominant culture leaving the latter unchanged. Rather we can expect both cultures to be transformed in the fusion of their horizons.

This will not be the case only within one democratic community but communities can learn from one another. "We British" can learn something from "you Germans," and vice versa, if we really take seriously our cultural encounter as a potentially edifying and educational experience. We will deepen our understanding not only of the others, but of ourselves as well. In this way, as our self-interpretation changes, so we change ourselves. We can think of the cultural aspects of closer European cooperation as an attempt to engage various European cultures in a mutually enriching and self-transformative dialogue. Nor need this experience be limited to Western cultures learning from each other. In fact, we might expect to learn more, on condition that we put in the more demanding efforts of listening required, from an encounter with non-Western cultures that aims at a genuine understanding, or a fusion of horizons.[98]

In seeking to give the best interpretation of what the substance of justice is for us, through our own internal debates as well as external encounters, we are therefore enriching our own tradition. As each participant in these encounters seeks to incorporate the better insights of the other, they are collectively striving to give the most adequate account of justice for them. This of course is always open to future revision and so is never given a definitive full stop. The fusion of horizons that we seek will enrich and develop our communal articulation of what justice demands of us. While this will not resolve all of our disagreements, the encounter itself will constitute a vibrant public culture where a passionate concern for justice can be expressed collectively.

A hermeneutic understanding of justice requires of each of us that we be open to our deepest shared moral convictions. To engage in a serious attempt to answer the question "What is justice for us?" inevitably involves us in the common project of facing up to the questions "Who are we?" and "What do we aspire to be?"[99] Our account of justice in part defines our identity as a community. In so far as we share a form of life at all, and this is surely not an option, then these questions are inescapable.

A dialogical understanding of substantive justice can claim to have important advantages over an account of justice that is derived through an abstract procedure. It does not deny the significance of historical and cultural traditions and so it can respect the particularity of different communities. It also reflects better the communal aspect of democratic deliberation that is essential to the derivation of legitimate, substantive principles of justice. This provides strong motivation for the shared effort to articulate and to adhere to such principles. It seems clear then that hermeneutics does not undermine the possibility of social criticism. Hermeneutic critique is grounded on the fact that we can be more or less true to our deepest shared moral convictions.

This defense of the critical potential of Walzer's stress on interpretation adds to our understanding of the holist aspects of an adequate liberal holist approach to justice. We will recall that in the discussion of the communitarian critique of Rawls, I suggested that while Rawls is a liberal holist, his attempt to isolate the political sits rather uneasily with that commitment. However, I have maintained throughout that the attempt to provide a philosophical conception of an impartial point of view is indispensable to a theory of justice. In fact, impartiality is a crucial aspect of the self-understanding of any political community that aspires to a just social reality in a context characterized by a plurality of conceptions of the good. This should become clear now as we turn to the most significant weaknesses in Walzer's work. In the following chapter I will argue that his rejection of the impartialist project is seriously misguided. Walzer is left with a hermeneutic approach to justice that is dangerously partial in that it obscures the key feature of any theory of justice that is to serve its critical task in a modern context.

4

The Limits of Walzer's Immanent Critique

In the last chapter I argued that Walzer's defense of connected criticism should not be dismissed as an apology for the status quo. Shared moral commitments can be articulated in ways that conflict with current social and political practices. In this chapter I aim to present a critique of Walzer's work by exposing the limits of interpretive social criticism as a theoretical approach to justice. I will argue that despite the critical role that hermeneutics does play, the form of immanent critique that Walzer actually advocates represents, at best, one important aspect of what is required of us with respect to our reflection on justice.[1] Its potential for rigorous social criticism is seriously undermined by Walzer's refusal to endorse the impartialist project. Without a philosophical articulation of an impartial point of view we are left without adequate resources for the necessary task of justifying substantive principles of justice. I will be suggesting that in the context of a modern society characterized by a plurality of individual conceptions of the good, the justification of principles of justice must depend on some conception of an impartial point of view. Hermeneutics could never on its own act as a substitute for some such conception.

SOCIAL POWER, MORAL UNIVERSALISM,
AND THE IMPARTIALIST PROJECT

The focus of the argument of this chapter is to show that Walzer's hermeneutics of justice is a form of immanent critique that is limited in at least two significant respects. First, it does not reveal a sufficiently firm theoretical grasp of the ways in which the operation of social power can have distorting effects on public reflection and debate about justice. Second, it does not provide a convincing account of the thin moral universalism that it endorses. In the early sections of the chapter I will argue that one of the consequences of Walzer's rejection of the impartialist project is that his interpretive approach to questions of justice is insufficiently sensitive to the effects of power in political discourse. In the later sections I will explore the tensions in Walzer's understanding of a thin moral universalist code. The conclusion of the chapter will lead us back to the impartialist project and to the search for a procedure of justification for substantive principles of justice in a modern context.

The first question to be asked, then, is whether or not an interpretive account of justice can be sufficiently sensitive to the operation of social power. Marxists will wonder how interpretation is expected to penetrate the ideological beliefs that serve to justify the power structure of capitalism's relations of production. Foucauldians will wonder how an interpretive account of justice can do anything but affirm, ever more deeply, the regime of truth that constitutes the configuration of power relations in any given modern society.[2] Can Walzer's hermeneutics adequately identify, explain, and overcome the effects of power in democratic deliberation as it is currently carried out? In order to begin to find an answer to these questions, we will return briefly, in the next section, to Walzer's rejection of Marxism, or indeed any critical social theory, for the sake of what he takes to be a sufficiently connected approach to social criticism. I will argue that this betrays a naiveté on Walzer's part with regard to the possibility of ideological distortion in actual processes of democratic deliberation.

We can develop this point further by considering, in the following section, Jürgen Habermas's critique of Gadamer's hermeneutics and his defense of a version of ideology critique based on the model of psychoanalysis. This debate can be related quite straightforwardly to some of the problems associated with Walzer's defense of immanent critique. Even if the psychoanalytic model depends on certain untenable assumptions, there is no good reason to abandon the search for a theoretically grounded model of critique. This will take us beyond Walzer's antitheoretical stance. Critical theory does not in itself offend our democratic sentiments, as Walzer seems to suggest. In fact only a critical theory of society, that is sensitive to democratic concerns while at the same time facilitating a critique of ideology, could actually be effective in the defense of legitimate and just institutions and practices.

We will then go on to consider the related question of moral universalism. Walzer presents a thin universalist code as a product of historical conjuncture, a moral minimum that just happens to be recognized in a wide variety of cultural contexts.[3] It seems to me that this stress on the contingency of the code represents Walzer's failure to acknowledge the far more significant role that moral universalism actually plays in his own approach to matters of justice. What the universalist code requires from a political theorist is not simply acknowledgment but rather rational grounds for its justification.

This criticism will be presented in the fourth section when I begin to assess the relationship between universalist moral principles, ones that are justified independently of any one context or tradition, and substantive accounts of justice that are particular to one context or tradition. I will argue that if we are to theorize adequately the relationship between a minimal universalist moral code, such as the one Walzer affirms, and the substantive accounts of justice that constitute the shared convictions of particular political communities, then we will need to look beyond Walzer's preferred form of immanent critique. The discussion will seek to provide further evidence in support of the view that philosophical theory plays an indispensable role in clarifying what is involved in the justification of substantive principles of justice. This is related to the fact that if the practice of social criticism is not to be undermined, we will need a clear moral-theoretical understanding of what is to count as rational deliberation about justice in a modern context. This is something that Walzer's hermeneutics does not provide.

In the final section I will argue that an adequate alternative to a hermeneutics of justice should clarify both the relation between the universal and the particular and the demands of rational deliberation. It should also show, more convincingly than Walzer manages to, that both individual rights and the democratic will are necessary and, indeed, complementary aspects of a theory of justice. Walzer's interpretive account of justice tends to submerge the individual by stressing the common will in a way that is inappropriate in a modern context. It is inappropriate in that it does not reflect adequately the variety of perspectives that we could expect individuals to bring to disputes about justice in a society that is characterized by a plurality of conceptions of the good. It sacrifices a concern for pluralism in our first sense with its overriding concern for the plurality of differently constituted political societies. In this way, despite its stress on real talk and on the importance of open democratic deliberation about the substance of justice, Walzer's approach is insufficiently discursive.

Before I present this critique, it is worth noting here the connection between the two important limitations that I am discussing in this chapter. Both of these, insufficient sensitivity to the effects of power in discourse and failure to recognize the need for a rational grounding of a universalist moral code, highlight the problems associated with Walzer's rejection of the impartialist project. Both reflect the fact that Walzer's account of interpretive justification fails to outline clearly a set of conditions of rational acceptability for principles of justice. The impartialist project is, in contrast, concerned with clarifying some such set of conditions so that our reflections on justice can act as an effective critical tool that could facilitate a rational challenge to the operation of social power.

We have already assessed, in the first part of the book, the role of a conception of impartiality as a challenge to power in public deliberation about justice. In discussing feminist criticisms of Rawls's procedural test for substantive principles of justice, we found that Rawls's test is seriously flawed because it involves an abstraction from all differing perspectives in disputes about justice. That discussion did affirm, however, the importance of some impartialist test for substantive principles if the marginalization of certain social groups is effectively to be confronted. By demanding impartiality in public discourse groups that have been marginalized can begin to find a voice for their own particular needs. This provides a self-critical test for any public discourse that could claim not to be arbitrarily biased in favor of some social groups over others. What philosophy can and should provide is an account of practical reason that outlines such a conception of impartiality. This conception must facilitate the justification of substantive principles of justice while encouraging the articulation of differences in a vibrant, critically self-questioning public encounter.

Rawls's main problem is that his conception of impartiality is too restrictive, depending as it does on the attempted isolation of the political as a means of overcoming difference. Walzer's problem, in contrast, is that he does not present any philosophically grounded conception of impartiality. In this sense his conception of democratic deliberation, or real talk, is not restricted at all. There are no procedural rules that act as constraints on that deliberation. There is, therefore, no adequate means of distinguishing between claims that can be defended on reasonable grounds and claims that are more or less entangled with relations of power. While Walzer stresses the importance of context by taking the plurality of differently constituted political societies seriously, he does not respond effectively to the differing bargaining positions among the plurality of social groups that characterize all modern societies.

If we are to ground a conception of impartiality in an account of practical reason then we can see how the impartialist challenge to power is linked to the justification of a universalist moral code. A universalist moral code, if it is to be grounded rationally, must be justified in a way that is independent of any one particular tradition or context. If it can be justified in this way then it can act as a critical test for principles of justice that can challenge relations of power in all contexts. We will see in the next part how Habermas's conception of impartiality is derived from an account of practical reason that he reconstructs from a theory of language that makes strong universalist claims.[4] In the later part of the book we will go on to consider how different uses of practical reason can allow us to offer an account of justice that can take sufficiently seriously pluralism in both of the senses with which we have been concerned.

What these two crucial limitations of Walzer's hermeneutics amount to is a failure to draw a line clearly between connectedness and partiality. As we saw in the last chapter, connectedness is an appropriate disposition of a critic who seeks to interpret the substantive demands of justice in a particular cultural context. Partiality, on the other hand, would represent an unreasonable and unjustifiable loyalty to dominant interpretations of those demands. In other words, it would represent a failure to take sufficiently into account the voice of the dissident, or the marginal, in disputes about justice in particular contexts. If we are to distinguish adequately between connectedness and partiality then we will need to engage in the philosophical task that Walzer had hoped to abandon. The only sufficiently rigorous test for principles of justice in modern societies is one that draws on a conception of impartiality that is philosophically grounded in an account of practical reason.

IMMANENT CRITIQUE AND IDEOLOGY

Marxism tends to be antagonistic toward hermeneutics since its stress on shared social meanings seems to obscure class conflict within capitalist societies. The locus of shared understandings for the Marxist is the social class and not the political community. The bourgeoisie of one political community share social meanings with the bourgeoisie of other communities and not with their own local proletariat and the same goes for the international proletarian movement. This is because social meaning will be determined by economic relations and interests. In fact, it is the ideological claim that meanings are shared across a community that serves to institutionalize the rule of the dominant class. The task for the proletariat is to overcome their own false consciousness and to penetrate bourgeois prejudices by becoming aware of their own interests, which will inevitably conflict with the interests of their local bourgeoisie.

In the last chapter we saw that Walzer used Antonio Gramsci's critique of bourgeois ideology as an example of connected criticism. This is controversial since we might expect a Marxist like Gramsci to deny that a political community could actually share social meanings across classes. As we saw, Walzer maintains that we should understand Gramsci's critique as a reinterpretation of the shared values of liberty and equality. The deeper interpretation he gives deprives the bourgeoisie of their privileges by showing that these values could only be institutionalized by destroying the capitalist economic system. The internal contradictions of bourgeois ideology provide the critical foothold for this challenge to bourgeois hegemony.[5] In this way ideas that are used to establish class rule always provide grounds for resistance to that rule.[6] This is the danger of using ideas that have a broad enough appeal to operate successfully as an ideology in the first place. Walzer maintains that Gramsci's social criticism presupposes the fact that political communities share social meanings, but that those meanings can be interpreted well or badly.

The next issue, of course, is how we distinguish between good and bad interpretations. We have already seen that Walzer suggests that a good interpretation will be one that gives a deep and inclusive account of the community's self-understanding. But what about the possibility of a false consciousness or ideological distortions in democratic deliberation, caused by the power relations that are always, for a Marxist, grounded in the economic base of the society? Is it not possible that power will distort citizens' reflection on justice and more generally on their own self-understanding in ways that they will not even be aware of? What if Gramsci's radical reinterpretation of bourgeois values is rejected by most workers? It might be possible, as Walzer puts it, that "the greater number of workers believe that the equality realized in capitalist society is genuine equality or equality enough."[7]

Unlike Gramsci, Walzer refuses to claim that workers could misinterpret their own objective interests, that they could be wrong about what would constitute "equality enough."[8] In this way he seems to be giving the workers the last word on what counts as a good interpretation of the demands of justice. He does not consider it likely that any theory could provide a cogent explanation as to why the conditions of democratic deliberation involve structural biases that distort decision-making processes by repressing the interests of the workers. While he accepts that workers could be mistaken because of a lack of information, he seems to deny that they could be mistaken in interpreting their own moral standards.

> The workers can indeed be wrong about the facts of their case, such as the actual extent of income differentials or the real chances of upward mobility. But how can they be wrong about the value and significance of equality in their own lives? Here criticism depends less on true (or false) statements about the world than on evocative (or unevocative)

renderings of a common idea. The argument is about meaning and experience; its terms are set by its cultural as well as its socio-economic setting.[9]

It seems clear therefore that Walzer's hermeneutics involves the rejection of any form of Marxian objectivism.[10] If we must choose between our theory and our connectedness to the community we criticize, it is obvious which choice Walzer would see as the better one. This is not to say, as we have already seen, that the connected critic must be blindly loyal to current practices. Connectedness is humanizing in that it ensures that the critic's theory continues to address the issues that really matter to fellow citizens.[11]

But the choice is not so straightforward if we do not follow Walzer in giving the last word on what counts as a good interpretation to the participants in democratic deliberation itself. He simply has not said enough about the ways in which structural biases can distort such deliberation and how critical theories might identify and explain such distortion. If a critic is convinced that such distortion is possible then the fact that a radical reinterpretation of shared meanings is rejected by most fellow citizens does not necessarily imply that the critic's views should be revised. Social criticism can lead to isolation despite the best intentions of a critic to remain connected. If this occurs then it is theoretical conviction, and perhaps the support of a few significant others, that for the most part sustains the lonely critic.[12] Social critics often face a real dilemma when their theoretical convictions force them to sacrifice much of their sense of connectedness to their political community.

On the other hand, Walzer does seem to accept that the majority of citizens "might well misunderstand the logic of their own institutions or fail to apply consistently the principles they professed to hold."[13] This must allow for the possibility that the critic is right and the majority of citizens wrong. It is not clear however, from what Walzer has to say about this possibility, how the critic's claim might be justified. How are we to distinguish between an ideological and a nonideological decision, a genuine and a pseudoconsensus, a fair and a warped conclusion, an impartial and a biased principle of justice? This remains something of a mystery.[14] While Leninist elitism is rejected by Walzer, and with good reason, he tends to assume that every critical theory of society must involve antidemocratic implications. This leaves him ill-equipped to offer a critically sound test for democratically worked out norms of justice. I believe that only some more sophisticated account of power, integrated with a philosophical conception of an impartial point of view, could possibly enable him to deal with these challenges.[15]

The effects of power might be considered as the exclusion from the democratic process of those whose real interests could not be satisfied within its particular structure.[16] This view of power allows us to think of the preferences and values of at least some of the participants, as they are expressed and acted upon in a democratic context, as products of a system that, behind their backs as it were, obscures their own real interests. Were they to experience a less repressive system they might well come to realize how their real interests had previously been obscured. This insight would therefore give them good reasons for acting differently. It seems to me that this would constitute a genuine achievement for them as it would give them a better self-understanding by enabling them to overcome illusions with regard to their own deepest aspirations.[17]

But if the people concerned were not to experience a less repressive system, thus leaving them blind to the ways that their interests are obscured, this does not make the critic's interpretation wrong. We might consider the claim Walzer makes in relation to the internal justness of a caste society.[18] Such a society is just, according to him, if the social meaning of ritual purity is integrated with that of many other social goods and if those meanings are genuinely shared. But it is possible for an internal, connected critic to argue that these meanings are shared precisely because the interests of the lower-caste members have been obscured. The critic might go on to point out that deliberation about the caste system has therefore been distorted and biased. Even if the majority are not convinced, the critic might support this claim empirically by indicating, for example, the level of conversions to other religions among lower-caste members.[19]

Susan Okin argues that Walzer's defense of the internal justness of a caste society shows up the dangers involved in an approach that "depends heavily upon what people are persuaded of."[20] She then argues that the gender system is in some sense analogous to a caste system. In both cases "an inborn characteristic determines dominant or subordinate status in relation to social goods over a whole range of spheres."[21] It certainly seems to make good sense to consider the ways in which women have been expected traditionally to perform domestic duties, leaving political matters for men, as ideological distortions that led to the interests of women being systematically obscured. The gains that have been achieved by the feminist movement must be thought of as examples of an overcoming of the effects of power. It has been a matter of dispelling patriarchal illusions that repressed and constrained women's self-understanding. The fact that women of earlier generations, and many women today, fail to see the injustice of patriarchy must be explained with reference to certain structural features of society of which they themselves are not sufficiently aware.

What is at issue here is whether or not we can give theoretical justifications for critical interpretations of a community's principles of justice even if that interpretation is rejected by a majority of citizens. Walzer's version of immanent critique is not helpful in this respect. I have been suggesting that one way of justifying this type of critical interpretation would be to provide a convincing explanation for the majority's rejection of the critic's interpretation. The explanation would attempt to reveal that rejection to be a mistake caused by some factor or other that the majority had failed to recognize at the time. In other words the justification of the critic's interpretation would depend on a successful explanation of an ideological distortion. This issue might be brought into a clearer focus if we consider Habermas's critique of Gadamer's hermeneutics.

HERMENEUTICS AND CRITICAL THEORY

While Habermas accepted many of the insights of the philosophical hermeneutics elaborated by Gadamer, particularly regarding the impossibility of transcending completely an historically effected consciousness, he was alarmed by what he saw as a tendency to absolutize the authority of tradition. It is the proper balance between the authority of one's tradition and the capacity for critical reflection on the prejudices of that tradition that is at issue in the debate between hermeneutics and critical theory.[22] From Habermas's point of view, if we are to be capable of critical reflection at all, then we must appropriate our tradition selectively, which means that we will repudiate or reject certain aspects of it. Habermas seeks to undermine the authority of tradition in an attempt to avoid the possible conservative implications of Gadamer's critique of the Enlightenment's "prejudice against prejudices."[23]

Of course, while we can acknowledge that some particular horizon of understanding is inescapable we must also recognize that all known historical traditions are repressive as well as enabling. Habermas stresses the power of critical reflection, our capacity to challenge what has been handed down through tradition and to replace dogmatism with rational insight. But how could critical reflection be grounded in a system of reference that is not context-dependent? Can any social theory guarantee a critical distance that facilitates a selective, and liberating, appropriation of tradition without taking certain unquestioned assumptions, or prejudices, for granted? If these assumptions actually underwrite repressive social practices then must we not accept that the promise of such a critical theory is in fact an illusory one?

The theoretical project that Habermas set for himself, against the claims of hermeneutics, was to detect and overcome systematic distortions in self-interpretations. For Gadamer all understanding is linguistic.[24] Our language discloses to us the truth of our world and of ourselves. Language is the horizon that enables us to ask questions and to participate in a dialogical encounter with another (text, person, culture) that we previously had not been capable of comprehending. As we saw in the last chapter, if we are to have any hope of understanding something unfamiliar, we must be genuinely open in anticipating a fusion of horizons. This fusion enriches our language and discloses to us new aspects of the world, and of ourselves. But if, as Habermas claimed, language can be systematically distorted by power, then it may represent not only the resources for an ever enriching self-understanding but also a force of domination and mystification. But what exactly had Habermas in mind when he spoke of systematically distorted communication?

A particular aspect of a tradition is systematically distorted if it is, in part, the result of nondialogical factors, notably social processes of labor and domination.[25] In other words the language of our self-understanding, in modern Western capitalist societies, is not simply the result of an open dialogue, a series of fusions bringing us to our present horizon. Other factors, such as the innovative technological exploitation of external nature and consequent changes in the system of labor, have shaped our language in a nondialogical manner.[26] Relations of power and authority have framed our dialogical encounters of understanding, without themselves being legitimated in an open dialogue where all participants are equally free to question the normative content of those relations. In this way language serves as a medium in which organised force is legitimated.

> Insofar as the legitimations do not articulate the power relationship whose institutionalization they make possible, insofar as that relationship is merely manifested in the legitimations, language is also ideological.[27]

Gadamer's hermeneutics is, according to Habermas, insufficiently aware of the need for a critique of ideology. The intention of such a critique is to distinguish between aspects of our language that emerge from open dialogue and aspects that are distorted by the effects of systems of domination.

For Habermas, hermeneutics pays insufficient attention to the objective context, constituted by labor and domination as well as open dialogue, in which all social action takes place. It therefore makes a false claim to universality.[28] But the crucial question remains: How can we get beyond hermeneutics to a critical standpoint that is not context-bound? In response to Gadamer's work, Habermas initially turned to psychoanalysis as an analogy for the critique of ideology. Psychoanalysis and the critique of ideology both deal with systematically distorted communication in a way that can be understood in terms of the general conditions of communication.[29] In both cases subjects fail to recognize the intentions that are actually guiding their expressive activity. This constitutes a distorted form of communication, one that cannot be fully comprehended by a purely hermeneutic inquiry since genuine understanding can only occur in these cases if the cause of the distortion is explained.[30]

Habermas invokes Alfred Lorenzer's use of Freudian psychoanalysis in explaining neuroses or specifically incomprehensible symptomatic expressions.[31] The analyst tries to reconstruct an original scene from the patient's early childhood that might account for the particular neurosis. A certain form of interaction that occurred at that formative early stage may have given rise to such intolerable conflict that it was unconsciously repressed. This led to it being split off from its corresponding linguistic symbol. The rejected form of interaction may, however, continue to motivate action at a subconscious level. This, Lorenzer suggests, can be the cause of neurotic compulsive reactions to certain stimuli that it may eventually become impossible to conceal with public rationalizations. The analyst's aim is to reintroduce the repressed form of interaction into public language and thereby to resymbolize it. Subjects overcome their neuroses if they can accept the analyst's theoretically guided interpretation by coming to recognize the original unconscious repression.[32]

In so far as this type of scenic understanding is guided by theoretical assumptions, it succeeds, at least from Habermas's perspective, in going beyond hermeneutics. The meaning of the systematically distorted use of language must be explained before it can be understood.[33] In the case of scenic understanding, this occurs under experimental conditions and the analyst's pre-understanding is directed at a specific set of possible meanings regarding early childhood. The analyst's interpretation is not, however, imposed but rather it must be accepted by the subject as an enlightening account of previously incomprehensible aspects of her own behaviour. We could then say that the analyst's theory led to the emancipation of the subject from some or other force of repression.

But there are some obvious problems with the model of psycho-analysis when it comes to the practice of social criticism in terms of the justification of substantive principles of justice. First, as Gadamer, in his response to Habermas, points out, the social critic is not a doctor dealing with patients who need therapy but rather a partner in dialogue, just another member of a social community.[34] The critic can claim no privi-leged vantage point in seeking to justify an interpretation of justice that is critical of current practice, perhaps against the view of the majority of citizens. Unlike the relation between the analyst and the neurotic in need of therapy, the social critic is on an equal footing with every other citizen.

Second, if we rely too heavily on our theory we may begin to suffer under the illusion that we no longer depend on the authority of any tra-dition at all, that we see beyond all horizons. We may even begin to believe that our own theoretical analysis convincingly demonstrates that all who disagree with us hold such distorted self-understandings that they are incapable of recognizing themselves in our (uniquely correct) explanatory account of the cause of their delusions. Of course, this con-flicts not only with any commitment to genuine democratic deliberation but with the most basic insight of hermeneutics, that we could not even engage in a dispute about justice if we did not do so in the context of some tradition or other, however broadly defined. The danger of show-ing contempt for fellow citizens is indeed a real one. It is this, as we have seen, that grounds Walzer's concern for connectedness and his suspicion of philosophy.[35]

Third, in the case of psychoanalysis, a precondition of successful therapy is that a patient has the desire and the determination to over-come and recover from whatever suffering the neurosis has caused. The patient must have a "passion for critique."[36] In a social context it seems that the analogy breaks down if the members of a social group are not sufficiently aware of some supposed pathology that has arisen from the systematic distortion of their language and that has caused them to suf-fer. Since it is behind their consciousness they may not be aware of their own suffering. They will therefore have no desire for any treatment and so it would appear that successful therapy is impossible.

Fourth, resistance to therapy and a struggle to work through insights is to be expected of a willing and cooperative patient who both accepts the authority of the analyst's theory and displays a resolute "passion for critique." If this is so, then we can be certain that the resistance that members of a political community, perhaps the majority, will offer to a social critic will be incomparably greater. This will be even more evident if the interpretation of justice that the critic rejects, as an effect of systematically distorted communication, is actually bolstered by institutional authority. In such a case we might imagine that the critic's interpretation is more likely to be dismissed by the majority as the result of a distorted personal self-understanding than to be embraced by them as a liberating explanatory account of their own collective pathology.[37]

Finally, Gadamer maintained that neither the system of labor nor relations of power are themselves outside of language, as Habermas seemed to suggest, but they too can be objects of hermeneutic reflection. Indeed, if we are to understand them at all we must do so linguistically. For this reason it is "absurd to regard the concrete factors of work and politics as outside the scope of hermeneutics."[38] If we are crudely to dismiss the authority of tradition, as always taking the form of dogmatic power, we will obviously be blind to the critical potential of hermeneutics. In this case, if we engage in social criticism at all, it must be on the basis of an unsustainable conception of critical reason that assumes falsely that it has freed itself from the authority of all tradition. Reason and tradition must not be opposed in this vulgar fashion but rather we should think of critical reflection as the selective appropriation of tradition.[39]

Now while many of these counterarguments do not do justice to Habermas's intentions, they do serve as salutary indications of the dangers involved in using psychoanalysis as a model for social criticism.[40] But where has this discussion brought us? It may seem that we are back at our point of departure in our assessment of the dispute between Gadamer and Habermas. It is now clear that both of them are concerned with critical reflection as the selective appropriation of tradition. While Gadamer initially seemed to Habermas to overemphasize appropriation to the detriment of necessary critical selectivity, Habermas's use of psychoanalysis seemed to Gadamer to overemphasize selectivity to the detriment of inescapable appropriation. This still does not provide much in the way of a theoretical guide as to how we might engage, as social critics, in this selective appropriation, distinguishing as we must between legitimate and illegitimate aspects of our tradition.

It seems to be highly implausible to deny that democratic deliberation can be distorted by the effects of power. A brief assessment of, say, the historical trajectory of the institutionalization of patriarchal power, should be sufficient to underscore this very real possibility. If this is so, then the theoretical project in which Habermas was engaged in his initial response to Gadamer is one that is of crucial importance to an adequate understanding of what counts as a justifiable principle of justice. This raises questions that have simply never been at the center of Gadamer's concerns.[41] Although there are obvious problems with a straightforward application of the model of psychoanalysis, the need for some alternative theoretical basis for grounding criteria of normative justification that can test substantive principles of justice has never been greater. What is clear is that such an alternative must take due care in ensuring that it does not undermine a commitment to democratic deliberation. In his work since the debate with Gadamer, Habermas has set about constructing a critical social theory that is grounded in a theory of communication that is not so dependent on the analogy of analyst and patient.[42] This theory of communicative action allows him to integrate a critical social theory with a moral-theoretical conception of an impartial point of view. The discourse ethics that emerged from this work will be the subject of the next two chapters.

Critical theorists must certainly remain connected to the community that is criticized in some significant sense since they cannot expect to be taken seriously unless it matters to them personally that the community lives up to its own deepest moral convictions. But, contrary to what Walzer suggests, there can be sound theoretical reasons for doubting the views of most of our fellow citizens. If those doubts are to be justified they will need to be supported by an explanation as to how these views are the result of the distorting effects of power on the self-understanding of democratic actors. If a social critic's interpretation of shared moral convictions is rejected by a majority of fellow citizens, as certain features of Walzer's own account of complex equality might well be in the United States, then the critic must choose one of two options. The first option is to admit that the interpretation was wrong while the second is to seek a deeper justification for the interpretation. This deeper justification must draw on some critical theory that can explain the original rejection of the interpretation by fellow citizens. There are often good reasons to take this second option. For this to be a possibility there can be no alternative for convincing social criticism but to draw on critical theories that go beyond Walzer's hermeneutics.

It would appear that, in modern pluralist societies, the effects of power can be much more subtle and pervasive than the type of immanent critique that we find in Walzer's interpretation of Gramsci's social criticism could possibly confront.[43] There are many possible structural biases that can obscure the interests of particular actors from their own self-understandings.[44] Since Walzer presents a theory of justice, he cannot be satisfied, as Gadamer is, to treat the development of a philosophically grounded critical social theory as somebody else's agenda. Nor should he reject the project out of hand as a return to Leninist vanguardism and an inevitable danger to democracy.

Walzer's antitheoretical stance leaves him bereft of an adequate account of the justification of substantive principles of justice. He has not dealt in sufficient depth with the real danger of democratic deliberation being systematically distorted by power. If we are to be in a position to test currently dominant interpretations as potentially arising from the effects of power, we would be wise not to be so dismissive of philosophically grounded theory. If it is possible that victims of injustice can acquiesce in their own suffering by failing to recognize the effects of power, then our need for some critical social theory seems to be beyond argument. A philosophical conception of impartiality would be a vital component of such a critical theory. This would act as a test to see whether or not some particular norm or institutional arrangement is biased in favour of some people's interests over those of some others. Before we return to assess Habermas's contribution on this point we must explore the second important limitation of Walzer's hermeneutics.

EXTENDING THE UNIVERSALIST MORAL CODE

The stress in Walzer's work has been on defending the particularity of substantive principles relative to the shared understandings of historical communities. He insists that "the critical enterprise is necessarily carried on in terms of one or another thick morality."[45] Nevertheless, his conviction, that we must be tolerant of the cultural creativity of other communities, is supported by a universalist meta-ethical principle. Each community is to respect the internal norms of all other communities. The point has been made with admirable clarity by William Galston.

> His [Walzer's] entire theory of justice is presented as a transcontextual metatheory, structurally valid for all communities (though substantively different for each). And the nerve of his relativism—the assertion that it is not possible to rank-order social worlds—is itself put forward, not as an interpretation of *our* experiences but as a universal truth.[46]

So there is, after all, within Walzer's scheme, a way of objectively rank-ordering communities. We can do so by assessing the extent to which they allow other communities to be true to their own deepest convictions, and refrain from imposing their moral standards as cultural imperialists.[47] Even though Walzer does not consider this rank-ordering to be of great relevance to a theory of substantive justice, we might bear in mind that, in modern pluralist societies, minorities are often culturally oppressed by a self-glorifying majority.[48] This rank-ordering might therefore be of great significance as a defense of the cultural rights of minorities, a point we will address later in our discussion of Northern Ireland's constitutional status.

This meta-ethical principle of cultural toleration is not, however, the only universalist principle that Walzer recognizes. He accepts that there is a minimal moral code that can be considered to be valid universally since it seems to be adhered to in almost all known cultures. This thin universalist code involves the recognition of the fact that the same kinds of things, political tyranny and the oppression of the poor, for example, are unjust in many different contexts. What the code recognizes is a partial commonality among "protagonists of different fully developed moral cultures."[49] The content of the code must be, for Walzer, an empirical matter, but it would appear that moral principles respecting the life and autonomy of human persons are to be included.[50] There are a number of important claims that Walzer makes however, that seem to indicate that the moral code he considers to be universal in scope is not as minimal as he tends to suggest. Indeed, within the context of modern pluralist societies, if we were to give a full account of all the aspects of social life that Walzer appears to treat as universally essential features of any just society, we may not have very much to add in determining the structural requirements of justice for any one political community.

What I am suggesting is that all modern pluralist societies work out what the substance of justice is for them by interpreting the same (or at least a very similar) code of universalist moral principles. Their interpretations will differ in the details and in various stresses and nuances, given the particularity of each society's history and culture. There may, of course, also be some substantive principles of justice that are unique to one society, because they have some problem or other that, for whatever reason, is not shared by other communities, but which rather reflects an idiosyncratic characteristic of that society's history. Nonetheless, it does seem to be the case that Walzer assumes that convincing accounts of justice for all modern societies share certain fundamental structural features.

But what are the claims that suggest that Walzer is, despite his own self-understanding, committed to this more extensive moral universalism? First of all, we might note that Walzer assumes that every just society defends rights and liberties for its members that go far beyond a respect for life and a commitment to individual freedom. In fact he must presuppose a universalist moral code that includes liberties of conscience and of critical thought and expression. It also includes rights of participation in the democratic process of deliberating about the substantive principles of justice that are to regulate the life of the community. These liberties and rights must be presupposed since all just societies are politically egalitarian for Walzer, in that it will be a necessary feature of them that "no one possesses or controls the means of domination."[51] This commitment to a universalist political egalitarianism is grounded in his conception of human beings as culture-producing creatures who seek to justify to each other their interpretations of the principles of justice for their shared way of life.[52]

Furthermore, in any society where social meanings of goods are complex and differentiated, and for Walzer that includes any modern society, "there is no alternative to democracy in the political sphere."[53] Democratic government depends on the outcome of deliberation among citizens and no social good (money, rank, status) that is irrelevant to the idea of deliberation is to have any influence within it.[54] We have already seen that Walzer's resistance to the use of philosophical theory for social criticism leads him into a position from which he seems ill-equipped to deal with the distorting effects of power on democratic deliberation. Yet it is clear from his discussion of democracy as the political sphere of justice that he is committed to an ideal of distortion-free deliberation himself.

> What counts is argument among the citizens. Democracy puts a premium on speech, persuasion, rhetorical skill. Ideally the citizen who makes the most persuasive argument—that is the argument that actually persuades the largest number of citizens—gets his way. But he can't use force, or pull rank, or distribute money; he must talk about the issues at hand. And all the other citizens must talk, too, or at least have a chance to talk. It is not only the inclusiveness, however, that makes for democratic government. Equally important is what we might call the rule of reasons. Citizens come into the forum with nothing but their arguments. All non-political goods have to be deposited outside: weapons and wallets, titles and degrees.[55]

While it is very obvious what Walzer considers to be the requirements of justice in the political sphere, he seems unwilling to offer the kind of theoretical support that this vision demands.

On the one hand, these two ideas, of human beings as culture-producers and a deliberative democratic form of government, do support Walzer's contention that morality is always potentially subversive of power.[56] Any citizen can argue that our current institutions and practices are failing to do justice to our deeper aspirations as a particular community. On the other hand, however, the structural features of democratic government are assumed by Walzer to have a universalist egalitarian thrust. This seems to demand a shift of focus from the particularity of substantive accounts of justice to the universality of the structural requirements of democracy for any modern society.

If Walzer's work does reveal a commitment to a much more extensive universalist moral code than he is happy to admit to, as I think it clearly does, then there is a serious tension between this implicit commitment and his explicit stress on interpretive accounts of justice as local narratives.[57] Hermeneutics simply does not have the theoretical resources that are necessary to ground this more extensive universalist moral code. The important point here is that some of the main features of Walzer's own interpretation of the substance of justice for a modern democratic society appear, contrary to his own claims, to be grounded independently of the particular historical traditions of any one modern society. These are features of a universalist moral code that is far from minimalist, but rather is the articulation of the most significant aspects of an adequate substantive account of justice for any modern society. These features include; respect for human life and individual autonomy, liberties of thought and expression, rights of democratic participation for all as an expression of their human creativity, a politically egalitarian conception of deliberative democracy. We might also include toleration of the different cultural creations of other traditions on condition that those traditions include these other features in their accounts of justice. These features taken together represent the structural characteristics of all possible valid accounts of justice in any particular modern context.

While this suggests that Walzer's stress on local narratives is inappropriate, it does not imply that a social critic who invokes this moral code is disconnected from the community to which the criticism is addressed. There should still be genuine loyalty and commitment to the common life of that community. More importantly such criticism is not derived from a totally abstract, ahistorical perspective, but rather from an open articulation of the demands of justice that must apply in any modern society. It is situated in the context of any society that has shared the historical experience of an ever more expansive globalization in terms of both economic markets and administrative bureaucracies. An appeal to this universalist moral code represents "situated criticism for a global community that does not shy away from knocking down the 'parish walls'."[58]

To be situated as a social critic within a modern context will at times demand an appeal to moral principles that represent structural features of all modern societies that could claim to be just. At other times it will demand an appeal to a local narrative that speaks directly and uniquely to the historical traditions of a particular modern community. Neither the universal nor the particular tell us all we need to know about the demands of justice in any particular context. There are at least four implications that can be drawn out of this critical assessment of Walzer's work before we bring this discussion to a conclusion.

AVOIDING PARTIALITY

The first of these implications is that the practice of effective social criticism requires, as we have seen, an approach to justice that is connected to a social-theoretical understanding of the effects of power. It also requires a moral-theoretical understanding of the way in which political communities, even culturally homogeneous ones, are made up of a plurality of widely divergent social groups all of whom are entitled to have their voice heard in any deliberation about the demands of justice. This means that we need a philosophically grounded conception of an impartial point of view, something that Walzer's antitheoretical stance rules out. This conception would provide us with a way of working out in a particular dispute, which account of the demands of justice is morally right. Every modern society, in so far as they share conditions of pluralism in this sense, also share this task of combining social-theoretical contributions and moral-theoretical insights in a way that gives us a critical understanding of the effects of power in a modern context.

Second, it seems quite likely that within the context of a modern pluralist society, a clash could emerge between the demands of the universalist moral code and the principles of justice that are legitimately accepted as a constitutive dimension of that particular form of life.[59] For example, a Dutch social critic may argue that the Dutch people, and all citizens of other relatively wealthy countries, treat those who suffer and die because of famine, say in Somalia, unjustly. In other words, she appeals to the fact that the failure to relieve famine when they have more than enough, violates for the Dutch people the moral code they have come to respect as being universally valid. But others might object that if they were to relieve famine, by themselves or in alliance with other wealthy countries, their carefully worked out arrangements for the distribution of wealth among their own citizens would have to be disregarded.[60]

In practice, of course, those who object almost always win out. In fact, it would appear that nothing short of a strongly coercive state could actually succeed in ensuring the redistribution of resources from North to South that could prevent famine. Is that too high a price to pay? The dilemma is a very real one. We might acknowledge everybody's right to life without thinking that it would be right to sacrifice the advantages of a less coercive state than would be necessary to protect that right. The point is that some local principles of justice do clash with the universalist thrust of other principles. Again Walzer, by leaving the universalist code on the margins of his concern, does not say near enough about this possibility.[61]

Third, the defense of the rule of reasons in the sphere of democratic politics is something that requires far greater attention than Walzer has given to it. Why should reason be privileged over other means of persuasion in the political sphere? Perhaps the rule of reasons is simply another regime of power/knowledge, as Foucault at times seemed to suggest.[62] It might even be asserted that to privilege reason is to endorse the repression and marginalisation of the "other" of reason, the emotional, the sexual, the irrational, or the zany.[63] Walzer does not say in detail what it is that is required of us if we are to argue in a rational way. Nor does he mount a defense of the rule of reasons. We would surely want to know what constraints or procedural rules are to be adopted if the rule of reasons is to preside over the political sphere. More importantly, we would want to know why these constraints are justified. This is, in part, the task of a moral-political theory that defends an impartial point of view.

Finally, I have already outlined how Walzer's stress on inclusivity ensures that nobody is prevented from participating in the democratic process. Indeed everybody is encouraged as a culture-producer to make their own unique contribution to the enrichment of the common life.[64] Despite this, however, his failure to endorse a theoretical conception of an impartial point of view is a cause for concern with regard to the rights of an individual who disagrees with the views of the majority on some fundamental principle of justice. What theoretical guarantee does Walzer provide that the process of democratic deliberation can afford to give that dissenting individual's say its due weight?[65]

One problem that Walzer has here is the fact that there may be some serious tension between majority rule and the rule of reasons. Even if no coercion is used in democratic deliberation, it is far from self-evident that these will amount to the same thing. Again we would need to know much more about the procedural constraints involved if we were to accept that this is in fact so. Another problem is that there is a danger that the democratic authority will constantly interfere in the regulation of our lives to such an extent that the private space, sacred to the tradition of liberalism, will be so shrunken as to leave each of us uncomfortably exposed in our chosen way of life. We will begin to feel morally quite vulnerable to the will of the majority.[66]

Walzer might respond by arguing that these fears fail to take into account the fact that the political sphere is only one sphere among many. While politics is of crucial significance, it does not define the shared meanings within each sphere, but only regulates the boundaries. Democratic authority is decisive "at but not within the boundaries."[67] This was the most important advantage of complex equality over simple equality. But what guarantees a limitation on the right of a majority of citizens to decide that the political sphere is to include ever more aspects of social life?[68] The rights of the individual seem to be insufficiently grounded in Walzer's work. This includes both rights in the negative sense, guaranteeing freedom from state interference, and in the positive sense, ensuring that each individual has a proper and fair political hearing. Again, some moral-theoretical account of the rules of democratic deliberation, incorporating a conception of an impartial point of view, would seem to offer the only effective route around these problems.

If we are to draw out the implications of the more extensive universalist moral code that Walzer seems to presuppose, then a number of problems in Walzer's approach to justice and social criticism rise to the surface. In the first place, this code is not an empirical matter of certain rights that all political communities just happen to recognize but rather it outlines the structural features of any legitimate account of justice, at least under the conditions of modern pluralism. While Walzer assumes these features, he does not do nearly enough to justify them. As I have stressed throughout, such a justification seems to point us back in the direction of a detailed philosophical defense of some procedure of justification that is to act as a test for our substantive principles of justice. It is the search for such a philosophical defense that will lead us in the next part to a detailed consideration of Habermas's work.

Our purpose in this part has been to assess the prospects of a theory of justice that abandons the attempt to justify a philosophical conception of an impartial point of view. Michael Walzer maintains that substantive principles of justice are embedded in a community's shared understandings of the meaning of social goods in their own particular context. From his perspective, abstract procedures of impartial justice, such as that advocated by Rawls, violate the self-understandings of particular historical communities. They fail to take sufficiently seriously the plurality of differently constituted historical communities.

Substantive principles of justice must be presented as interpretations of shared meanings that are constitutive of a community's way of life.

With the stress he places on cultural particularity, Walzer captures a crucial aspect of an adequate theoretical account of justice. His hermeneutics highlights the self-interpretive dimension of communal disputes about substantive justice within particular contexts. Just institutions are constitutive of the identity of individual citizens. They embody the community's efforts at living up to its own deepest moral convictions. They represent critical standards that articulate the community's deepest aspirations. These critical standards can change and develop as the community engages in dialogue with other forms of life and so ethical reflection on identity will be an important feature of any public deliberation about justice in a particular context.

On the other hand, we have discovered in this chapter that Walzer fails to acknowledge the fact that, within the context of particular modern societies, we cannot afford to abandon the philosophical project of grounding a conception of impartiality in an account of practical reason. There is, in fact, an extensive universalist moral code at work in Walzer's approach to justice, despite his attempts to obscure it with an almost exclusive stress on cultural particularity. The moral principles of justice that are to be included in this universalist code cannot be justified in terms of the traditions of one particular form of life. In a modern context any community that is just must allow ethical reflection on its identity to be shaped and directed by the moral demands of this universalist code. Otherwise hermeneutically grounded social criticism will be dangerously partial. It is for this reason that I suggested that hermeneutics could never act as a substitute for the project of justifying a philosophical conception of an impartial point of view.

There are other good reasons for rejecting Walzer's hermeneutic approach to justice. Most importantly, it cannot draw on a critical social theory that could provide a rational challenge to the possibility of ideological distortion or the unjust effects of power in democratic deliberation. Furthermore, it does not justify its apparent commitment to rational deliberation nor does it clarify what this demands. Finally, its stress on the common will leaves the individual with a vulnerable moral status that should cause serious concern. Philosophical theory is necessary to, and not as Walzer implies, a danger to our understanding of democratic deliberation. This theory must inform us as to how the rational acceptability of substantive principles of justice is to be tested.

We must return therefore to the impartialist project. It is important that the project is pursued in a way that avoids the problems associated with Rawls's attempt to isolate the political. The concern for context that characterizes a hermeneutic approach to matters of justice must also be taken on board. We want to combine a liberal defense of individual autonomy and the priority of right with a holist acknowledgment of the importance of political institutions as a constitutive aspect of the personal identity of each citizen. We need, in other words, a theory of justice that builds both on Rawls's impartialism with its concern for the plurality of conceptions of the good in all modern political societies and on Walzer's contextualism with its concern for the plurality of differently constituted political communities. By conceiving of impartiality in terms of an open dialogical encounter, Habermas's discourse ethics provides the most fertile ground available for a theory of justice that can combine these concerns while also overcoming the different problems we have found in Rawls's impartialism and in Walzer's contextualism. We can now, finally, turn to an exploration of that fertile ground.

III

Jürgen Habermas's Discourse Ethics

5

The Priority of Communicative Action

Jürgen Habermas has developed a highly impressive and comprehensive approach to philosophy and social theory. Few, if indeed any other contemporary theorists, have studied so thoroughly, with such diligence and imagination, the problems associated with the justification of social criticism in a modern context. From his earliest reformulations of critical theory through numerous wide-ranging and far-reaching scholarly disputes and political controversies, to his most recent contributions to contemporary thought, Habermas has worked through a systematic critical defense of the Enlightenment and its hope for emancipation based on human reason.[1] In this part I hope to show that in Habermas's work we find the most fruitful theoretical resource available to us in dealing with the problems of justification that are central to our concerns in this work.

THE THEORETICAL ROOTS OF DISCOURSE ETHICS

Habermas's discourse ethics represents a procedure of justification for substantive principles of justice that is built on a conception of dialogical impartiality. While Habermas shares with Rawls the project of justifying an impartial procedure that can act as a test for competing principles of justice, he rejects the restrictive account of moral-political reasoning that is represented by the original position. For Habermas, norms are not valid unless they could be accepted by all affected by them as participants in a real discourse.[2] The discursive test must be thought of as a cooperative venture among the members of a community who are practically engaged in deliberation. Valid norms are grounded in a shared conviction that is collectively achieved and so these norms express a common will. They cannot therefore be justified by an aggregate of solitary individuals choosing principles in isolation from one another under theoretically designed conditions.

This discursive emphasis enables Habermas to avoid the problems that Rawls encounters in insisting that we isolate political aspects of our morality from our more comprehensive moral commitments before we can consider impartial reflection to be even possible. More significantly, it allows for the participants in discourse to assess critically and, if necessary, to revise their moral intuitions in the light of the encounter with others. Within this procedure of justification the participants really do differ from one another, and the critical flexibility required of them ensures that there is a real possibility that they will experience the discourse as a moment of uncoerced self-transformation.

Habermas insists that it is not for the philosopher to derive or to justify substantive principles of justice.[3] This must be left to the participants in real discourses. The principles and norms that are to be tested are thrown up in the context of the real disputes that arise in any shared form of life. By keeping the philosophical task of justifying an impartial point of view strictly separate from the political task of justifying substantive principles of justice, Habermas can address Walzer's concern that the democratic will should not be overridden by philosophical theory. The procedure that discourse ethics defends does not violate the self-understandings of historically particular communities. Habermas is every bit as concerned as Walzer that the justification of substantive principles of justice be characterized by a public encounter of cooperative deliberation. But what Habermas does provide, and Walzer does not, is a justification for specific rules of argumentation that act as procedural constraints on that deliberation. In this way he takes us far beyond Walzer in detecting the more subtle distorting effects of power on democratic deliberation.

The first task of this part will be to present an overview of Habermas's critical defense of the Enlightenment. With this in mind, I will explain how the theory of communicative action is to be understood, at least in part, as Habermas's response to the debate with Gadamer. This theory provides a basis for critique that makes it abundantly clear, in ways that the psychoanalytic model could not, that Habermas is not interested in any vanguardist form of elitism that is hostile to genuine democracy. Habermas grounds his criteria of justification for principles of justice in a theory of language and in the claim that communicative action has priority over strategic action. In this chapter, we will see why this claim is fundamental to Habermas's defense of reason, modernity, and Enlightenment and how it relates to the paradigm shift from the philosophy of consciousness to the philosophy of intersubjective understanding.[4] This claim, of the priority of communicative action, grounds both Habermas's critical social theory, which will be considered very briefly here, and his discourse ethics, which will be discussed in detail in the next chapter.

The role of this chapter is to enable us to place discourse ethics in its proper context so that its advantages over the theoretical accounts of justice given by Rawls and Walzer can be made clear. The central argument of the book is that discourse ethics furnishes us with the theoretical resources that can allow us to present an approach to justice that takes seriously both the plurality of individual conceptions of the good in each modern society, and the plurality of different historically constituted political societies. As a dialogical conception of impartiality, it can avoid the restrictions that Rawls's attempted isolation of the political places on our reflection regarding justice. It therefore yields a better way of showing how an impartialist test for principles of justice can fully respect the plurality of individual conceptions of the good.

By leaving an account of substantive principles of justice to participants in real encounters, Habermas's discourse ethics also shows a hermeneutic sensitivity to context that can appreciate the plurality of historically unique political societies. But since discourse ethics articulates an account of impartiality that is grounded in a conception of practical reason, Habermas tempers his respect for differing contexts with a theoretical perspective that challenges effectively the ways in which dominant interpretations of justice can be entangled with the subtle operation of social power.

The next chapter will focus directly on the distinctive features of discourse ethics. Habermas presents this as a cognitivist ethic. This means that the norms or principles of justice that are justified as valid according to its procedural test have a status analogous to truth. This claim is defended against sceptics in a complex argument that I hope to clarify. In doing so, I intend to show how, in conceiving of an impartial point of view dialogically, Habermas can make a much more convincing case for the impartialist project than Rawls could. Once the advantages of this approach have been indicated, it should then become clear that discourse ethics incorporates the better insights of communitarianism and feminism without making Walzer's mistake of rejecting altogether the task of providing a philosophical justification for a procedural test of impartiality.

Habermas's encounter with contextualists will be dealt with more explicitly in the final part of the book. While discourse ethics makes significant concessions to the concerns of a variety of contextualists, Habermas never succumbs to the temptation of abandoning his strong universalist moral claims. I will defend the universalist thrust of Habermas's discourse ethics in chapter 7 by considering his moral theory in relation to three recent contributions to the ongoing debate about universalism and contextualism. I will also suggest there that Habermas himself has not yet developed fully the potential of certain context sensitive features of his own approach. What I will offer is a modified version of discourse ethics that gives a more central political role to a hermeneutics of communal self-interpretation. In Habermas's own terms, I will be highlighting the political significance of ethical discourses of self-clarification by showing the ways in which they complement moral discourses of normative justification.

Finally, in chapter 8, I will seek to stress the advantages of this version of discourse ethics over the antiprocedural contextualism of Walzer, by looking in some detail at a particular dispute about justice. My concern there will be to show how this dialogical conception of impartiality throws light on the demand for justice in relation to the dispute about the constitutional status of Northern Ireland. This gives us an opportunity to work through the claims of dialogical impartiality in one particular context. The discussion of Northern Ireland's constitutional crisis will allow us to assess both Walzer's and Habermas's approaches to the theory of justice. This example will expose the limitations of Walzer's approach while also indicating the ways in which discourse ethics takes us much further in clarifying what justice demands in this case.

First of all, we need to show now how Habermas's overall project makes the theoretical resources available for an account of justice that situates the concerns of impartiality in particular contexts. The discussion that follows here, of the claim for the priority of communicative action, is motivated by our need for a more adequately discursive conception of impartiality than we found in Rawls's work. As we will see this is made possible by the way in which Habermas grounds his account of normative justification in a theory of language.[5] We are also motivated by our need to avoid the danger of partiality that undermines Walzer's hermeneutics of justice. We will see how the universalist thrust of Habermas's reconstructive theory of communicative action promises an approach to disputes about justice that is more adequately critical than hermeneutics, while remaining sufficiently sensitive to differing historical contexts. Before we explore these theoretical resources, a few brief preliminary remarks are in order.

Habermas's work is best situated in the tradition of critical social theory that aspires to ground our hopes for an emancipated future on a real basis. That people want to be emancipated from whatever causes them to suffer unnecessarily is, for Habermas, not just a contingent fact. It is rather, as he puts it,

> so profoundly ingrained in the structure of human societies—the calling
> into question, and deep-seated wish to throw off, relations which repress

you without necessity—so intimately built into the reproduction of human life that I don't think it can be regarded as just a subjective attitude which may or may not guide this or that piece of scientific research.[6]

While the idea of an emancipatory cognitive interest does not feature explicitly in his most recent substantive social theory, there can be no doubting that this critical attitude continues to constitute the dominant characteristic of his self-understanding as a theorist.[7] Habermas now grounds our emancipatory hope in a theory of communicative action. More specifically, his later work suggests that the claim that communicative action is the original mode of language use provides us with a theoretical basis for social criticism that can help to sustain our hope in a better future.

Both Habermas's social-theoretical diagnosis of modern society and his discourse ethics, are built on the theory of communicative action. While his social theory aims to identify and explain the repressive features of advanced capitalist societies by revealing the ways in which our communication can be distorted by power, his moral theory, or discourse ethics, articulates the criteria by which we can distinguish between valid and invalid moral norms or principles of justice. Discourse ethics facilitates constructive social criticism by articulating standards of legitimacy, while critical social theory helps us to realize the conditions of fulfilment for a legitimate social order.

What follows then in the remainder of this chapter is a broad outline of Habermas's overall project that will help us to grasp the theoretical roots of discourse ethics as an approach to disputes about justice. The main aim of Habermas's project is to present a critical defense of reason, modernity, and the Enlightenment. The focus of this outline is on Habermas's crucial claim that communicative action is the original mode of language use. This is the key argument of the theory of communicative action. I want to suggest that we should think of this theory as a response to the insufficiently critical stance of hermeneutics. This requires a brief discussion to introduce the idea of a reconstructive science, the key theoretical feature that enables discourse ethics to avoid the problems I have outlined in Walzer's contextualism.

PHILOSOPHY AND RATIONAL RECONSTRUCTION

In his social theory, Habermas accepts much of the hermeneutic critique of the unwarranted objectivist claims of positivist social science. However, in building a framework for a critical theory, he is concerned to avoid the implied relativism of radical hermeneutics.[8] While the role of the social theorist must indeed be thought of as that of a participative interpreter rather than that of neutral observer, the conclusion that we must therefore give up on the idea of objectivity altogether does not necessarily follow. We can certainly give up our privileged observer status and our pretensions to context-independence. We can also extend our inquiries beyond claims of propositional truth to include nondescriptive claims of normative rightness and sincere self-expression. But we can still derive objective standards of social criticism by drawing out and theoretically reconstructing the rational assumptions implicit in all possible interpretations of social actions and phenomena.[9]

What is at issue here is the possibility of making explicit the conditions of validity for expressions and actions that intuitively guide all social actors in distinguishing the valid from the invalid. It is an attempt to give a theoretical account of the intuitive knowhow that we all take for granted in everyday communication. Since this intuitive knowhow is thought to be universal, and not dependent on being situated in any particular context, it is clear that Habermas sees this as a theoretical means of transcending hermeneutics. This then is the first step in providing standards of justice that can avoid the danger of partiality that we discovered in Walzer's work.

At this stage we are examining Habermas's efforts to seek support for his theory of communicative action by turning to what he calls reconstructive scientific research. Reconstructive scientific procedures are distinguished from empirical-analytical procedures by the fact that they attempt to "systematically reconstruct the intuitive knowledge of competent subjects" rather than seeking to "develop nomological hypotheses about domains of observable events."[10] The rational reconstruction of communicative action is concerned with the deep structure of the symbolically structured reality of the social world.[11] It seeks to render explicit the practical, pretheoretical knowhow of all communicatively competent subjects. The deep structure that it reconstructs is the implicit rule consciousness that underlies the possibility of competent subjects generating meaningful expressions within the context of the surface structure of a language. For the reconstructive scientist

> the object of understanding is no longer the content of a symbolic expression or what specific authors meant by it in specific situations but the intuitive rule consciousness that a competent speaker has of his own language.[12]

What this type of analysis aims to uncover are the presumably universal standards of rationality that can be thought of as conditions for the validity of meaningful expressions.[13]

In this way rational reconstruction goes beyond the concerns of a hermeneutic approach that limits itself to the attempt to understand the content of expressions within the context of the surface structure of a language. In contrast, Habermas is interested in defending a general theory, insofar as the knowhow that is reconstructed expresses a universal capability or a "species competence."[14] In clarifying the general conditions of the validity of a symbolic expression, Habermas hopes that his theory of communicative action will secure a critical foothold with regard to particular invalid expressions.

The theory maintains that making a statement that can be understood necessarily involves participation in processes of communication where all participants (speakers, hearers, and observers) adopt a performative attitude. This attitude, as opposed to an objectivating attitude, enables "a mutual orientation toward validity claims . . . designed for critical assessment so that an intersubjective recognition of a particular claim can serve as the basis for a rationally motivated consensus."[15] Before examining this idea of communicative action in more detail, we should note that Habermas sees rational reconstruction as a key feature of his critical defense of the Enlightenment.

Habermas argues that in the light of the prevalent critiques of foundationalism, philosophy must find a new role.[16] It must humbly accept that it can no longer play the authoritative role that Kant had hoped for it, that of clarifying "the foundations of the sciences for once and for all, defining the limits of what can and what cannot be experienced."[17] This attempt by philosophy to usher the sciences to their proper place is, Habermas admits, unacceptable.[18] The same can be said for philosophy's self-appointed role as judge of all cultural matters such as the differentiation of value spheres (science, morality, art), with its implicit claim to confer legitimacy on these spheres within their own limits. This represents a task that philosophy cannot achieve. The reason for this is because these structures of rationality do not need to be grounded or justified in a modern context, since the fact of their cultural generation is what characterizes modernity itself. The task of giving these differentiated value spheres a philosophical justification is simply redundant.[19]

So even though philosophy can no longer claim the roles of usher and judge, it can still, despite the ironic laughter of its contemporary gravediggers, claim to function as the "guardian of rationality."[20] If it is to do so, it must steer a course between the discredited tradition of foundationalism on the one hand, and the flight to irrationality of a totalizing critique of reason on the other.[21] This is where Habermas sees the importance of reconstructive science. Philosophy can enter into a cooperative relationship with certain research projects in the human sciences by playing the role of "stand-in" for "empirical theories with strong universalistic claims."[22] In other words philosophy can furnish reconstructive hypotheses that are to be used in empirical settings. In turn, the empirical research may offer indirect confirmation of the reconstructive hypothesis.

Philosophy then continues to make universalist claims, but ones that are fallibilistic in orientation. They are offered without any pretence to support them with a foundational grounding. Nor is there any attempt to provide ultimate justifications for these hypotheses independently of any empirical corroboration. The hypotheses involved would be used in empirical research that might, for example, seek to explain, from the intuitive knowledge of competent subjects, "the presumably universal bases of rational experience and judgement, as well as of action and linguistic communication."[23] Habermas's own philosophical work is to be thought of in the context of this cooperation with the reconstructive human sciences.[24]

Similarly, while philosophy can no longer set itself up as judge, above and beyond the value spheres of culture, it can take on the more modest task of helping us to find a balance between these separated moments of reason in communicative everyday life.[25] Philosophy can be the mediating interpreter between the spheres of science, morality, and art, so that, while the regional rationality of each sphere is respected, they are no longer isolated from each other. These spheres are conceptually distinct, yet they are constantly interpenetrating and overlapping. It is for this reason that Habermas sees a necessity for a general theory of communicative action that can thematize validity claims in each of these spheres, while at the same time fulfilling this role of interpreter on behalf of the lifeworld. As mediating interpreter, philosophy can help us to identify and to challenge the dominance of one of these spheres over the others.[26]

Habermas understands these new roles for philosophy as being characteristic of a paradigm shift from the philosophy of consciousness to the philosophy of intersubjective understanding. The philosophy of consciousness sought to secure its foundations in the lone, isolated, autonomous subject standing apart, rationally disengaged and disembodied, independent of all historical and social contingency.[27] Even though these foundations would seem to have crumbled under our feet, we need not be paralyzed philosophically by accepting the contingency of our situatedness in real historical and cultural contexts. We can be rescued from the fate of such a paralysis by refusing to see reason as necessarily pure and disembodied, but rather by seeing reason as historically situated in the communicative practice of everyday life.

Habermas's philosophical project is the task of clarifying, with a fallibilistic consciousness, the pragmatic presuppositions of rationality in everyday processes of reaching understanding, presuppositions that he presumes to be universal in so far as they are unavoidable. He seeks confirmation for his hypothesis in a cooperative venture with empirical theories of universal competences. Within the contours of this project neither paralyzing anxiety, nor ecstatic celebration, are appropriate responses to the demise of the ultimate foundations of a philosophy of consciousness. Philosophy as guardian of rationality has not ended but rather it has been transformed

> so as to enable it to cope with the entire spectrum of aspects of rationality—and with the historical fate of a reason that has been arrested again and again, ideologically misused and distorted, but that also stubbornly raises its voice in every inconspicuous act of successful communication.[28]

It would appear then that philosophy, from Habermas's perspective, takes a far more humble role than that which was such a cause of worry to Walzer. All he claims philosophical theory can offer for a critical social theory is, at best, a reconstruction of the pragmatic presuppositions of everyday attempts to use language as a means of achieving a mutual understanding. For our concerns, this reconstruction can then, as we will see, offer a theoretical basis from which we could work out a conception of impartiality. This is the route Habermas takes to overcoming the dangers of a hermeneutics of justice by grounding a stringent and universally valid discursive test for competing principles of justice.

In the next chapter I hope to show clearly how discourse ethics develops out of the paradigm shift to a philosophy of intersubjective understanding. In this way it provides us with a dialogical conception of impartiality that constitutes, or so I will argue, the best guide available to us in seeking criteria of justification for principles of justice. It is the reconstructive theory of communicative action that is the theoretical resource that allows Habermas to offer a more convincing version of the impartialist project than that of Rawls. By drawing his conception of impartiality out of a theory of language, Habermas presents a discursive basis for his criteria of normative justification. We will discover later how this thoroughly intersubjectivist grounding allows Habermas's impartialism to avoid the attempt to isolate the political that led to the most serious flaws in Rawls's procedural test for substantive principles of justice. But now we must examine more closely some of the main features of the theory of communicative action.

COMMUNICATIVE AND STRATEGIC ACTION

The theory of communicative action gives us an account of the pretheoretic knowledge and the intuitive command of "rule systems by means of which competent subjects generate and evaluate valid expressions and performance."[29] What distinguishes Habermas's approach from the hermeneutics of Gadamer, or Walzer, is the claim that whenever we seek to reach an understanding we must implicitly appeal to universal standards of rationality. He is not concerned only with the interpretation and explication of meaning but rather also with the rules of language use that are intuitively known by all communicatively competent subjects. The identification of universal conditions of validity that is the object of a process of rational reconstruction produces theoretical knowledge of the general structures of communication that transcends the limiting horizon of a particular tradition.

In communicative action validity claims, that are in principle criticizable, are raised. There are, according to Habermas, three separate validity claims that correspond to three different relations to the world; a claim to truth relates to an existing state of affairs in the objective world; a claim to normative rightness relates to the regulation of interpersonal relationships in the social world; a claim to truthfulness relates to the speaker's lived experience in the subjective world.[30] Every speech act could therefore be criticized from three different perspectives, even though "only one of the three validity claims can be thematically emphasized in any explicit speech act."[31]

What is distinctive about communicative action is the performative attitude that is adopted in any attempt to reach an understanding with somebody else about something in the world. The formal-pragmatic features of this attitude can be analyzed in terms of speech acts, where one participant says something to which the other participant takes a yes or no position. This is the simplest form of communicative action but this attitude is not unique to speech acts and it can also characterize many forms of nonverbal action in everyday communicative practice.[32] This includes action that can easily be given a linguistic form, such as that involved in a game of charades, and action that cannot be given a verbal form at all, like certain gestures that an orator might use to emphasize a point. If we are to analyze what is involved in the process of two or more subjects reaching a mutual understanding, however, then we must refer to the model of speech. Habermas therefore reconstructs the formal-pragmatic presuppositions of communicative action through an analysis of speech acts.

When we engage in communicative action there are certain necessary and unavoidable presuppositions involved in our speech acts. If, in communicating with you, my attitude is solely oriented to reaching an understanding with you about something, then I have to presuppose that you will be motivated to accept the validity claims I raise by nothing but the force of reason. In other words, I presuppose that the understanding we seek will be rationally motivated. This can be contrasted with a mere *de facto* accord since any communicatively achieved agreement must be accepted or presupposed by the participants and not just imposed.[33]

A *de facto* accord can be imposed by whichever participant is in a stronger bargaining position. We can differentiate between a communicatively achieved agreement and an imposed accord, as illustrated in the following examples. It seems clear that somebody looking for work in Britain today is, in normal circumstances, in a weaker position than is a prospective employer. In any negotiations that might arise in this context, the person seeking employment might be inclined to come to an agreement or even to sign a contract not because of the force of reason alone but rather because it may represent the best offer available at the time. Getting off the dole is sufficient motivation for the employee not to question the normative claims entailed in the contract. While an employer may act benevolently, the basic inequality in bargaining positions is not altered since the employer has the power to decide whether to be benevolent or not.

A rather different example that demonstrates that a mere *de facto* accord is not the same as a communicatively achieved agreement might arise on an occasion where I am having a quiet drink in a pub with one friend and a large and boisterous group wrongly accuse me of having spilt one of their drinks. I am not likely to engage in communicative action in order to come to a rationally motivated agreement with them about whether or not I did spill the drink. It seems much more likely that I would cut my losses and accept that buying them a drink is the best offer available to me at the time. The advantages of avoiding violence, which may implicitly or explicitly be threatened in the encounter, would prevent me from questioning their truth claim.

Habermas is clearly not claiming that all linguistically mediated interaction is communicative action. He is primarily concerned with distinguishing between communicative action and what he refers to as strategic action.[34] These represent two types of interaction that might be used in coordinating plans of action. It is of course true that we often engage in social action with an attitude that is not oriented to reaching understanding but rather with an objectivating attitude that is oriented to consequences, to the success of our private goals. For Habermas the latter constitutes strategic action. Linguistically mediated strategic action involves the use of speech acts to instrumentalize our fellow participants as we seek to succeed in our own individual goals.

It must be noted that communicative action often serves to link individual participants' teleologically structured instrumental plans of action. However a distinctive feature of communicative action, as a form of coordinating interaction, is that it cannot be reduced to teleological action that could only be analyzed by reference to the intentions and aims of the individual actors. Of course, action oriented to reaching understanding does have a goal, but it would be a mistake to think that this necessarily means that the distinction between the two models of action must break down. This is because the "medium of language and the telos of reaching understanding intrinsic to it reciprocally constitute one another. The relation between these is not one of means and ends."[35] While strategic action aims to intervene causally in the world, the aims of communicative action are situated at a different level. That level is the linguistically constituted lifeworld.

> The telos of reaching understanding, inherent in linguistic structures, compels the communicative actors to alter their perspective; this finds expression in the necessity of going from the objectivating attitude of success-oriented action, which seeks to effect something in the world, over to the performative attitude of a speaker who seeks to reach an understanding with a second person about something.[36]

Communicatively achieved agreement always proceeds cooperatively "within the dimension of world-disclosing language itself" and is therefore never "at the disposal of an individual party to interaction."[37] The end of communicative action is so interwoven with the intersubjective form of life which makes all linguistically mediated interaction possible that it cannot be treated as a contingent end but rather, it is an end that cannot be bypassed.[38]

Communicative action must therefore be analyzed independently of the intentions and purposive activity of individual actors. Since in communicative action our speech acts are oriented to reaching understanding, it must be possible to "clarify the structure of linguistic communication without reference to structures of purposive activity."[39] For Habermas, this is the central feature of the paradigm shift from a philosophy of consciousness to a philosophy of intersubjective understanding. In attempting to derive the general pragmatic presuppositions of communicative action from the structure of processes of reaching understanding, Habermas is hoping to provide a reconstructive theoretical account of the

> pretheoretical knowledge of competent speakers, who can themselves distinguish situations in which they are causally exerting an influence upon others from those in which they are coming to an understanding with them, and who know when their attempts have failed.[40]

While there are numerous important issues that would have to be addressed in any serious consideration of the notion of communicative action, it would take us too far from the central focus of this present work to pursue many of them here.[41] For our purposes we need only address one question that bears directly on the justification of discourse ethics as an impartialist test for principles of justice that can avoid the problems we discovered in Rawls's account. Since Habermas admits that linguistically mediated interaction could be communicative or strategic (as he defines them), then why is it that he takes speech acts to be a model for communicative and not strategic action? In other words, why should communicative action have priority over strategic action as a mode of language use? Habermas needs to justify this priority if the presuppositions of communicative action are to provide the basis for both his moral theory and his critical social theory. What is so special about the use of language with this orientation to reaching understanding?

ILLOCUTIONS, PERLOCUTIONS, AND
COMMUNICATIVE ACTION'S PRIORITY

At one point in his attempt to justify the priority of communicative action over strategic action as a mode of language use, Habermas puts the matter quite straightforwardly; "the use of language with an orientation to reaching understanding is the original mode of language use, upon which . . . the instrumental use of language in general, [is] parasitic."[42] After making this strong claim he immediately goes on to assert that Austin's distinction between illocutions and perlocutions shows us that this is indeed so.

For Austin, to say something that expresses a state of affairs is a locutionary act, to perform an action in saying something is an illocutionary act, to bring about an effect on the hearer through saying something is a perlocutionary act. When we pursue only illocutionary aims in our speech acts then it can be considered to be self-sufficient in the sense that "the communicative intent of the speaker and the illocutionary aim he is pursuing follow from the manifest meaning of what is said."[43] On the other hand, perlocutionary effects can result "whenever a speaker acts with an orientation to success and thereby instrumentalizes speech acts for purposes that are only contingently related to the meaning of what is said."[44] We can only describe these effects in "a context of teleological action that goes beyond the speech act."[45] Furthermore, while illocutionary aims have to be openly expressed to succeed, the opposite is true of perlocutionary aims that must be kept concealed in order to be successful.[46]

I might say to a student, "That essay is particularly difficult." I am pursuing the illocutionary aim of warning the student of problems that would lie ahead if she were to choose to write that essay. I may have no other aim except that of reaching an understanding with the student. However, in another case, I may say exactly the same thing but with the hope of putting the student off doing the essay because it would be more difficult for me to assess it than any of the other alternative essays. This desire to save myself work would represent a necessarily concealed perlocutionary aim that is obviously related to the meaning of what is said in a contingent and not a necessary sense. Success of the perlocutionary aim depends on the success of the illocutionary one. What this means in this case is that if I am successfully to save myself work then the student must understand the meaning of my speech act.

How does Austin's distinction help to justify Habermas's claim that strategic action is parasitic upon communicative action, and that the latter is the original mode of language use? As in the example just given we could only use speech acts to pursue perlocutionary aims if they could achieve illocutionary aims.

> If the hearer failed to understand what the speaker was saying, a strategically acting speaker would not be able to bring the hearer, by means of communicative acts to behave in the desired way. To this extent . . . "the use of language with an orientation to consequences" is not an original use of language but the subsumption of speech acts that serve illocutionary aims under conditions of action oriented to success.[47]

What communicative action amounts to, then, is any linguistically mediated interaction where all participants pursue only illocutionary aims.

Austin's distinction does not give as neat a result as Habermas would have hoped for in making his claim for the originary nature of communicative action. He recognized himself that a simple imperative is a case where the speaker pursues unreservedly illocutionary aims and yet acts with an orientation to success rather than understanding. If I say "Shut the door!" I do not conceal the perlocutionary aim involved, to get somebody else to close the door simply because I want it closed. In order to take imperatives into account, Habermas argued that it is only illocutionary acts that raise criticizable validity claims that should be considered as constitutive of communicative action.[48]

It would appear therefore that since the distinction between illocutions and perlocutions is not the same as the distinction between communicative action and strategic action, then demonstrating the dependence of perlocutions on illocutions will not provide Habermas with the conclusion that communicative action is originary as a mode of language use while strategic action is parasitic. Astute critics have not been slow to point that out.[49] More recently, however, Habermas has modified his view on this point so as to defend his central claim that communicative action has priority over strategic action. He now argues that simple imperatives are also parasitic on the use of language with an orientation to understanding, in that they must refer to potential sanctions. This makes up for a deficit in illocutionary force but again this could not be understood if the hearer did not know what the demand would mean in a normatively authorized context. The validity claim to normative rightness is replaced by a power claim of threatened sanctions or perhaps violence.[50]

Furthermore, Habermas realizes that, since the distinction between illocutions and perlocutions is not the same as that between communicative and strategic action, he will have to differentiate between perlocutionary effects that are strategically intended and those that are not. While strategically intended perlocutionary effects are undeclared, nonstrategically intended effects arise in the context of an interactive success. The acceptance of a validity claim may well lead the hearer to "take on obligations which are relevant to the further sequence of interaction."[51] An interactive success therefore goes beyond the narrow sense of an illocutionary success that simply involves the hearer's understanding the speaker's utterance. It also involves a success in the more far-reaching sense of achieving a consensus on a validity claim that can effect coordination of action. Such an effect would be a nonstrategically intended perlocutionary effect of successful communicative interaction.

It should be noted that these revisions do not in any sense undermine the distinction between communicative action and strategic action itself. As we will recall, these types of interaction are to be distinguished in terms of their structural characteristics.

> In communicative action the structure of language usage oriented toward reaching understanding is superimposed on the underlying teleological structure of the action, and subjects the actors to precisely such constraints as compel them to adopt a performative attitude that is more laden with presuppositions than the objectivating stance of the strategic actor. Interaction mediated through acts of reaching understanding exhibits a both richer and more strictly limiting structure than does strategic action.[52]

Austin's work undoubtedly provides Habermas with useful tools for a formal-pragmatic analysis of speech acts that allows him to study the structure of processes of reaching understanding without reference to purposive activity. We have seen however that it does not in itself justify the priority of communicative action. But just because Austin's distinction between illocutions and perlocutions does not ground this priority, it does not follow that it cannot be grounded.

Habermas might, for example, draw explicitly in this context on Wittgenstein's analysis of the concept of following a rule. He discusses this in his account of Mead's work on symbolic interaction. The basic point is that we can only learn to use language if we develop a rule-consciousness. As Wittgenstein noted, it is not possible to obey a rule privately. Rather he

> emphasized the internal connection that holds between the competence to follow rules and the ability to respond with a "yes" or "no" to the question whether a symbol has been used correctly, that is, according to the rules. The two competences are equally constitutive for rule-consciousness.[53]

If this is true of learning a language then the original mode of language use must have an orientation to intersubjective understanding among those who together become conscious of rules genetically. Before a language can be used with an orientation to success, rule-consciousness must already have been developed among its speaking subjects and this could only occur through action oriented to reaching understanding. It seems that communicative action could in this way be shown to be originary and strategic action parasitic as uses of language.[54]

If we are to appreciate fully the strength of Habermas's case for the priority of communicative action however, we must shift our focus away from the formal-pragmatic analysis of speech acts so as to take into account the fact that communicative action always takes place in the context of a concrete form of life, or a lifeworld. This analysis of the possible arguments for the priority of communicative action is crucial to our overall project in seeking a sufficiently context-sensitive account of impartiality. As we will see later, the theoretical grounding of discourse ethics in everyday communicative action makes it possible for us to provide a conception of impartiality that can take seriously not only the plurality of individual conceptions of the good, but also the plurality of differently constituted political societies. It yields an impartialist procedure that is always already situated in particular contexts.

THE REPRODUCTION OF THE LIFEWORLD AND CRITICAL SOCIAL THEORY

The lifeworld is a background resource that represents a "culturally transmitted and linguistically organized stock of interpretive patterns."[55] This stock of interpretive patterns is the horizon within which communicative actors are always already moving. It represents the taken for granted background assumptions that shape the contexts of all processes of reaching understanding. The conception of the lifeworld, as the shared background knowledge of participants in everyday practices of communication, helps to explain how successful interaction is possible at all. In every act of communication the participants depend on the resources of a prereflexively known form of life over which they have no control. They always find themselves within a shared interpretive horizon that is taken for granted. Interactive success is therefore achieved autonomously in a qualified sense.[56]

Processes of reaching understanding, in turn, maintain and reproduce the symbolic structures of the lifeworld. As a resource the lifeworld is not merely "routed through" communicative action but it is "saddled on" the interpretive accomplishments of the actors.[57] As Habermas puts it, "the network of communicative actions is nourished by resources of the lifeworld and is at the same time the medium by which concrete forms of life are reproduced."[58] The concepts of communicative action and the lifeworld are therefore complementary. Habermas supplements his analysis of action oriented toward reaching understanding with his analysis of the lifeworld. In communicative action, participants stand in a cultural tradition that they simultaneously use and renew. The symbolic structures of the lifeworld are reproduced through the practices of communicative action.

> Under the functional aspect of mutual understanding, communicative action serves to transmit and renew cultural knowledge; under the aspect of coordinating action, it serves social integration and the establishment of solidarity; finally under the aspect of socialization, communicative action serves the formation of personal identities.[59]

The processes of cultural reproduction, social integration and socialization constitute the reproduction of the symbolic structures of the lifeworld and communicative action is the medium through which this reproduction takes place.

This two-way relation between the lifeworld and communicative action provides Habermas with the basis for an alternative justification for the priority of communicative action. In fact, he develops this argument in response to the claim that it might be possible to avoid the performative attitude oriented to reaching understanding altogether by consistently adopting the objectivating attitude of the strategic actor.[60] Habermas claims that this would require the disengagement of the individual from the lifeworld.[61] As we have seen, the lifeworld can only be reproduced through the medium of communicative action and not in accord with the rational purposive activity of isolated individuals. The individual can only form her personal identity in the context of a web of mutual recognition and intersubjective understanding that is provided by the lifeworld.[62]

Insofar as the actor's personal identity depends on the structures of the lifeworld, the option of consistent strategic action is only available in the abstract, in individual cases, and not as a long-term disengagement from contexts of communicative action. Habermas maintains that

> opting for a long-run withdrawal from contexts of action oriented to reaching understanding, and thus from communicatively structured spheres of life, means retreating into the monadic isolation of strategic action; in the long-run this is self-destructive.[63]

Strategic action presupposes an identity of a self whose formation is dependent on the symbolic structures of the lifeworld. There is therefore no substitute for communicative action from the perspective of the lifeworld to which the individual belongs and on which her identity depends. There is a high price to be paid by the individual for long-term withdrawal from this context, be it the self-destructive monadic isolation of the compulsive strategic actor, schizophrenia or suicide.[64] This conception of the lifeworld shows how the claim that communicative action is prior to strategic action is directly connected to the paradigm shift from the philosophy of consciousness to the philosophy of intersubjective understanding.

But it is still not clear how the priority of communicative action relates to the realm of politics. While we might accept, for example, that since our personal identity depends on the symbolic structures of the lifeworld and these are reproduced in a necessarily communicative way, communicative action certainly does have priority in the sphere of intimate relations, but what about matters of political and social policy? Why is strategic action not adequate as a medium of coordinating action in these realms?

We have already seen that the reproduction of the lifeworld is constituted not only by the socialization of individuals but also by the transmission and renewal of cultural knowledge and processes of social integration and the establishment of forms of solidarity. The coordination of action through social and political institutions, no less than the socialization of the individual, is anchored in the lifeworld. While strategic action may well play an ineliminable role in political and social life, our political and social institutions must also act in the service of social integration and solidarity formation. To this extent these institutions cannot be detached from communicatively structured domains of action. If the symbolic structures of the lifeworld are to survive the atomizing effects of pervasive strategic action and its instrumental rationality, then communicative action must also have priority in the realm of politics.[65]

It should now be clear how Habermas's theory of communicative action can be thought of as a reformulation of critical social theory. It is intended to facilitate both the explanation and the critical assessment of the institutional patterns of late capitalist societies. It is not strategic action as such, but rather the functionalist reason of social systems that promote it, that constitutes the greatest threat to the communicative structures of the lifeworld. In complex modern societies the material reproduction of the lifeworld becomes systematically organized through the development of economic markets and state bureaucracies. These systems and their corresponding nonlinguistic steering media, money and power, have encroached into domains of the symbolic reproduction of the lifeworld. Functionalist reason, in the form of systemic mechanisms, has suppressed communicative reason, in the form of social integration.[66]

One of the effects of this one-sided process of rationalization has been to promote rational purposive strategic action and its objectivating attitude in domains of social life where this type of interaction cannot perform the task required of it, that of the reproduction of the lifeworld.[67] With his theory of communicative action, Habermas hopes to explain "why modern societies cannot be held together exclusively or even primarily through money and power."[68] Put slightly differently, it shows that "money and power can neither buy nor compel solidarity and meaning."[69] The suppression of communicative action constitutes a crisis, or a pathology for the lifeworld, one that can be diagnosed in terms of the colonization of the lifeworld by systems.[70]

Habermas's colonization thesis recasts the notion of reification. His critical social theory is concerned to articulate the necessary conditions for a communicatively rationalized society. It suggests that we need to reclaim for the public sphere those aspects of our politics that have been colonized by systemic imperatives.[71] The priority of communicative action both grounds a critical social theory and offers us a normative guide for political protest and resistance to the domination of the current configuration of power. It is with the justification of his discourse ethics that Habermas makes the normative aspects of this theory explicit.

We have seen how the argument for the priority of communicative action is related to the task of rational reconstruction, the concept of the lifeworld and the elaboration of a critical social theory.[72] These are the key features of the paradigm shift that Habermas claims his work to represent, from the philosophy of consciousness to the philosophy of intersubjective understanding. My intention in this chapter has been to lay the ground for my argument that Habermas's work enables us to theorize justice in a way that can overcome the weaknesses of both Rawls's restricted conception of moral-political reasoning and Walzer's anti-impartialist contextualism. Habermas's conception of impartiality is given a thoroughly intersubjectivist grounding in his analysis of everyday processes of reaching mutual understanding through communicative action. This means that he does not have to restrict the subject of justice in advance of a public assessment of competing principles. Furthermore, since the analysis of communicative action is presented as a rational reconstruction of universal capabilities, his account of discourse ethics can transcend the limits of hermeneutics. Having provided some necessary theoretical background in this chapter, we can return directly to our task of working out a theory of justice that can take seriously pluralism in both the senses we are concerned with. It is to the elaboration of discourse ethics as a dialogical conception of impartiality that we must now turn.

6

Discourse and Impartiality

We have seen how Rawls's impartialist project is designed to present a theoretical account of justice that responds to the fact that modern societies are characterized by a plurality of individual conceptions of the good. On the other hand, Walzer's contextualist hermeneutics of justice stresses the significance of the plurality of differently constituted, historically unique, modern political societies. Neither theory takes sufficient care to present an approach to matters of justice that can give both senses of pluralism their due weight. In the previous chapter we saw how the theoretical roots of Habermas's discourse ethics are to be found in his analysis of everyday communication, more specifically in the priority of communicative action. In this chapter we will see how this grounding furnishes us with the theoretical resources we need so as to situate our concern for impartiality in particular historical contexts. This then clears the way for the next part, where I hope to show how discourse ethics allows us to theorize justice in a way that can give both senses of pluralism their due weight.

Discourse as Reflective Communicative Action

Habermas's contribution to current debates in moral and political theory constitutes the most compelling case for resisting the conclusion that the insights of a variety of contextualists have, for once and for all, undermined the attempt to justify a conception of an impartial point of view. In defending a discourse ethics that claims to be valid universally, Habermas is swimming against the tide, stubbornly refusing to be carried away in the contemporary drift toward relativism.

Habermas sets about reconstructing an impartial point of view with two principal concerns in mind. First, he wants to refute the views of sceptics and relativists by using his theory of communicative action to argue that advocates of such views are inevitably enmeshed in a performative contradiction.[1] Second, he hopes to defend a modified version of Kant's categorical imperative from the contextualist criticisms that have dogged Kantian moral theory since Hegel's celebrated critique.[2] While discourse ethics follows Kant in its most significant features, Habermas draws on Hegel's distinction between morality (*Moralität*) and ethical life (*Sittlichkeit*) in his characterization of moral discourse as a reflective form of everyday communicative action.[3] Although morality is always embedded in ethical life, "the unrelenting moralizing gaze of the participant in discourse" weakens the power of norms that had previously enjoyed a naive social acceptance.[4]

Habermas's encounter with contextualism will be the subject of the next chapter, but the aim here is to outline the way in which discourse ethics elaborates a dialogical conception of impartiality. Our concern is with the project of justifying an impartial procedure that can act as a test for competing substantive principles of justice. It is with regard to questions of political and social justice, rather than moral theory in a wider sense, that we will evaluate Habermas's discourse ethics.[5] First of all, we need to account for the distinctive features of discourse ethics. Second, we will analyze the important role that idealization plays in rational discourse concerning normative validity claims and principles of justice. Third, we will assess Habermas's justification for the impartial procedure implicit in this approach to moral-political theory by examining the arguments he presents against those who are sceptical of his rational reconstruction of rules of discourse. Finally, I hope to make clear the advantages of a dialogical conception of impartiality over Rawls's conception by showing how discourse ethics is not vulnerable to the criticisms, outlined in the first part, that undermine the attempt to isolate the political. The thrust of the chapter's argument is that Habermas's work offers an approach to questions of justice that successfully combines a concern for impartiality with a sensitivity to the particular contexts in which disputes about justice might arise.

Discourse ethics is Kantian in the sense that it shares the following attributes with Kant's moral theory.[6] First, it is deontological, concerning itself with the validity of norms, which in providing a legitimate ordering for the satisfaction of interests, can act as a basis for the justification of our actions. It therefore limits itself to questions of moral rightness, rather than dealing with full conceptions of a good life. Habermas, like Rawls, affirms the priority of right but, as we will see, he does so in a significantly different way. Second, it is cognitivist in that it treats normative rightness as a claim to validity that is analogous to a truth claim. Third, it is formalist in that it defends a procedure of moral argumentation rather than any substantive moral principles. This procedure embodies a moral point of view that explains how competing substantive principles can be judged impartially, or in a way that expresses a common interest. The rules of argumentation that Habermas elaborates represent a dialogical procedure that can be contrasted with the monological procedures of Kant and Rawls. Furthermore, Habermas, unlike Rawls, leaves the justification of substantive principles of justice to the participants in a real discourse. Fourth, discourse ethics is universalist, in that it claims to justify its procedure of moral argumentation independently of the prejudices or biases of any particular tradition or culture.

Habermas grounds discourse ethics in his analysis of communicative action, or action oriented toward reaching understanding. As we saw in the last chapter, this involves at least two participants who seek to harmonize their individual plans of action on the basis of a communicatively achieved agreement that is rationally motivated. An agreement is generated if all participants can affirm, at least implicitly, some criticizable validity claim that has been raised.[7] The actors share as a background a lifeworld that forms the context for communication while at the same time providing the resources that the actors need to engage in this process.

In the context of a modern lifeworld, according to Habermas's reconstruction, all competent communicative actors can differentiate between three different relations to the world and three corresponding validity claims. As we will recall these are, first, the objective world (existing states of affairs) and a claim to truth, second, the social world (regulation of interpersonal relationships) and a claim to normative rightness, and, third, the subjective world (the speaker's lived experience) and a claim to truthfulness.[8] We can also differentiate between the unquestioned intersubjectively shared certitudes of the lifeworld and the content on which participants in communicative action reach agreement. Participants reach agreement about something in a world (objective, social, or subjective). This content has become detached from the diffuse background of the lifeworld and has taken on "the character of knowledge linked with a potential for reasoning, knowledge that claims validity and can be criticized, that is, knowledge that can be argued about on the basis of reasons."[9] Our capacity to make these differentiations constitutes for Habermas a decentered understanding of the world.

With this decentered understanding of the world the lifeworld is put at a distance as the objective, social, and subjective worlds are problematized.[10] For example, the objective world is theorized in that propositions that had been unquestioned may now be true or false. Similarly, the social world is moralized in that norms that were previously taken for granted can now be valid or invalid. This means that the normativity of existing institutions becomes open to question. A hypothetical attitude has been introduced to the domain of social interaction that allows for a move to discourse, a more reflective form of communicative action.[11] These validity claims, to truth and to normative rightness, must be redeemed discursively, that is, with the support of reasons, if the participants are to continue to orient themselves toward reaching mutual understanding.[12] If they do not resort to strategic action or to brute force, they will become involved in a discourse that anticipates a rationally motivated consensus. The participants will then be engaged in a procedure of argumentation that tests a disputed validity claim's worthiness to be recognized.

> The rationality proper to the communicative practice of everyday life points to the practice of argumentation as a court of appeal that makes it possible to continue communicative action with other means when disagreements can no longer be repaired with everyday routines and yet are not to be settled by the direct or strategic use of force.[13]

Discourse ethics relates specifically to the moralization of the social world that occurs when the normativity of existing institutions is brought into question. These can no longer enjoy a naive social acceptance but are potential subjects of a practical discourse.

If a normative validity claim is called into question then the background consensus that plays an important action coordinating function in everyday communicative practice is broken. Practical discourse is a procedure of moral argumentation in which "participants continue their communicative action in a reflexive attitude with the aim of restoring a consensus that has been disrupted."[14] Agreement is produced if the participants collectively become convinced of something. This might involve the restoration of the intersubjective recognition of the old norm that had become controversial or, perhaps more likely, its substitution with another norm that is newly recognized as valid. This new norm could then facilitate continuing disagreement on the substance of the old norm, which, in that case, would no longer be morally justified.

Habermas's insistence that discourse ethics is cognitivist amounts to the claim that it represents a procedure of argumentation that satisfies the conditions for making impartial moral judgments. In other words, it maintains that norms can be given a rational justification. This is what it means to say that a claim to normative rightness is analogous to a claim to truth. It does not, however, require that we deny the important differences between the two claims.[15] While both can be redeemed discursively, there are no moral facts as such. Normative validity claims do not therefore reflect a moral "truth" in the same way that assertoric validity claims reflect propositional truth. We might also note that while the reality of nature does not depend on validity claims to truth, the social reality of an intersubjectively regulated form of life is dependent on the recognition of validity claims to normative rightness.

This asymmetry between claims to truth and normative rightness is highlighted if we contrast the unequivocal relation between existing states of affairs in the objective world and true propositions about them, and the relation between socially accepted norms and the question of their validity.

> We must distinguish between the social fact that a norm is intersubjectively recognized and its worthiness to be recognized. There may be good reasons to consider the validity claim raised in a socially accepted norm to be unjustified. Conversely, a norm whose claim to validity is in fact redeemable does not necessarily meet with actual recognition or approval.[16]

The validity of a norm does not depend on its social currency but rather on the fact that it could rationally be justified in a practical discourse.

Finally, the differences between the validity claims to truth and to normative rightness reflect the fact that while both empirical knowledge of the objective world and moral knowledge of the social world are fallible, in that they acknowledge the "critical potential of superior future knowledge," our moral knowledge is provisional in a more far reaching sense.[17] This is because of the intrinsic historicity of the social world. Social reality throws up unforeseen situations that then become objects of our moral knowledge. Unlike the objective world, the social world is constituted by historical and cultural processes that shape the interpretations we give to morally valid norms.[18]

By grounding discourse ethics in the theory of communicative action Habermas wants to make it clear that an impartial assessment of claims can only proceed dialogically, in terms of a real argumentation where the individuals concerned reach an agreement cooperatively. Norms are not justified through a rational procedure that an isolated individual could undertake in solitary reflection. It is not a matter of what an individual moral agent could will, without self-contradiction, to be a universal maxim. Nor is it a matter of representative parties in an original position choosing rationally principles of justice in isolation from each other behind a veil of ignorance. For Habermas, unlike Kant and Rawls, the justification of norms is necessarily a matter of whether or not a disputed norm is acceptable to the participants in a practical discourse that is actually carried out.

Real argumentation is required not only because it equalizes power among the participants, though as we will see it does that, but because it is the only way in which a genuinely common will, generated by moral insight, could be expressed.[19] In discourse we do not simply seek a fair compromise between participants, though we may often have to settle for a fair compromise if no norm that expresses a common will can be affirmed. What is highlighted in the shift from a monological to a dialogical moral point of view is the fact that the aim of a practical discourse goes well beyond the task of accommodating the initial moral intuitions of the participants. The aim is rather to clarify a common interest. Each of us involved in this real process of argumentation is called on to adopt the perspective of all the other participants.[20]

To adopt an impartial point of view requires that we engage critically in a process of interpreting our individual needs and interests so as cooperatively to reach an agreement on norms that satisfy shared interests. Needs and interests are always interpreted in the light of cultural values and so this can only be undertaken dialogically, in an intersubjective, public encounter.[21] This may well involve a moment of moral transformation for some, or perhaps all, of the participants, since the dialogical encounter engages them in a self-critical revision of their own need interpretations.[22] Indeed, such a moral transformation might also be necessary even if, while no norm is accepted as being in the common interest, the participants are to agree on a fair compromise. We can now see how the dialogical conception of impartiality in discourse ethics draws out the moral-theoretical implications of the paradigm shift from a philosophy of consciousness to a philosophy of intersubjective understanding. What we now need to assess is the argument that Habermas offers as a justification for this view of impartiality.

IDEALIZATION AND RATIONALITY

The justification of Habermas's procedure of moral argumentation as a universally valid impartial point of view takes as its starting point the unavoidable presuppositions of communicative action.[23] In raising a validity claim a speaker takes on the obligation to support that claim with reasons if called on to do so.[24] By entering into a discourse about a disputed norm the participants must also presuppose rules of argumentation that guarantee that the only motivation driving the discourse is the rational force of the better argument.[25] Habermas suggests that the normative content of these rules ensures that no subject capable of speech and action is excluded from the discourse, that all participants are allowed to question any assertion, to introduce any assertion and to express their attitudes, desires, and needs, and that the exercise of these rights is not to be prevented by coercion, whether internal or external.[26] These presuppositions, expressed as rules, represent the general conditions of a cooperative search for a rationally motivated agreement.

These presuppositions have been characterized in terms of an "ideal speech situation."[27] It is more appropriate to speak of the idealizing presuppositions that must be made by participants if they are communicatively to restore a disrupted normative consensus. They must assume that nothing but the force of the better argument is going to influence the outcome of the discourse.[28] This is how Habermas derives the rules of argumentation outlined above.

> Every speaker knows intuitively that an alleged argument is not a serious one if the appropriate conditions are violated—for example if certain individuals are not allowed to participate, issues or contributions are suppressed, agreement or disagreement is manipulated by insinuations or by threat of sanctions and the like.[29]

Now, of course, when we actually engage in communicative action our idealizing assumptions may not always be objectively correct. Indeed, they may never be correct in a strict sense.[30] The point is that if we do not assume that the conditions under which we engage in argumentation at least approximate, to a sufficient degree, ideal conditions, that is conditions where these rules of argumentation are adhered to, then we could not be participating in a discourse at all. These presuppositions therefore make possible "the practice that participants understand as argumentation."[31] In cases where something other than the force of the better argument is actually in play, we will be acting under a counterfactual presupposition.

Habermas is not guilty here of presupposing the possibility of a fully transparent, rationalistic, homogenized society.[32] In fact, he assumes that much of the background taken-for-grantedness of any intersubjectively shared lifeworld will remain opaque. He also assumes that modern societies will continue to be characterized by a plurality both of interest positions and of comprehensive conceptions of the good. Discourse ethics is a response to pluralism and not an attempt to eradicate it. Idealization does not demand of participants in discourse either a change of worldview or of identity. The particularity of each participant's identity is not effaced but is rather to be given full play in discourse. In contrast with the logic of Rawls's original position, discursive impartiality requires not abstraction from, but rather, explicit articulation of difference. Of course, our need for the justification of norms to regulate our social world actually increases with an ever greater diversity of lifestyles. Habermas is aware that this need "must be satisfied at higher and higher levels of abstraction. For this reason the consensual norms and principles become ever more general."[33]

Just as Habermas is not guilty of seeking to eradicate pluralism, neither is he guilty of assuming that any discourse could ever be completely free from the effects of power. The reconstruction of the pragmatic presuppositions of communicative action is intended to enable us to identify the use and abuse of power in actual discourses. We may accept the outcome of some particular discourse as rational since it appeared, at the time it took place, to approximate sufficiently ideal conditions. In other words, none of the participants had noticed any clear breach of the rationally reconstructed rules of discourse. We may, however, come to realize that the discourse was in fact distorted by some subtle form of manipulation that had been hidden from most of the participants. It may, for example, be revealed at a later stage that somebody had withheld a vital piece of information from the other participants so as to ensure that some new claim would not be introduced into the discourse. It is the reconstruction of the rules of argumentation that in this way enables us to reject the rationality of the outcome to such a discourse. These rules represent conditions of the possibility of distinguishing between more or less reasonable processes of deliberation.

Rational discourses exist like "islands in the sea of everyday practice," serving as they do important social functions, not least of which is the justification of principles of social and political justice.[34] We must institutionalize such discourses in accordance with rules that regulate our public deliberations "with the goal of ensuring the probability of adequate fulfilment of demanding communicative presuppositions under temporal, social and practical limitations."[35] The institutionalization of such discourses, in the form of legal norms, is intended to facilitate an approximation to ideal conditions. Such an approximation would seem to be impossible, for reasons of the motivational and cognitive burdens involved, if argumentation were thought of simply in terms of the spontaneous outbursts of participants engaging in everyday communicative practice. It is the rule of law that allows the conditions of rational collective will-formation to take on a concrete institutional form.[36]

In the next stage of the argument Habermas derives from these presuppositions, or rules of argumentation, a principle of universalization (U). This is to act as a bridging moral principle that will allow us to clarify the condition of normative validity.[37] Whether or not a norm could be discursively redeemed will depend on the satisfaction of (U), that

> all affected can *freely* accept the consequences and the side effects that the *general* observance of a controversial norm can be expected to have for the satisfaction of the interests of *each individual*.[38]

The justification of (U) as part of the logic of practical discourses is intended to refute the sceptic who maintains that norms cannot be justified rationally. This allows Habermas to introduce the principle of discourse ethics itself (D).

> Only those norms can claim to be valid that meet (or could meet) with the approval of all affected in their capacity as participants in a practical discourse.[39]

This is the test of justification that discourse ethics demands of any substantive principle of justice that is raised as a normative validity claim within the context of a particular form of life. So there are four layers here: first, there are the unavoidable presuppositions of argumentation expressed as rules; second, the moral principle (U) that is grounded in those presuppositions; third, the principle of discourse ethics (D); and fourth, substantive principles that are the subject matter of argumentation.[40]

One important question that must be addressed is whether or not there are any substantive norms, or principles of justice, that could pass the universalizability test involved in discourse ethics. Perhaps there are no principles of social and political justice at all that would be equally good for all. This has been the basis for much of the contextualist criticism that has been directed against Habermas, and we will confront it more directly in the next chapter.

For now we can note that justified norms need not be equally good for all in the strict sense of being of equal benefit to all. Norms of equal benefit are not the only ones that could rationally be justified in a practical discourse. "Do not kill another human being" is an obviously plausible candidate for a norm that is good for all in the sense of being of equal benefit to all. There are other norms, however, that might be rationally acceptable to all while offering greater benefit to some than to others. For example the norm "everybody should receive from the state a basic income" may be rationally acceptable to some, because it seems fair, even though they themselves might lose out financially because of the higher taxes that the institutionalization of such a norm might involve. On the other hand, this norm would be rationally acceptable to others in a more straightforward sense since they may not have to weigh the gain of the general observance of this norm against any significant loss. Now this norm, were it to be acceptable to all participants in a real practical discourse, may be said to articulate a shared interest without being equally good for all in terms of the benefits that accrue from its general observance.[41]

Furthermore, a norm that is rationally justified from a dialogically impartial point of view may demand that some social groups give up certain privileges that they have come to recognise as being unjustifiable. The fact that justice benefits some social groups more than others should come as no surprise since it rectifies injustices that have clearly had consequences that have been to the advantage of some groups while causing others to suffer unnecessarily. The rectification of injustice need not, indeed, could not be of equal benefit to everyone.

The fact that norms can rationally be justified as being equally good for all, without having consequences that are of equal benefit, underscores the fact that impartiality demands the political articulation of, and not the denial of, differences between social groups. If a political claim to a right is to be made, say for example, the right to a "basic income," then this normative validity claim will have to be supported with reasons. An actual discourse about this possible norm would presumably involve those social groups who currently have a less than basic income, however that is defined, seeking to reveal the ways in which their experience of citizenship really differs from those who enjoy a greater than basic income. Since it is those real differences that provide the context for the generation of this normative validity claim in the first place, it would seem rather strange if the ensuing discourse were not to involve a public articulation of differing experiences and contexts of identity formation.

In this initial response to the possibility of no norm being found to be equally good for all, it is also important to note that Habermas differentiates between moral questions, which can in principle be decided rationally in terms of justice or the universalizability of interests, and evaluative questions, which are accessible to rational discussion only within the context of a concrete historical form of life, or a prior commitment to a particular conception of the good.[42] While evaluative, or ethical, questions, call for a distinctive use of practical reason, Habermas restricts the moral domain to matters of justice, or the generalizability of interests.[43] This distinction between moral and ethical questions is central to the possibility of grounding impartial justice in particular historical contexts. We will examine the relation between these two sets of questions in the final part of the book.

ARGUING AGAINST SCEPTICISM

Our central concern just now is whether or not Habermas has successfully defended a discursive, or dialogical, conception of impartiality that grounds a universally valid, cognitivist ethic. Is his moral theory really built on inescapable presuppositions of argumentation, or does it merely reflect his own view of an ideal form of communication? If this challenge, typical of the claims of contemporary sceptics, is convincingly to be deflected, much will depend on the arguments that have already been discussed. These include Habermas's claim about the priority of communicative action and his reconstruction of the idealizing presuppositions of communication as rules of argumentation that are intrinsic to the structure of language itself. But in defending his position against sceptical objections Habermas has also drawn on an argument first used by his colleague, Karl-Otto Apel. If sceptics are to put forward their views as arguments, then they cannot avoid the pragmatic presuppositions of communicative action and these contradict, as a matter of fact, the content of their arguments.[44]

In order to convince, and not merely to cajole, manipulate, or demand assent, the sceptic cannot escape the normative presuppositions of the practice of argumentation itself. Sceptics must presume that the position they defend is supported with the force of reason. This means that they will not convince their interlocutors by excluding certain people from the discussion, or by preventing certain claims from being discussed, or by using threats or sanctions to ensure that the discussion proceeds in the manner that they would favor. If the use of power is to be avoided, and it must be when we are considering matters of conviction, then the idealizing presuppositions that Habermas reconstructs do indeed seem to be inescapable as rules of argumentation. The objections of sceptics therefore involve performative contradictions.[45]

Habermas disagrees with Apel however with regard to the status of the transcendental-pragmatic argument they both use against sceptical objections. For Apel it counts as an ultimate justification (*Letztbegrün-dung*) that is absolutely secure. For Habermas, however, the argument is fallible. According to him the identification of the inescapable pragmatic presuppositions of argumentation relies on a maieutic method that seeks to explicate the pretheoretical intuitive knowhow that the sceptic relies on even when denying it. What is required, as we have already noted, is a hypothetical reconstruction of presumably universal intuitions and competences.[46] This reconstruction, as opposed to the intuitive know-how itself, is fallible in the sense that we cannot dismiss a priori the pos-sibility that the human life-form, within which the practice of argumen-tation is interwoven, will undergo future changes.[47] The reconstruction is also dependent on maieutic confirmation, that is on subjects coming to explicate their own pretheoretical intuitive knowhow for themselves. Within the paradigm of the philosophy of intersubjective understanding, an ultimate philosophical justification is neither warranted nor neces-sary. Habermas's moral theory is rather to be thought of as a recon-structive science that is susceptible to indirect corroboration.

In the last chapter we saw how reconstructive scientific research projects engage philosophy and the empirical sciences in a cooperative venture.[48] Empirical theories can use fallible philosophical reconstruc-tions, of presumably universal bases of rational experience, in particular contexts of research. The success of the empirical theory can then safe-guard the validity of the philosophical reconstruction. It is Lawrence Kohlberg's work on moral development that Habermas sees as the prin-cipal source of empirical corroboration for discourse ethics.[49]

On the basis of his empirical research, Kohlberg claims to identify cer-tain universal forms of moral reasoning that can be understood as a six-stage sequence in the development of the individual's capacity for moral judgment.[50] The first two stages are at what Kohlberg calls the preconven-tional level, the next two at the conventional level and the two highest stages are at the postconventional level. The moral judgment of a child at the pre-conventional level is oriented only to immediate consequences of action. At the first stage this is simply a matter of avoiding punishment, while at the second stage it extends to a straightforwardly instrumentalist view of all human relations. An identification with others, such as family, social groups, the political community, takes priority over immediate consequences at the conventional level. At the third stage this is a matter of making judgments on the basis of what others approve of, while at the fourth stage it is more particularly oriented toward the maintenance of the social order.

There is a shift in moral judgment at the postconventional level toward moral principles that do not depend for their validity on the individual's identification with particular social groups. At the fifth stage this is a matter of adhering to a legal system that facilitates each individual's pursuit of their own personal values. At the highest stage, moral judgment is guided not so much by concrete legal norms but rather by universal principles of justice that affirm the equal rights of each individual. Legal norms would be judged in accordance with the demands of these universal principles. This can be thought of in terms of a procedural test of the validity of substantive principles from an impartial point of view.

In constructing this account of moral development in terms of six successive stages, Kohlberg is guided by moral-theoretical assumptions as to the superior moral adequacy of a higher stage. For example, a higher stage should be more adequate in taking the claims of others into account. But his empirical research provides indirect confirmation for those philosophical assumptions, since these assumptions would be called into question if they did not fit with the psychological facts of the moral development of the subjects of his empirical investigations. This is a good example, according to Habermas, of the way in which philosophy and empirical research can complement each other, since it shows us one way in which a reconstructive science can indirectly be corroborated through such a coherence test.[51]

Habermas also believes that the theory of communicative action can add support to Kohlberg's theory by grounding his moral stages in a logic of development. Conceiving of discourse as a more reflexive continuation of communicative action involves reconstructing stages of interaction in terms of perspective structures. It is with the moralization of the social world that norms of action are subordinated to principles and eventually, at the highest stage of moral development, to procedures for testing substantive principles. This requires of the participants the higher-level cognitive structures involved in adopting a hypothetical attitude to socially accepted norms.[52] Such a progressively decentered understanding of the world accounts for the learning process involved in the shift from conventional to postconventional levels in Kohlberg's theory.

Habermas maintains that the development of higher-level cognitive structures characterizes the process of tradition becoming reflexive in general and should not be thought of in terms of the historical development of one particular tradition. If the members of any culture begin to take a hypothetical stance toward their own traditions, then the processes of learning and adaption required of them involve the same logic of development as they would in any other culture.[53] At the postconventional level, socially current norms and expectations are brought into question and assessed from an impartial point of view. In this sense morality at the postconventional level becomes autonomous from ethical life.

What if a sceptic were to refuse to engage in argumentation at all, anticipating the performative contradiction trap that Habermas has laid for all who are foolish enough to enter into his language game? I have already argued that Habermas quite convincingly maintains that the sceptic cannot withdraw entirely from the communicative practice of everyday life, at least not without embarking on a path of self-destruction.[54] But while communicative action cannot be bypassed, is there any reason why the sceptic must move beyond the certitudes of ethical life? Why shift from conventional moral reasoning to accept the abstract formalism of postconventional morality?[55]

It must be noted that it is only those norms that are called into question that become subjects of moral argumentation. This leaves many other aspects of our ethical life as taken for granted certitudes of the life-world. We need not, indeed we cannot, question all norms at once. Nonetheless any norm can be problematized, including Habermas's reconstruction of the normative content of the pragmatic presuppositions of argumentation. When a norm is questioned it would seem that the shift to discourse is inevitable. The refusal to adopt a hypothetical attitude toward such a norm (take any norm that discriminates on the basis of race or gender) endorses a conservative attachment to a discredited tradition that can no longer serve as a basis for rational agreement.[56] Insofar as we seek to restore the background normative consensus within a modern lifeworld, there is no alternative to postconventional moral reasoning over disputed norms.

THE ADVANTAGES OF DIALOGICAL IMPARTIALITY

I have been suggesting that it is the fact that discourse ethics conceives of an impartial point of view dialogically rather than monologically that supports the central argument of this book. Discourse ethics provides the most adequate moral-philosophical basis available to us for the necessary task of grounding a procedural test for the justification of substantive principles of justice. The impartialist test involved is grounded in the context of everyday practices of communicative action. This discursive grounding allows Habermas to defend the centrality of a conception of impartiality while also taking seriously, as we will see in the next part, the plurality of historically unique, differently constituted, modern political societies. My overall argument is that discourse ethics combines the concerns of Rawls's impartialism and Walzer's contextualism while avoiding the most serious weaknesses of both of these rival approaches to the theory of justice.

We will return to the question of the plurality of historically unique political communities in the next chapter. In the remainder of this chapter, however, I want to show how discourse ethics gives a more adequate conception of impartiality than the conception we found in Rawls. It seems to me that, on the basis of the paradigm shift from the philosophy of consciousness to the philosophy of intersubjective understanding, Habermas's version of the impartialist project is more successful than Rawls's in achieving its end of theorizing justice in a way that takes seriously the plurality of individual conceptions of the good.[57] There are, I think, a number of reasons for favoring Habermas's approach over that of Rawls, as the best theoretical articulation of the demands of postconventional moral reasoning. Since they both defend the centrality of a conception of an impartial point of view, it is clear that they agree that the justification of principles of justice in modern societies depends on citizens' capacity for postconventional reasoning.[58]

Discourse ethics represents an attempt to redeem Hegel's aspiration to overcome both the abstract individualism of Kant's moral universalism and the concrete particularism of Aristotelian moral contextualism.[59] Habermas achieves this to the extent that morality is grounded in the intersubjective understanding of participants in moral argumentation. This allows him to link justice with solidarity and concern for the common good by elaborating certain structural features of the good life. These are the social bonds of an intersubjectively shared web of mutual recognition that constitute the well-being of any and every community. The protection of these social bonds is a necessary condition of respect for the dignity of each individual.[60] As well as grounding the individual's equal right to respond freely to the offer of a normative validity claim, discourse ethics at the same time requires that each participant overcome an egocentric perspective by adopting the perspective of all relevant others. Solidarity and empathetic sensitivity among all participants is thereby built into this conception of an impartial point of view. One implication of this is that autonomy is reformulated in intersubjectivist terms since according to this account "the free actualization of the personality of one individual depends on the actualization of freedom of all."[61] Private autonomy can only be secured for an individual if the bonds of solidarity that constitute the context in which that individual's identity is formed receive some protection.

By clarifying the interdependence of justice and solidarity, Habermas can reckon with the ways in which differences between social groups cut deeply into the fabric of modern societies. Modern societies do not only have to deal with a plurality of individual conceptions of the good as such, but each modern society also has to come to terms with the generation, and the regeneration, of different socio-cultural forms of life. This plurality of forms of life reflects multiple dimensions of group difference including race, gender, ethnicity, nationality, language, class, religion, sexual preference and orientation, age, and physical capacity. These group differences constitute the forms of life that provide, within modern societies, the cultural context in which the identities of individuals emerge. As we saw in the discussion of holism in the first chapter, these forms of life engender in individuals a sense of belonging that is constitutive of their own personal identities. The interdependence of justice and solidarity shows how the claims of individuals can only be taken seriously if attention is paid to the identity forming context from which those claims emerge. We will return to the ways in which discourse ethics is sensitive to group difference when we analyse the relation between moral and ethical discourses in the next chapter.

For now we must show how the interdependence of justice and solidarity brings into focus one of the most important theoretical differences between Habermas and Rawls. By grounding his procedure in everyday communicative practices, Habermas sees no need to introduce a veil of ignorance into his conception of an impartial point of view. The idealizing presuppositions that participants actually do make already require them to adopt a hypothetical stance toward their own interpretations of their needs and interests. In argumentation, characterized as a real encounter with others, we adopt the perspective of all participants, or as Habermas puts it, we engage in the practice of ideal role-taking.[62] The notion of an original position is therefore redundant. The lifting of the veil of ignorance means that nothing is excluded as a potential subject of discourse. It also means that the participants can bring to the encounter knowledge of everything that particularizes them, including their experiences within the variety of identity forming contexts that are constituted by social group differences.

Earlier on, in concluding the assessment of feminist objections to Rawls's impartialist procedure, I suggested that the original position can, at best, act as a test to determine whether or not a public discourse has actually succeeded in achieving a rationally justified consensus on some principle of justice. It cannot itself further the quest for agreement. By explaining an impartial point of view in terms of a real discourse,

Habermas shows us how an encounter with collective concrete others facilitates and makes possible shared moral insight. An agreement has to be worked through dialogically out of the multiplicity of perspectives that could be brought to bear in a discourse about principles of justice in a modern context.

Participants in argumentation do not choose principles in isolation from each other by asking themselves what they would find acceptable if they did not know the position they were to occupy in society. Habermas's explanation of an impartial point of view involves a much more radical break from an egocentric perspective than is achieved by the parties to Rawls's original position. The logic of the original position presents a scenario where the parties choose principles on the basis of a calculation of private interests. In contrast, a participant in discourse can only make a moral judgment socially, in a cooperative venture with all relevant others. An impartial point of view must therefore be thought of as a reflective form of communicative action, where the presuppositions of argumentation constrain all the participants to ideal role-taking.[63]

Thomas Scanlon presents an alternative version of contractualism to that of Rawls. He argues that in choosing principles of justice, the parties to a contract are moved by "the desire to be able to justify one's actions to others on grounds they could not reasonably reject."[64] This, Scanlon maintains, requires that they adopt the perspectives of the other parties to the contract.[65] But, again, the ideal role-taking that Scanlon discusses is, according to Habermas, something that is always already taking place once we engage in discourse. Since this involves the unavoidable pragmatic presuppositions of communication, it takes us beyond the perspective of contractualism altogether.[66] The basic assumption of contractualist theory is that we begin with an aggregate of individuals who come together to find norms that will regulate their social interaction. Habermas, in contrast, takes as his theoretical starting point the necessary conditions for the communicative reproduction of the lifeworld. If we also consider the fact that, in Scanlon's approach, real argumentation does not necessarily have to take place, it seems that Scanlon's account of a moral, or an impartial, point of view only partially overcomes the problems associated with Rawls's procedure and its failure to account adequately for the generation of collective insight.

It is clear in Rawls's more recent work that he understands the rationality of the choosing parties to be framed by the reasonableness of the conditions of choice that constitute the original position. These conditions are themselves justified in relation to certain ideas that are thought to be fundamental to any political culture that could claim to be democratic.

Procedures of rational justification are grounded in the deeply held convictions that are embedded in every modern democratic society. Habermas's procedure of rational justification is, in contrast, grounded in the rational reconstruction of the idealizing presuppositions of communicative action as such.[67] In this sense Habermas builds his conception of impartiality on a theoretical framework that is more forcefully universalist. The theory of communicative action seeks to explain the significance that democratic procedures have as key structural features of any form of life that could claim to be rational. They represent the outcome of a process of communicative rationalization in all modern societies that are characterized by a plurality of individual conceptions of the good. Rawls's political constructivism, in contrast, assumes, and does not explain, the rational significance of a democratic form of life in an attempt to secure agreement on certain general principles of justice.

It seems plausible that Rawls begins with certain fundamental ideas that he takes to be embedded in democratic political culture because he is seeking not only to clarify the rational demands of impartiality, but also to advocate particular substantive principles of justice that could regulate social interaction in all modern democratic societies. But, as we have already seen, Habermas maintains that this task of advocating substantive principles must be kept strictly separate from the philosophical task of clarifying an impartial point of view. He insists on leaving open the substantive principles of justice, or the moral-political norms, on which agreement could be achieved in any particular context.[68] The substance of agreement must be left to actual participants in a discourse where everything, including the rational reconstruction of the rules of discourse themselves, can be called into question. By trying to secure a substantive basis for agreement, Rawls runs a risk of relying in his account of justice on certain fundamental ideas that could not actually be discursively redeemed. This was the critical thrust of our assessment of the feminist challenge to Rawls's procedure in chapter 2.

Habermas's conception of impartiality is therefore both more strongly universalist and more sensitive to differences of context than Rawls's. The procedural framework of discourse ethics is itself built on a theory of communicative rationality that claims universal validity. This strongly universalist procedure allows, however, for more flexibility with regard to the substance of possible agreements about principles of justice in each modern democratic society. The rationally reconstructed rules of discourse provide us with a procedure of rational justification that can test the validity of substantive principles but it leaves the generation and the testing of those principles up to participants in particular contexts. Habermas could therefore agree with Walzer's rejection of Rawls's substantive principles as being insufficiently sensitive to particular contexts. But he would do so without following Walzer in giving up on a universalist procedure of rational justification that represents an impartial point of view.

Most importantly discourse ethics theorizes impartiality in a way that can overcome the difficulties that Rawls's project encounters when faced with the challenges of communitarianism and feminism. In other words it can yield an impartialist basis for principles of justice without attempting to isolate in advance political aspects of our morality from our more comprehensive moral views. Rawls is forced into this attempted isolation of the political because his conception of an impartial point of view is designed to avoid moral controversy. His strategy of avoidance implies that we must exclude from our public deliberations anything about which it is presumed that we will not agree.

In contrast, discourse ethics allows the participants themselves to decide where to draw the line between the political and the comprehensive. This makes explicit the possibility of a transformation of the initial moral intuitions of the parties and offers us a dynamic model of the demands of impartiality. It also explains how a genuinely collective insight can emerge in public deliberation about justice. Without such collective insight it is difficult to see how any progress can be made in our attempts to ground a normative justification for principles of justice that are to regulate the institutions and practices of a modern democratic society. Rawls's invitation to the citizens of a democratic society to enter the original position would certainly not lead to any significant political achievements without some such collective insight.

We might point out that Habermas's theory is itself a comprehensive doctrine in Rawls's sense since its theoretical roots are far deeper than Rawls thinks necessary for securing political agreement about justice.[69] As should be clear from the main argument of the first part of this work, however, Rawls's own attempt to secure agreement fails because of the impossibility of isolating the political. In this sense, the comprehensiveness of Habermas's account is a virtue. It gives a deeper analysis of the fact that agreement on norms is a requirement of the rational reproduction of the lifeworld. This comprehensiveness has other advantages since it means that the theory of communicative action allows for a clear link to be made between a discursive conception of impartiality and a critical social theory that explains the operation of systemic power in modern societies. The analysis of communicative action shows both how the demands of discursive impartiality are continuous with everyday communication and also how the rational reproduction of the communicative structures of the lifeworld depends on such discourses actually taking place.

The fact that the demands of discursive impartiality are, in Habermas's conception, continuous with everyday communication also makes a clear link between the role of a vibrant public sphere and the justification of principles of justice. Since the attempt to isolate the political is eschewed in this approach, we can see how the diffuse processes of opinion formation in the background culture of a society, or within the variety of public spheres, can inform discourses about justice. As we will discover in the next chapter, deliberation in the background culture can facilitate the articulation of differences in a multiplicity of ethical discourses among diverse social groups. These discourses can then inform the more formal processes of deliberation concerning norms and principles of justice.[70] Again, this underlines the fact that it is the deliberations of participants themselves that are central to the rational justification of substantive principles of justice.

Habermas affirms the priority of right by reconstructing the rules of moral argumentation. But this in no way restricts the potential subject matter of a discourse since he acknowledges the fact that we can only separate moral questions, that admit of a rational consensus in terms of common interests, from ethical questions, through the clarification of an actually carried out public discourse.[71] It is through ongoing deliberation within a vibrant public sphere that we will be enabled to test and to reflect on each others' moral intuitions in a way that protects the social bonds of an intersubjective web of mutual recognition while respecting the dignity of each individual.[72] The potential biases of the theorist have nowhere left to hide once impartiality is reconceptualized in terms of a public dialogue.

With regard to the feminist challenge, there is no good reason for not considering the internal justice of the family to be a subject of discourse. Furthermore by stressing the intrinsic link between justice and solidarity, Habermas reiterates the need for actual discourses taking place if we are to achieve shared moral insights. These insights could not be generated by accommodating initial moral intuitions but only by putting those intuitions to the test in a real encounter with collective concrete others. Since discourse demands that we adopt a hypothetical stance toward our own interpretations of our needs and interests, each participant engages in argumentation in full awareness of the fact that the encounter itself could represent a moment of moral transformation.

It would seem to be the case therefore that by leaving the substantive principles of justice open to the particular contexts in which disputes might arise, Habermas gives a more context-sensitive account of impartial justice than does Rawls. His procedure rejects the attempt to isolate the political and it encourages the public articulation of group differences. We still have to assess the extent to which discourse ethics really does take seriously the plurality of differently constituted, historically unique, modern political societies. There are also a number of contextualist criticisms that could be aimed directly at Habermas's work. It is these issues, concerning the ways in which impartiality can be grounded in particular contexts, that we must now, in the final part of the book, address.

IV

Impartiality in Context

7

Morality and Ethical Life

Discourse ethics represents a project that reconstructs a conception of impartiality on the universalist grounds of the theory of communicative action. I have been suggesting, in the last part, that as a procedure of normative justification for principles of social and political justice in modern pluralist societies, discourse ethics exhibits a number of crucial features that reveal it to be highly sensitive to particular contexts. In this chapter I will develop this argument further so as to make clear the ways in which discourse ethics can take seriously the plurality of differently constituted, historically unique, modern political societies. In order to do this, I will consider, at different stages of the argument, three significant contributions to the ongoing debate about universalism and contextualism in contemporary moral and political theory. All three of the theorists whose work I consider find Habermas's discourse ethics to be insufficiently sensitive to context. I will argue that a suitably modified version of discourse ethics not only overcomes the relevant objections that are made by these theorists, but that it provides the best available grounding for principles of justice in each historically unique modern society. This defense of Habermas's approach involves an increased emphasis on the role of ethical discourse, as a complement to moral discourse, in public deliberation about the demands of justice in modern societies.

HABERMAS AND THE CONTEXTUALIST CHALLENGE

As we have noted, Habermas insists that discourse ethics is valid universally. Contextualists, from a variety of perspectives, argue that any attempt to defend moral universalism not only fails to fulfil its promise to provide impartial standards or a critical foothold beyond all particular perspectives, but that it conceals from itself its own cultural prejudices, totalizing tendencies and male biases. In our current cultural climate, the recognition of difference is undoubtedly a matter of real concern. We have already considered, in the first part, the ways in which this concern is articulated theoretically in the work of communitarians and feminists. In such a climate, universalist moral claims appear so controversially strong that they carry with them a dauntingly onerous burden of proof. Habermas does not flinch from the challenge of carrying this burden, despite the perilous state of the theoretical terrain that must be traversed. In the last part I argued that by grounding discourse ethics in the pragmatic presuppositions of everyday communication Habermas justifies convincingly an impartial point of view that can transcend the ethnocentric prejudices of a male, liberal, white, Western bourgeois worldview.

Habermas is able to overcome the contextualist challenge more effectively than Rawls because of the way in which he incorporates contextualist insights into impartialist moral theory, most notably in his characterization of moral discourse as a reflective form of communicative action. But since, according to Habermas, morality is indeed embedded in ethical life, this means that we must make a crucial distinction, one that I referred to briefly in the last chapter. This is the distinction between a moral employment of practical reason, one which deals with questions that can in principle be decided rationally in terms the universalizability of interests, and an ethical employment of practical reason, one which deals with evaluative questions that are accessible to rational discussion only within the context of a concrete historical form of life or a particular conception of the good.[1] Habermas restricts the scope of the moral domain by limiting it to questions concerning the universalizability of interests.

While moral discourses seek to justify norms that are equally good for all in terms of the universalizability of the interests involved, ethical discourses involve a particular community or social group in an interpretive project of self-clarification. As we saw in chapter 3, it is this kind of encounter that Walzer understands as the interpretation of shared meanings regarding the demands of justice in particular contexts. In an ethical discourse a group of people who share a collective identity assess how they are to do what is best for them, given their history and traditions, their hopes and aspirations and the problems and issues they now face. There is an impartialist dimension to ethical discourses in so far as they aim at an outcome that is equally good for all members of the collectivity. Depending on the collectivity involved, this is a more or less limited sense of impartiality since it extends only to those who share the particular identity that is in question. In chapter 4 we saw the dangers involved in Walzer's efforts to theorize justice only in terms of ethical discourses of communal self-interpretation. Habermas, in contrast, recognizes the significance of both these forms of discourse, ethical and moral, as feeding into processes of rational will-formation that constitute the legislative politics of a legitimate, democratic, constitutional state.

In our discussion of the discursive justification of moral norms or principles of justice, we saw, in the last chapter, how moral discourses may often require the articulation of differences among social groups. Ethical discourses, of course, necessarily involve the expression of the particularity of a collective identity. Within the context of a democratic state, an ethical discourse concerns itself with a conscious, self-critical appropriation of the contingent history of a particular political collectivity. Ethical discourses take place at two levels within each modern pluralist state, at state level and at intrastate level.[2] In a state-level ethical discourse the political collectivity involved is inclusive of each and every citizen.

In Great Britain, for example, one issue that might fall into this category is the question of the monarchy: Does that institution represent something distinctive about Britain that is worth carrying forward? This obviously raises other more general questions related to the British identity: What is it to be British? What kind of society does Britain aspire to be? How is the particular history of British democracy best to be celebrated? Given the history of Britain and the current problems that British citizens face, what is the most appropriate form of political constitution for such a multicultural society at the end of the twentieth century? How is Britain best to flourish? These questions can be dealt with in an impartial manner only to the extent that they are conducted in such a way as to aim at an outcome that is equally good for each and every British citizen.

In contrast, the political collectivity involved in an intrastate-level ethical discourse is a particular group of citizens. Again taking Britain as an example, there is an indeterminate number of these intrastate ethical discourses. Such discourses could take place, for example, among citizens who are gay, or among citizens who are Scottish, or Roman Catholic, or Bangladeshi, or among women, or among Bangladeshi women, or among gay Roman Catholics. A citizen could participate in such an ethical discourse within every social group that provides one aspect to the identity forming context of that citizen. Taking the gay community in Britain as an example, the questions that are addressed within such a discourse might include: What does it mean to be gay in contemporary Britain? Given present circumstances what are the needs of gay British citizens today? How is the gay identity best to be celebrated in this context? What

are the political aims and aspirations of gay citizens? How is the gay identity within Britain best to flourish? These questions can be dealt with in
an impartial manner only to the extent that they are conducted in such a
way as to aim at an outcome that is equally good for each gay British citizen. Of course, as we will see later, the ways in which these two levels of
ethical discourse, state and intrastate, are related to each other raises very
important questions for a discursive impartialist approach to democratic
deliberation.

Habermas insists that at state level the task of self-realization that a
political community pursues in dealing with ethical questions must be
brought into harmony with the demands of moral discourse in a modern
society. Justice requires that each democratic constitutional state institutionalize those moral norms that have a political relevance, including, for
example, basic human rights. These norms would represent the substantive content of the more extensive universalist moral code that is
obscured in Walzer's hermeneutic account of justice. Habermas thinks of
the set of norms involved as a system of rights that state "precisely the
conditions under which the forms of communication necessary for politically autonomous law-making can be legally institutionalized."[3]

So while each state can continue to express its own identity through
its political institutions, this identity must be compatible with a system
of human rights that is universally valid. Furthermore, the ongoing project of clarifying the distinctive political identity of a particular constitutional state can only be carried out legitimately if these human rights
are effectively guaranteed. As we will see toward the end of this chapter,
it is the interplay of moral discourse and state-level ethical discourse in
democratic states that allows for both the recognition of the validity of
universalist principles of justice and the political expression of a distinctive, and unique, collective identity. This will enable us to fulfil the
promise that was made back in chapter 1: to offer an account of liberal
holism that eschews Rawls's attempt to isolate political morality in our
reflections on justice.

Before we can return to this alternative account of liberal holism, we
will be concerned to assess some of the issues at stake in the debate
between Habermas and contemporary contextualists, an encounter that
updates the agenda set by Hegel's celebrated critique of Kant.[4] We will
consider the implications of Habermas's distinction between moral and
ethical employments of practical reason in relation to the arguments of
three recently influential contributions to this debate. These arguments
raise important questions for discourse ethics as a theoretical account of
justice that could take seriously both of our senses of pluralism.

Seyla Benhabib advocates a "postconventional *Sittlichkeit*," a vision of ethical life thought of from the standpoint of a universalist morality. This involves a rejection of Habermas's strict separation of moral and evaluative questions.[5] Georgia Warnke advocates a hermeneutic conception of political philosophy, where an interpretive pluralism about appropriate principles of justice in any given society is thought to be inevitable. No procedure therefore, discourse ethics included, could possibly guarantee a moral consensus on any given principle.[6] Charles Taylor advocates a "politics of recognition," where the importance of the cultural survival of certain, particular, collective goals can, at times, legitimately outweigh the importance of the state's uniform treatment of all its citizens. Taylor argues that Kantian proceduralism, in contrast to his own view, is insufficiently hospitable to cultural difference.[7]

It would appear then, that despite the paradigm shift from the philosophy of consciousness to the philosophy of intersubjective understanding, many of Habermas's critics maintain that his universalist moral theory has not gone far enough in incorporating contextualist insights into the impartialist project. There are at least two remaining sets of contextualist objections that we must consider. The first set concerns the formalism of impartialist moral theory. Given its exclusive stress on proceduralism, is discourse ethics devoid of moral content? If it is to avoid this emptiness, must it make some substantive moral claims that are inconsistent with formalism? I will deal with these objections in relation to Benhabib's work by stressing the importance of maintaining a clear distinction between moral and ethical questions. The second set, which I will consider in relation to Warnke's work, concerns the idealizing abstraction from ethical life that is involved in moral discourse. Does this render it insensitive to the real context of particular moral disputes? Can discourse be practically effective given its separation of rationally motivated insight from empirical attitudes? My defense of Habermas on these points will lead us to discuss the ways in which ethical discourses, at state level and intrastate level, play a key role in rendering this discursive approach to impartial justice sensitive to the differences among the plurality of historically unique, modern, political societies. Finally, in relation to Taylor's work, I will discuss more explicitly the ways in which the moral and ethical employments of practical reason are best to complement each other in the discursive grounding of substantive principles of justice.

What the chapter aims to do is to assess the extent to which these rival positions undermine the claim that Habermas's discourse ethics offers the best available theoretical resource for the necessary task of justifying substantive principles of justice in modern societies. I will argue that the complementary roles of moral and ethical discourses provide a basis for the contextually sensitive impartialist approach to justice that we are seeking to ground in this work. The discussion of the work of Warnke and Benhabib clears the way for the chapter's concluding contrast between discourse ethics and Taylor's politics of recognition. Having shown how the plurality of differently constituted modern political societies is dealt with in discourse ethics, we can then underline, in the final chapter, the theoretical strengths of Habermas's discursive impartialism over Walzer's hermeneutics by analyzing the demands of justice in the troubled political context of Northern Ireland.

THE SCOPE OF THE MORAL DOMAIN

The moral theory Seyla Benhabib develops in *Situating the Self* is a form of interactive universalism that draws heavily on Habermas's work. Despite this, I think it will prove to be instructive for our purposes to highlight the significance of the ways in which her version of discourse, or communicative, ethics differs from that of Habermas. The point here is to underline the importance of making a clear distinction between moral and ethical discourse. Benhabib's project is a post-Enlightenment reconstruction of the modern ideals of moral and political universalism through a dialectical engagement with the sceptical concerns of communitarians, feminists, and postmodernists.[8]

Benhabib interprets the objection to Kantian formalism as the claim that any procedural moral theory faces an unavoidable choice between triviality and inconsistency. Critics might suggest that the norms that are justified by such a procedure are either self-evident or of little consequence or else that the procedure of justification is itself more substantive than is explicitly admitted. Benhabib argues that, as a testing procedure for moral norms, communicative ethics can evade this dilemma.[9] As we will recall, Habermas himself notes that norms are generated not by philosophy but by real life.[10] He is, however, insistent that philosophy can explain and ground a procedure of moral argumentation that could allow us to test the intersubjective validity of disputed norms that are thrown at us in everyday communicative practice. According to Benhabib, what this procedure achieves is the placing of substantive limitations on our moral intuitions. It yields standards of what is morally permissible or impermissible, without telling us what is the most morally meritorious norm of action in any given context.

Benhabib argues that Habermas unnecessarily relies on the idea of consensus as a guarantee of the validity of a norm. According to her version of discourse ethics, the moral principle (U) is redundant. Its consequentialist formulation renders it too indeterminate to be of use even as an adequate universalizability test for negative duties. For example, given the existence of masochists, the principle "Do not inflict unnecessary suffering" could not be justified as a morally valid norm, or indeed as a principle of social justice. She maintains that we could overcome such counter-intuitive outcomes if (U) were abandoned along with its guarantee of consensus. The norms of universal respect and egalitarian reciprocity, which can be established as the normative content of the rules governing discourse, along with the principle (D), are adequate in themselves as a moral test. The infliction of unnecessary suffering would then have to be ruled out if the procedure of moral argumentation is not itself to be undermined. This shifts the emphasis from consensus as an outcome of discourse to the moral relationships that could sustain the practice of reaching reasoned agreement as a way of life.

It is on this basis that Benhabib calls for a "postconventional *Sittlichkeit*." One implication of this is that Habermas's distinction between a moral and an ethical use of practical reason can no longer be maintained. There is no longer the possibility of distinguishing between a moral norm that expresses a generalizable interest and an agreement that is premised on a prior commitment to the good of a shared way of life. In Benhabib's version of communicative ethics the scope of the moral domain is extended to include practical reasoning concerning particular conceptions of the good. While accepting that a universal, rational consensus is unattainable on such issues, we can, Benhabib maintains, allow for intersubjective moral debate and reflection on evaluative questions.[11]

The restriction of the moral domain to questions of universal justice in Habermas's sense, that is questions that admit of a rational consensus, is, from Benhabib's perspective, untenable. Unfortunately, this overlooks an important and distinctive feature of valid moral claims. For Habermas these moral claims can be given a strong cognitive justification. They are not validated simply with regard to the procedure of argumentation but rather because of the fact that they express a common will. This reflects a communicatively achieved moral insight into a generalizable interest as all participants come to share this conviction together. We know that any norm that passes (U)'s test is right because the grounds that support it are rationally justified. Benhabib claims to defend ethical cognitivism in that valid norms must be supported with reasons, but this claim is weakened since these norms need not express a common will.[12] She must accept this consequence as the price to be paid for such an extensive moral domain.[13]

Benhabib also suggests that her concern to distance herself from strictly formalist Kantianism leaves her less vulnerable than Habermas to the sting of contextualist criticism. Her weak deontological moral theory commits her to certain substantive presuppositions. She maintains that such a commitment is unavoidable.[14] Communicative ethics is justified as an "historically self-conscious universalism" that establishes the principles of universal respect and egalitarian reciprocity as "our philosophical clarification of the constituents of the moral point of view from *within* the normative hermeneutic horizon of modernity."[15] She presents this as an alternative to Habermas's strategy of reconstructing presumably universal competences of all communicative actors in the context of a modern lifeworld.

But in fact Benhabib's position is hardly distinguishable at all from Habermas's own views on this matter. Benhabib's defence of post-conventional morality and the conception of modernity that informs it depend very much on Habermas's reconstruction.[16] While she maintains that other interpretations of the requirements of postconventional moral competence cannot be ruled out in principle, this has also been conceded by Habermas. It was precisely this point that he was making in presenting his reconstruction as fallible while rejecting Apel's notion of an ultimate justification. Furthermore, he has stressed the fact that his defense of discourse ethics as against other postconventional moral theories, such as those of Rawls and Scanlon, is based on philosophical arguments that are "fuelled by historical experience" and not with reference to empirical science.[17] As we have seen, these arguments turn on the shift from a monological to a dialogical conception of an impartial point of view. We will recall that if the individual's dignity is to be respected then the social bonds of the intersubjectively shared web of mutual recognition on which that individual's identity is dependent must also be protected.[18] This elaboration of the structural features of a good life that Habermas includes in his deontological conception of justice can be thought of as the articulation of substantive presuppositions that take him, with Benhabib, beyond the strict formalism of Kant.

There is another important matter at issue between Benhabib and Habermas regarding the scope of the moral domain. This relates to the sensitivity of discourse ethics to particular moral contexts and to morally relevant differences between individual actors. According to Benhabib, Habermas's conception of an impartial point of view is too rationalistic and not situated enough in the context of gender and community.[19] We saw in the second chapter how Benhabib, in presenting her criticisms of Rawls, draws on Carol Gilligan's feminist critique of moral theories that privilege justice and rights over care and concern for particular concrete others.[20] Habermas is also accused of relegating care to the margins of a moral domain that is centered on issues of justice.[21] The conception of moral maturity implied depends on a male bias that emphasizes "our dignity and worth as moral subjects at the cost of forgetting and repressing our vulnerability and dependency as bodily selves."[22] While not wishing to underestimate the importance of our moral concern for justice in political and socioeconomic arrangements (the focus of the present work), Benhabib maintains that the moral disputes most likely to preoccupy us relate to personal decisions demanded of us in relationships, at work, in the social interaction of our everyday lives.[23]

I have already outlined the way in which justice and solidarity are considered to be two sides of the one coin in Habermas's defense of discourse ethics. Our concern with both individual rights and the care of the other have the same root, the protection of the social bonds that constitute a web of intersubjective recognition. Moral reflection is impossible without empathetic sensitivity among the participants.[24] Strangely enough Benhabib admits, quite rightly, that Habermas has incorporated this concern for the other into his conception of an impartial point of view, but without withdrawing her criticisms.[25] I suspect that her continuing unease is due to Habermas's restriction of the moral domain to questions that admit of rational justification in terms of generalizable interests. Benhabib could, I believe, relieve herself of this unease by considering the fact that, in Habermas's recent work, evaluative questions do admit of a rational solution although this will be arrived at through an ethical, and not a moral, employment of practical reason.

Evaluative questions do not yield an answer that is valid for everyone. In seeking rationally to answer the question "What is right for me?" or "What is right for us as a particular group sharing certain ideals?" we must appeal to certain standards that are constitutive of the identity in question. As we have noted, this involves a critical task of hermeneutic self-clarification. What is at stake is a matter of identity that depends on a prior commitment to a particular consciously pursued way of life. Moral questions on the other hand are not resolved in relation to any particular form of life but they are concerned with the justification of principles that could be acceptable to all.[26] We can only work out whether a question is moral or evaluative after we have engaged in argumentation and not, as Rawls would have it, by restricting the scope of possible shared moral commitments in advance.

Let us once again take the issue of abortion as an example. Despite the fact that this has been a subject of public debate for some time, it would appear that there is little prospect of reasonable agreement with regard to the rights involved in this matter. While the question is usually posed in moral terms the answers given seem to depend on an ethical employment of practical reason. This is because different answers are given from the variety of ethical perspectives that reflect the plurality of competing conceptions of the good in modern political societies. From a political point of view, however, there is also, at a different level, another moral question involved. It is the issue as to how the forms of life that give different solutions to the question, "Is abortion right?" can coexist under conditions of equal rights.[27]

It is through our political failure to resolve the dispute about abortion as a moral question that leads us to accept two points. First, this question can only be given an ethical solution, an answer that will not be universally shared, even among the citizens of one modern society, but one that is rational from a particular ethical perspective. From a political or legal perspective, we can no longer treat the substantive question of abortion as one that could yield a moral solution. The only rational way of dealing with this question is to ask, from a particular ethical perspective, "Is abortion right for me? / for us who share this conception of the good?" Of course, many of the personal decisions that Benhabib is concerned to bring in from the margins of traditional moral theory will admit of a rational solution, but often this solution would have an ethical, and not a moral, character.

Second, the acceptance of this ethical diversity in turn gives rise to another moral issue, the question of coexistence of rival ethical perspectives on the question of abortion.[28] The implication here is that modern societies that are bitterly divided over moral disputes such as this one need to find norms of reasonable coexistence rather than a moral consensus on such divisive matters. They need a framework of justice that facilitates a respect for ethical diversity on such questions. From Habermas's point of view, this realization can only come about collectively as a mutual recognition of the failure of exhaustive attempts to reach a moral consensus. Participants recognize the fact that they have reached the limit of self-transformative dialogue on this substantive dispute. They have listened to each other, engaged in ideal role-taking, done everything that could be required of them by discursively impartial reflection, and still they cannot agree. At this point they reach the shared conclusion that, in spite of a genuine willingness on all sides to reach a reason-driven agreement, they have failed and they must now think of the question of abortion as a matter to be addressed from within their particular, diverse, ethical perspectives. Politically the focus of their attention is now the discovery of a moral norm that will facilitate the coexistence of their differing ethical perspectives.

There is an important shift of levels here. Participants begin with an anticipation of a moral consensus on a substantive moral issue such as abortion. In time they, or those who follow on defending the substantive position, come to accept, through public interaction, that consensus is not possible and so the moral focus shifts to the norms of reasonable and just coexistence.[29] It is important to note that from Habermas's perspective this shift is always necessarily a collective achievement. It could never be assumed to be a just outcome prior to an exhaustive public discourse about the substantive moral dispute. This shift of levels within public discourse is obscured by Rawls's attempt to isolate political morality and thereby to exclude from the political agenda matters on which he presumes that we cannot agree, including, as we saw in chapter 1, the morality of abortion.

Discourse ethics insists that this shift of levels can only be instigated by participants in actual moral disputes. The shift reflects an aspect of the self-transformative dynamics of discourse. While the participants do not change to the extent that would make a substantive moral agreement possible, they change their perspective on the issue in dispute to the extent that they can all accept that agreement must be found on a norm of coexistence that respects ethical diversity on the substantive issue. In this way they may alter the manner in which they hold certain fundamental moral beliefs. The experience of discourse can lead, for example, to some citizens accepting for the first time the fact that other citizens have good reasons for doubting the validity of their own deep conviction that abortion is morally wrong in all circumstances. In this way the dynamic of discourse can facilitate collective insight on certain moral norms of just coexistence for a modern pluralist society.

Returning to the apparent disagreement between Habermas and Benhabib, in fact it seems that both agree that ethical questions, which by Habermas's definition do not admit of a normative consensus, can nonetheless be answered rationally. Furthermore, even though they define the moral in different ways, they also agree on the deontological point that moral norms constrain reasonable conceptions of the good.[30] Given this, it is not clear that Benhabib gains anything by abandoning the distinction between the moral and the ethical, nor indeed does it appear to be necessary. What remains to be seen however is the extent of the gains that Habermas makes by holding on to the distinction. We will return to this matter later in the chapter when we attempt to explore further the ways in which the moral and the ethical are related to each other with respect to questions of democratic justification. What is clear here is that Habermas, no less than Benhabib, has incorporated many of the better insights of contextualists into his account of discourse ethics. In doing so he has shown his moral-political theory to be premised on a more situated, and less pure, conception of reason than many critics suppose.

Hermeneutics and Discourse

In *Justice and Interpretation* Georgia Warnke stresses the self-interpretive dimension of mutually educational conversations about justice within the context of a particular tradition.[31] Warnke traces the impulse for the recent interpretive turn in moral and political theory to a dissatisfaction with the abstract formalism of Kantianism.[32] She maintains that while political philosophy can encourage these self-interpretive conversations in a democratic society, a certain interpretive pluralism about the principles of justice that would be appropriate to that particular society is unavoidable. This rules out the possibility of a consensus on any moral principle. Despite this apparent subordination of morality to ethical life, Warnke is aware of the possible dangers involved in the implied relativism of her position. She seeks to defuse these dangers by insisting that hermeneutic conversations presuppose conditions of fairness.[33] It seems to me that this cannot be done without a more explicit appeal to Kantian impartialism than Warnke seems willing to make.

The interpretive understanding of principles of justice that has followed from this hermeneutic turn in recent political philosophy reflects a shift from Kant toward Hegel in its conception of a theory of justice as an "attempt to uncover and articulate the principles already embedded in or implied by a community's practices, institutions and norms of action."[34] From the perspective of hermeneutics, morality and justice do not have to be constructed or discovered independently of particular cultures since they themselves are embedded within the ethical context of historical communities. Moral principles must therefore be interpreted rather than derived from any abstract idealizing procedure. We have already considered this position, and exposed its serious weaknesses, in our critical discussion of Walzer's work in chapter 4.

Warnke is concerned to provide theoretical resources that would defend the hermeneutic approach to matters of justice from the charge that it must inevitably yield either a conventionalist or a subjectivist reading of our ethical life. A conventionalist reading would lead to an uncritical, conservative attachment to tradition with the consequence that the moral protection of minority rights and individual autonomy become dangerously inadequate. A subjectivist reading would reflect the personal biases and preferences of an individual interpreter thus undermining any claim to justify moral principles for the whole community.[35]

Warnke considers whether or not there are rational standards of interpretation that might enable hermeneutics to escape from the shadows of conservative conventionalism and partisan subjectivism. Discourse ethics, with its claim to provide a context-independent procedural test for substantive norms, is an obvious starting point in the quest for such critical standards. Warnke shares Benhabib's doubts about the ideal of consensus that is so crucial to Habermas's procedure of justification for moral norms. She wonders whether (U)'s test is simply too strict for any norm to pass or indeed whether there are any generalizable interests at all.[36] Warnke notes Habermas's acceptance that under conditions of pluralism, and an ever greater diversity of lifestyles, morally justified norms become ever more general and abstract and that, furthermore, many disputes will turn out to reflect particular and not generalizable interests.[37] In such a case what is called for is not a substantive moral consensus. What is in fact needed is either an agreement on a moral norm of coexistence, as in the example of abortion I gave above, or else some form of fair compromise. Fair compromise of course requires morally justified procedures for compromising.

Warnke responds to this by claiming that it is unlikely that we would even agree on what would constitute fair conditions of compromise. However it must be noted that, according to Habermas, moral theory itself can never guarantee a consensus, either on a norm or on a procedure of compromise. It can tell us what a morally justified procedure of justification involves, but it does not inform us as to the content of that procedure nor, as we will see, could it ever ensure that the participants will act morally.[38] Warnke's criticism is not altogether convincing for another reason. In the case of reasonable yet conflicting particular interests, it seems plausible to argue that a fair compromise would constitute a generalizable interest, in protecting the conditions for a democratic form of life, for example, on which a rational consensus could certainly not be ruled out in principle. This helps us to understand the shift of moral focus to norms of just coexistence that is likely to be called for in the ongoing disputes about abortion.

With regard to Habermas's view, that moral norms become more abstract and general in modern societies, Warnke maintains that this occurs to such an extent that, if these norms are not to become entirely irrelevant, the concrete disputes in which they are brought to bear will enmesh us once again in the interpretive problems from which discourse ethics promised an escape. Habermas does, however, insist on a distinction between the justification of a moral norm and its application.[39] The application of a norm requires a hermeneutic effort to undo the decontextualization that was necessary to give it a rationally grounded justification.

While justification does not depend on any particular ethical context, impartial application proceeds interpretively in the light of all information relevant to the context of the actual dispute. Nonetheless, application, no less than justification, requires the use of practical reason and must be carried out from a moral point of view. The idea of impartiality expressed in justificatory discourses as a principle of universalization appears in a discourse of application as a principle of appropriateness.[40] The cognitive operation involved in applying the appropriate valid norm in a given case is integrated with empathetic concern for those affected in the particular circumstances of the situation. This further strengthens Habermas's claim to have given care for the concrete other its due in his interpretation of an impartial point of view.

But what norms could possibly be justified independently of any concrete context? What Habermas seems to have in mind here is a set of moral norms, the validity of which has already provisionally been established, that we must choose between in seeking to apply the appropriate norm in a concrete context. He mentions human rights as examples of such norms since they clearly embody generalizable interests.[41] These can, he maintains, be given a strong cognitive grounding, one that Benhabib has, perhaps inadvertently, given up on. For example, murder is wrong because the norm "Do not kill" expresses a common will in protecting a generalizable interest in life. The justification of this norm is in no way dependent on a particular conception of a good life.[42] This is all that it means to say that justification is not context-dependent.

Habermas assumes that there are a number of moral norms, for example, those expressing negative duties such as "Do not deceive" or positive duties such as "Keep your promises," that have *prima facie* validity since they appear to represent norms that all could will. We might also include "Do not inflict unnecessary suffering," to return to one of Benhabib's objections that Warnke endorses, and another norm "Do not interfere in the sexual practices of consenting adults."[43] Now the existence of masochists no longer seems to invalidate the former norm, since in a discourse of application it might be decided that the latter and not the former is appropriate in a concrete case, say of a particular type of sadomasochistic sex. The former norm retains its validity even if it is deemed to be inappropriate in this particular instance.[44]

The fact that moral justification must be supplemented with a contextually sensitive discourse of application further emphasizes the fallibilism of Habermas's account. In acknowledging the critical potential of superior future knowledge, Habermas admits that our interpretations of morally valid norms must be provisional as they can change in the light of new circumstances. This awareness of the historical nature of the social world reveals the extent to which Habermas has appropriated the insights of hermeneutics.[45]

We must return to the Hegelian objection that discourse ethics is practically ineffective because its abstraction from ethical life leaves it with a serious motivational deficit. Rationally motivated insight is separated from empirical attitudes. I already pointed out that Habermas limits moral theory to the justification of valid norms and so freely admits that it could never guarantee that participants will act morally.[46] It must be borne in mind however that if it is successful in the former task then it will have achieved much. While his self-limiting conception of moral theory may be disappointing to some, the expectation that philosophy could provide sufficient motivation for moral action on its own would seem to overburden philosophy with a task that, given the demise of metaphysical worldviews, it can no longer accomplish.[47]

Habermas accepts that moral insight is compatible with a weakness of will and so its only motivating power is that an actor will have no good reason to act otherwise.[48] The gap between moral judgment and moral action must be compensated for with the anchoring of moral insight in the participants' internalization of the authority of the abstract principles embodied in discourse ethics. Ultimately the internalization of the authority of principles will depend on processes of socialization that are constitutive of a form of life that can meet discourse ethics halfway. There must be a "modicum of congruence" between morality and practices of socialization that could promote this internalization as well as sociopolitical institutions that will embody to some extent postconventional ideas about law and morality.[49]

These achievements are the result of an historical social struggle. It would be absurd to think that they were the tasks of the moral-political philosopher. This is the reason why Habermas refrains from advocating particular substantive principles of justice. Such concrete decisions must, as we have stressed time and again, be left up to the participants in a particular form of life. The ethical use of practical reason can guide the action of those who seek to ensure that their particular form of life better supports a universalist morality that respects human rights. Furthermore, the motivation to act morally can be anchored in an ethical concern for the flourishing of some particular form of life. After a recognition of the impossibility of moral consensus on matters of irreconcilable difference, participants to such disputes can focus their energy on the construction of a framework that allows for the flourishing of nonviolent ethical diversity. An ethical discourse at the state level will ask how moral norms of coexistence are to be grounded in a way that can do justice to the variety of intrastate ethical perspectives on these divisive matters. Participants are motivated to shift their attention from their substantive disagreements to the achievement of agreement on norms of coexistence because they are motivated by a concern to secure just institutions that will regulate fairly their own culturally unique form of life. Finally, as we will see below, moral and ethical reflection are complementary and, very often, we will be required to use both in the context of a particular dispute about justice.

This discussion of the work of Benhabib, with her concern for personal decision making, and of Warnke, with her focus on the interpretation of substantive principles of justice in particular contexts, makes it clear that the ethical employment of practical reason is of great political significance. Until recently Habermas had stressed moral discourse to such an extent in his work that the significance of ethical matters seemed to have been overlooked.[50] Both Warnke and Benhabib have, however, in different ways, abandoned the distinction between moral and ethical questions. I have argued that they are unwise to do so. The relevance for modern ethical life of the distinctive form of moral discourse elaborated in Habermas's work has certainly not yet been exhausted.

It seems to me that the shortcomings of Warnke's proposal for a hermeneutic conversation can be drawn on to illustrate this point. Such a conversation foregoes the aspiration to a normative consensus but aims rather at an ongoing dialogue, one that does not attempt to overcome interpretive pluralism. This dialogue will be mutually educational if we are to be genuinely open to other interpretations of the principles of justice that are to regulate our social interaction. Warnke is explicit in maintaining the need for some constraints on interpretation so that the conditions of the conversation are fair.[51] She turns to Habermas in elaborating the procedural rules of discourse ethics and also in pointing toward his social theory as a way of identifying and overcoming distortions in such conversations. She even invokes the idea of a reconstructive science as an empirical support for such a theory.[52] What she fails to recognize, however, is the extent to which this brings her away from Hegel back toward Kant. She stops short of accepting fully Habermas's conception of moral discourse, but it seems to me that if we are concerned to protect the conditions for a democratic form of life, then nothing less than this can finally save us from the dangers of conventionalism and subjectivism. While no substantive principles of justice are offered, discourse ethics retains its critical function as a fallible, yet universally valid, procedure of moral argumentation.

ETHICAL DISCOURSE AND CULTURAL DIFFERENCES

Having defended Habermas's distinction between moral and ethical uses of practical reason, we now need to know more about how this allows discourse ethics to be sensitive to the contextual differences among the plurality of historically unique political societies. As we have noted above, Habermas also distinguishes between the justification of a norm and its application in concrete contexts. On the one hand, moral norms are justified independently of any particular ethical context. Their validity is not grounded in a prior commitment to a particular conception of the good. On the other hand, norms are applied interpretively in the light of all information relevant to the concrete context.[53] The application of a norm, therefore, requires a hermeneutic effort to contextualize a moral norm that is rationally justified. But application, no less than justification, is to be carried out from an impartial point of view. A norm is justified impartially if it expresses an interest that can be shared by all participants in a practical discourse. A norm is applied impartially if, in the light of a consideration of all relevant particular facts, it is deemed to be the most appropriate norm in those circumstances.

It seems to me that this distinction between discourses of justification and application allows for sensitivity to cultural difference in two respects. First, it should encourage the political expression of the actual differences among social groups in one particular state. This will depend on a vibrant network of intrastate ethical discourses. It would appear that some such vibrant network is a prerequisite to the possibility of the impartial application of a valid norm in that context. Second, it can allow one democratic state to differ from others in the application of

universally valid norms to its own particular historical context. In this
way it respects the plurality of historically unique political societies. This
will depend, however, on a lively state-level ethical discourse's playing a
central role in democratic politics.

If we want to secure the equal right of each individual to pursue an
autonomous life-project, then we will also have to encourage the political articulation of the differing need interpretations of social groups to
which those individuals belong. Norms could not be applied in an impartial manner unless the political culture of a democratic state reflects the
different perspectives of all the collective identities that exist within the
state. This could only happen if social groups, particularly those at the
margins of that particular culture, begin to organize themselves politically. Political organization generates solidarity among the members of
those groups and facilitates the articulation of their difference and of
their differing political needs. This underlines once more the interdependence of justice and solidarity, of private and civic autonomy. As Habermas puts it "the realization of basic rights is a *process that secures the private autonomy of equally entitled citizens only insofar as citizens actively
exercise their civic autonomy.*"[54] If a democratic state is to concern itself,
through its legislation, with the impartial application of valid norms, then
it must encourage the political articulation of the different needs of all of
the social groups that provide an identity forming context for its citizens.

Consider, for example, legislation regarding equal opportunities,
career development, and child care. These are three general areas that
are relevant to, among other matters, the struggle for real equality
between women and men. This legislation is intended, let's say, to apply
the norm that each individual has an equal right to pursue an
autonomous life-project. With respect to the very real problems of gen-
der-bias, impartial application would depend on the existence of a
vibrant political movement that represents women and that articulates
the ways in which their needs differ from those of men. Such a movement must become part of the political culture of a democratic state if
that state is to have any chance of applying norms in an impartial manner. The same can be said of any political movement that represents a
social group with a different perspective to bring to political discourses
that feed into the legislative process. This reiterates once again the need
for the articulation of difference in our reflections on justice. As we saw
in chapter 2 Rawls's conception of an impartial point of view tends to
obscure this dynamic, dialogical aspect of justification.

There are numerous other examples of the way in which impartial
application of norms depend on the articulation of the particular per-

spective of distinct social groups. Think of the articulation of the needs of Muslim girls in France with respect to the proper limits of an expression of religious identity in the public sphere of the classroom.[55] Or the articulation of the needs of Sikhs who want to join the Royal Canadian Mounted Police but who could only do so on the basis of an exemption regarding the required headgear.[56] Or the needs of gays and lesbians who assert their rights not to be discriminated against within the structures of recruitment to the military. If we are interested in the impartial application of an appropriate norm in such circumstances then we will need to encourage intrastate ethical discourses that involve the articulation of the particular needs of the social groups who will be most affected by the application.[57]

One important implication of this is that the collective identities of particular social groups that are articulated in intrastate ethical discourses must be recognized publicly by other citizens. If they are to enjoy equality of respect as citizens then their identities must not be hidden away. What this means is that if one group of citizens has different needs to other citizens (because of their race, their sex, their religion, their sexual orientation, or whatever) then these must be taken into account in any public discourses that feed into the legislative process. In this regard, needs are relative to context. The needs of racially defined social groups will vary depending on the extent to which the struggle against racism has been successful in their own particular political context. This is also true of the needs of religious minorities and the struggle against sectarianism, the needs of gays and lesbians and the struggle against homophobia and so on. In this way intrastate ethical discourses feed into state-level ethical discourses. They demand an ever more inclusive articulation of the particular shared identity of the citizens of one state. The emergence of some such shared identity facilitates the achievement of just institutions by grounding them in the bonds of solidarity that are generated by an inclusive ethical discourse at state level.

This leads us to a consideration of the second respect in which a sharp distinction between justification and application facilitates discursive sensitivity to cultural difference. I have argued throughout that theories of justice must reflect the plurality of differently constituted, historically unique political societies. Democratic states will differ in the ways in which they apply universally valid norms in their own particular contexts. They will obviously differ in that no two states will have exactly the same constellation of social groups that constitute the identity forming contexts of their citizens. Some states will have more gypsies than others, some will have a significant national minority, some will have more immigrant workers, in some the gay liberation movement is at a more advanced stage of political development, some have made greater strides in the actual realization of equality between the sexes. This means that different legislation is required in each democratic state if there is to be a serious attempt to guarantee both private and civic autonomy for citizens. In some states special minority rights regarding the use of a certain language might apply.[58] In other states special rights might be granted to religious minorities.[59]

More generally states can give a set of basic human rights different patterns on the basis of their histories and traditions. This means that a norm guaranteeing religious freedom could be interpreted in a number of different ways. While some states might insist on strictly secular political institutions, others might grant a special institutional role to a particular church, or to the celebration of a particular religious feast. In these states the role of that church or the celebration of that feast would be thought of as an important aspect of the expression of the state's cultural identity. This could only be legitimate if it were acceptable to all religious minorities, thus ensuring that all citizens of that particular state would be treated in an impartial manner. While this seems unlikely to be possible within a large multicultural state, it certainly remains a possibility in smaller states and within the context of a federal state. In the latter case constituent states could have differing special guarantees for a particular religious practice or a particular language. This would be seen as a way of their continuing to express their cultural distinctiveness.

Political rights of participation are patterned in the history and traditions of particular states in so far as the development of political institutions, the choice of national flag, the celebration of state holidays, all of these will always reflect the particular struggles of the people of that state and those who went before them. These are the issues that can and do become subjects of state-level ethical discourses in concrete contexts. State-level ethical discourses therefore play a similar role to the hermeneutics of communal self-interpretation that Walzer draws out in his account of justice. They reflect a fact that is emphasized by all holist perspectives on justice, that just institutions are constitutive of the identity of each citizen in a particular society.

As we have already noted, these state-level ethical discourses must be sensitive to the intrastate ethical discourses of particular social groups. To return to the example of Muslim schoolgirls wearing headscarves in the classroom, we can understand the controversy here in terms of an ethical discursive challenge of a religious minority to the self-understanding of the French people with regard to their commitment to secular public education. The political articulation of the differing needs of Muslim girls raises a question for the actual practices of a secular education. An ethical discourse at intrastate level makes a certain demand on other citizens in that it impresses on them the fact that their self-understanding as citizens of a particular state is not yet inclusive enough to allow for the impartial treatment of all its cultural minorities. This can lead to a critical self-questioning ethical discourse at state level where all citizens can participate in the attempt to articulate what it means now to be a citizen of a state that has a certain history, a distinctive set of traditions, a unique constellation of social groups and a particular set of problems facing it at present.

Discursive impartiality demands no less of our public spheres than the expression of cultural differences among all social groups in a vibrant network of ethical discourses at both state and intrastate levels. According to the approach I am defending, communal reflection on the demands of justice involves not only moral discourses but also state-level ethical discourses of communal self-interpretation. They are in this way a struggle for clarity about the particular shared identity of the citizens of one historically unique political society. The motivation to engage in discourses about the demands of justice can therefore be drawn from a feeling of belonging and a deep concern for the flourishing of a particular way of life. Insofar as citizens care about the demands of justice in their own context, they will care about the demands of a discursive impartiality that can ground norms of coexistence while facilitating the articulation of differing needs among all concerned social groups. Such state-level ethical discourses respond to the call for recognition that emerges from the intrastate ethical discourses of particular social groups. At this stage it should be instructive to contrast the impartialist approach of discourse ethics defended here with the position outlined recently in the work of Charles Taylor.

AN IMPARTIALIST POLITICS OF RECOGNITION

In his essay "The Politics of Recognition" Taylor raises the question of Kantian moral theory's sensitivity to cultural particularity. He begins with a clear and convincing holist account of personal identity. According to this account, the identity of an individual is constituted by relations with others.[60] We come to a self-understanding dialogically, dependent as we are on a web of intersubjective recognition. Modern politics is characterized by the fact that individual citizens demand equal recognition from the state. This demand has come to be articulated theoretically in at least two different ways. A politics of equal dignity, inspired by Kant, demands equal rights for all citizens by virtue of their all having the potential to live an autonomous life. On the other hand a politics of difference, inspired by poststructuralism, demands that we acknowledge the particular identity of an individual, group, or culture. In its strongest versions, this implies that we must acknowledge the equal value not just of each citizen's potential for autonomy but "the equal value of what they have made of this potential in fact."[61]

Advocates of the politics of difference charge defenders of the politics of equal dignity with insensitivity to cultural particularity, a charge that Taylor supports. He finds Kantian moral theory, with its stress on equal individual rights, to be ill-equipped for the important task of safeguarding collective identities. Taylor gives two reasons for this. First, Kantianism tends to advocate a procedure of impartiality as a set of rules for defining individual rights. It insists that these rules must be applied in a uniform manner across all cultures. Second, this kind of proceduralism asserts a priority of right that is suspicious of collective goals.[62] He presents an alternative "politics of recognition" that respects basic rights while also allowing for a liberal state to espouse a strong collective goal, such as the survival of its own distinctive cultural tradition.[63]

But Taylor also seeks to maintain a scathingly critical distance from the "subjectivist, half-baked neo-Nietzschean" judgment that all cultures are of equal worth.[64] He finds this strong poststructuralist claim, that all cultures are of equal value not only in potential but in fact, to be somewhat ridiculous. He argues that we certainly must be open to the potential value of learning something new from a dialogical encounter with a different culture. We must respect other cultures by approaching them with an initial presumption of equal worth.[65] Indeed, in this way we actually acquire an enriched self-understanding. However, we must also accept that we do in fact learn more from some cultures than from others. What could be more homogenizing than to demand that we must find all cultures to be of equal worth?[66] It is surely absurd to expect that encounters with each other culture would be equally significant in enriching our own self-understanding? Taylor suggests that if our recognition of other cultures and collective identities were granted so cheaply, it could hardly count as the authentic expression of respect that is sought by groups and cultures who wish to have the particularity of their identities acknowledged.

There are a number of difficulties with Taylor's approach. He neither establishes the claim that Kantian moral theory is insensitive to cultural particularity, nor can the alternative he presents successfully avoid facing some serious objections. While his criticisms of Kantianism may carry some weight with regard to the proposals of those liberals who conceive of impartiality in a monological way, they are not at all convincing when leveled at discourse ethics.

As we have seen, Taylor suggests that the safeguarding of collective identities competes with the uniform treatment of citizens in relation to equal individual rights. Certain basic rights, though not the most fundamental liberties, can be trumped for the sake of ensuring that a distinctive cultural form of life will be carried forward by future generations. This might for example legitimately restrict citizens to the use of a particular language in business or in relation to their children's education.[67]

In response to Taylor, Habermas argues that collective rights could only be thought to be in competition with equal individual rights if the internal relation between private and civic autonomy were overlooked. According to him

> private legal persons cannot even gain equal individual liberties unless they themselves, by jointly exercising their autonomy as citizens, arrive at a clear understanding of the legitimate interests and standards involved and reach agreement on those aspects and criteria according to which equal things should be treated equally and unequal things unequally.[68]

Any and every legitimate system of rights must be implemented by democratic means. Legal subjects have an intersubjectively constituted identity so any system of rights must protect both individual liberties and "the integrity of the individual in his or her identity forming life context."[69] For this reason cultural and social differences must be taken into account if rights are to be implemented democratically. This presupposes the fact that the particular needs of distinctive cultures and social groups must be articulated and justified in an open public discourse.[70] The democratic implementation of a system of rights must be sensitive to the different life contexts in which the identities of individual legal subjects are secured. Taylor is therefore wrong to claim that Kantian moral theory must ignore cultural and social differences in implementing equal individual rights. He is also mistaken in his implication that there is no internal relation between collective rights and the protection of individual liberties.[71]

Taylor also suggests, in presenting his alternative, that policies that aim at the survival of a distinctive culture should not be seen as "just providing a facility to already existing people."[72] These policies seek to ensure that the collective identity of that particular culture be carried forward in the future and so they are designed actually to create new members of a community. It is not enough to guarantee the protection of the life contexts in which the particular identities of existing persons are secured, but rather we must ensure that the distinctive culture survives through "indefinite future generations."[73]

But why should this be so? Certainly, there is a sense in which the protection of the life context in which the identities of existing persons are secured might involve the support of their attempts to impart to the next generation the value of keeping their distinctive culture alive. But it might be the case that the next generation do not share the same passion for maintaining that distinctiveness. In other words, the earlier generation might fail in its attempt to instill in its children the conviction that their distinctiveness should be cherished. In this case the particular culture may indeed fail to survive but surely this loss cannot be avoided. The protection of identity forming life contexts is not to be thought of as "an administrative preservation of cultural species."[74] There can be no legitimate guarantee of success for citizens' efforts to protect the culture of a particular social group.

One further problem with Taylor's approach is that the right that each of us has to equal respect in our identity forming context seems to depend, in his account, on the initial presumption that our distinctive culture is of equal worth with other cultures. It is presumed to be of equal worth in relation to its having "something important to say to all human beings."[75] Why should the recognition and respect of our distinctive collective identity have anything to do with such a contribution? Again Taylor's difficulty here seems to be connected to his overlooking the way in which individual rights and the respect of collective identities are internally related. It is not because a particular culture might have something of value to say to all other cultures that the individuals who identify themselves with that culture should be treated equally by the state. It is simply because that culture represents the identity forming life context of those individuals that we must recognize and respect the distinctiveness of that culture as a necessary requirement of the equal treatment of all citizens.[76] The appeal to an initial presumption of equal worth is simply not necessary to the recognition and protection of collective identities in modern constitutional states.[77]

This issue of the recognition of collective identities clears up a number of questions regarding moral and ethical employments of practical reason in relation to the dynamics of democratic politics. It is now clear that Habermas does not consider it possible for any constitutional state to be ethically neutral. The ongoing democratic implementation of any system of rights depends on the incorporation of political goals "including those goals which are articulated in collective struggles for recognition."[78] In other words, the particular collective identities that are represented in any one state give a certain ethical shape to the political culture of that state. Intrastate ethical discourses feed ethical discourses at state level. Legal norms always apply in a particular political form of life, to the citizens of a specific state, within a certain geographically delimited territory. They must therefore depend on a particular society's networks of interaction.

Habermas argues that we can continue to maintain that impartiality is the core of justice, that ethical considerations are subordinate to moral questions, and that the right has priority over the good, while at the same time accepting that in the medium of law

> setting normative rules for modes of behaviour is receptive to the goals set by the political will of a particular society. For this reason, every legal system is *also* the expression of a particular form of life and not merely a reflection of the universalist features of basic rights.[79]

From this it seems clear that for Habermas state-level ethical discourse, in the form of hermeneutical self-interpretive reflection, does play an important role in procedures of democratic legitimation. The citizens of any specific constitutional state must clarify for themselves their own ethical self-understanding. Of course this will involve, as we saw above, an ongoing struggle for recognition of those groups that have been marginalized in the past. Immigrant cultures challenge the majority culture to broaden their horizon of self-understanding.[80] Gay activists challenge citizens to see themselves not just as a collectivity of heterosexuals. National minorities challenge majorities to reinterpret their identities so as to allow for the equal treatment of all the state's citizens.[81]

So while collective identities must be allowed to flourish in their particularity, the challenge to the citizens of any specific constitutional state is to engage in a critical process of hermeneutic self-clarification so as to achieve an integrated political culture.

> This political integration of the citizens ensures loyalty to a shared political culture. The latter is rooted in an interpretation of the constitutional principles from the perspective of a nation's historical experience; thus, the interpretation cannot be ethically neutral.[82]

The self-understanding of a political community is disputed within a common horizon of interpretation. Basic rights are always interpreted within a concrete historical context. The citizens' commitment to basic rights must be underpinned by their loyalty to a shared political culture

> for without such a motivational base, they cannot become the driving force for the project—understood here in a dynamic sense—of establishing an association of free and equal subjects. For this reason, the common political culture in which the citizens identify themselves as members of their community is *ethically patterned.*[83]

Habermas is advocating a form of constitutional patriotism that involves a commitment to the implementation in a particular political culture of universally valid norms, or basic rights, that can rationally be justified in a moral discourse. This moral commitment must be alloyed to an ethical commitment to a particular, historically unique, political culture.[84] Processes of democratic legitimation do not depend only on citizens shared commitment to justice but also to the flourishing of a distinctive and unique political way of life.

Ethical discourses at state level celebrate the substantive value of a particular political culture. If they are to respond to the challenges of intrastate ethical discourses they must also recognize the substantive value of the variety of forms of life that articulate their differences in these discourses. If impartiality is to reign then these intrastate ethical discourses must flourish. It is not, therefore, a case of balancing the good of impartiality with the good of cultural survival. It is rather the case that we could not seek to have impartial political institutions if we did not recognize the value of the full variety of forms of life that provide identity forming contexts for each and every citizen.[85] Any concern about the necessary conditions for impartial institutions then must lead us to highlight, to a greater extent than Habermas himself has done, the important role of ethical discourses at both state and intrastate levels.

Only when democratic processes are informed by a vibrant network of ethical discourses as well as moral discourses and fair bargaining processes could politics be founded on a shared commitment both to basic rights and to a particular political culture. This form of democratic politics, in celebrating substantive identities as well as guaranteeing basic rights, generates and reinvigorates stronger bonds of solidarity than a shared commitment to moral norms could in itself. The greater the extent to which citizens of particular states can achieve both a shared moral commitment to basic rights and an ethical commitment to their own distinctiveness, the greater the prospects for impartial state institutions that can do justice to cultural difference.

We have already explored in detail the way in which Habermas grounds the procedure of moral discourse in the pragmatic presuppositions of communicative action. Ethical discourse at state level complements such a procedure by allowing legal principles that express generalizable interests and universally valid moral norms to be embedded in the context of a particular form of life. We can now, at last, see how Habermas's work presents us with that more adequate version of liberal holism that was anticipated in the discussion of the communitarian critique of Rawls. While moral discourse grounds the liberal concern with just institutions that guarantee individual rights, ethical discourse reflects the holist nature of a commitment to the historical embodiment of particular just institutions.[86] Ethical discourse also takes into account the fact that deliberative democracy requires both the critical assessment of political identity and the articulation of particular needs that the feminist challenge to Rawls's procedure demanded.

Hermeneutic theories of justice are partial in that they limit themselves to reflecting on justice in purely ethical terms. I believe that the alternative discussed in this chapter effectively overcomes the weaknesses of such an approach. This is because Habermas's dialogical conception of impartiality presents moral and ethical reflection as complementary employments of practical reason in our attempts to resolve disputes about justice. Finally, I now want to show how discourse ethics is superior to Walzer's hermeneutics in helping us to clarify the demands of justice in the context of one particular deeply divided society: Northern Ireland.

8

The Case of Northern Ireland

We have seen, in part three, how Habermas's theory of communicative action involves a paradigm shift from a philosophy of the subject to a philosophy of intersubjective understanding. This enables him to justify a discursive conception of impartiality that is sensitive to particular contexts. Having looked in some detail at this justificatory grounding, I argued, in the last chapter, that discourse ethics can draw on a wealth of argumentative resources in its own defence against the challenges of some of its most astute critics. In this final chapter I will examine a concrete dispute about justice in the context of one particular modern society. This concrete issue is one that dominates the public agenda in that society. The discussion will, I hope, support my claim that Habermas's theory of justice has important advantages over the main contextualist alternative that we have considered in this work, that of Walzer. The concrete issue I refer to is the question of the legitimacy of the constitutional status of Northern Ireland.

Justice and Pluralism in Northern Ireland

If we wish to tie justice to the traditions of particular communities, as Walzer does, then a divided society like Northern Ireland should prove a challenging test case. One reason for this is because the notion of community is particularly problematic in such a context. By trying to apply Walzer's hermeneutics to this case I want to highlight the limits of that approach as an interpretive guide in assessing actual demands for justice in Northern Ireland. The real test here is whether or not the theory enables us to clarify the conditions that must be satisfied if a normatively justified solution to the particular conflict being analyzed is to be achieved. It seems to me that Habermas's discourse theory attains a considerably higher degree of success than Walzer in relation to this test. My claim is that an analysis of this particular dispute about justice supports my contention that Habermas's discourse theory can both incorporate the best insights of Walzer's hermeneutics and also indicate the ways in which its limits might be transcended.

181

While I will be emphasizing the strengths and weaknesses of the theoretical contributions of Walzer and Habermas, I also hope to say something constructive about Northern Ireland. I will offer a critique of one argument for the maintenance of the Union that at first glance appears to have much in common with Habermas's approach. What emerges from this critique is the suggestion that the problem of justice in Northern Ireland can adequately be resolved only through the engagement of the members of each community in a critically reflexive, self-transformative process of reinterpreting their identities. While this conclusion certainly promises no easy road ahead, it may provide some reasons for cautious optimism.

Rawls, like many other contemporary liberals stresses the plurality of individual plans of life. Walzer, as we will recall, draws our attention to the cultural dimensions of pluralism. It is the social meaning of goods that determines their just distribution. This meaning cannot be grasped outside of the concrete context of a particular historical tradition. There is, he argues, no ahistorical idealized perspective from which we could derive general substantive principles of justice. It is the plurality of political communities in the present and through history that is central to Walzer's concerns. He is critical both of atomistic individualism and of the cultural imperialism involved in the claim to universal validity for substantive standards of justice that have been derived from particular perspectives. Both liberalism and Marxism have been guilty of generalizing universally from assumptions that have a limited cultural relevance.[1]

For Walzer of course "every substantive account of distributive justice is a local account."[2] Standards of justice are embedded within the shared understandings of particular historical communities. Individuals still choose to pursue certain goods in their life plans but the meaning of those goods and the norms of distribution appropriate to them can only be interpreted and understood within the concrete social context in which the individual is embedded. From Walzer's perspective, demands for justice make no sense except within the context of a particular community that is constituted by the shared understandings of its members about the meaning of social goods.

Walzer respects the particularity of local communities and is hermeneutically sensitive to the context of other traditions and their moral worlds. He does not see the plurality of political communities as an unfortunate modern dilemma that we must learn to tolerate but rather as a cause for celebration as we contemplate the infinite multiplicity of possible cultures and possible human lives.[3] This celebration of the plurality of cultures, each with their own norms of justice, makes us more sensitive to otherness and to the need for us to limit our own conception of what the substance of justice demands to its finite and limited context. We must respect both the boundaries that separate the spheres of justice within our own community and also the boundaries that separate our community from communities of others.

We have already examined some of the main problems with Walzer's hermeneutics of justice. There is another set of problems that emerges in relation to the politics of a deeply divided society like Northern Ireland. The idea of community on which Walzer's theory of justice depends is based on the notion of shared understandings of the meaning of social goods. This is a conception of a moral or an historical community bound together by shared cultural traditions and practices. The argument of *Spheres of Justice*, however, is set in the context of the political community.[4] This leads to difficulties wherever historical and political communities do not coincide. It is questionable whether or not Walzer's approach to issues of justice has much to say, for example, in a political setting where two or more distinct historical communities are uneasily intermingled. It is for this reason that it seems worthwhile to return to Walzer's approach at this stage so as to assess the problems that are raised for his theory in this particular context.

Northern Ireland is a deeply divided society in the sense that it is constituted by two fairly distinct historical traditions that have lived very uneasily with one another over a long period of time. In cases like this what is often at stake is not an interpretation of just distributive norms within a political community but rather the very legitimacy of the boundaries of that political community. If we think for a moment of the turbulent regions in the contemporary world of international politics, we will realize that this is not an altogether unusual phenomenon. In the political entity of Northern Ireland, there is no agreement on what the constitutional status should be, even indeed if it should constitute a separated political entity at all.[5] While the Unionist majority defend the legitimacy of the link with Britain, the Irish Nationalist minority aspire to a United Ireland. It seems clear that there is not one historical community, nor is there one sense of national identity, nor one cultural tradition within Northern Ireland. There are two historical communities sharing the territory of one political entity.[6] An added difficulty is the fact that the two communities do not live in neatly separable geographical regions. If they did then it might be possible for one community to secede leaving two separated culturally homogenous political communities. Given the intermingling of the population in Northern Ireland, it is highly questionable that partition (or, in this case, repartition) would be a desirable option.

So to what extent can Walzer's theory of justice be applied to a political entity like Northern Ireland where the very legitimacy of the entity is itself in question? One of the features of the conflict has to do with the fact that Nationalists do not feel themselves to be recognized as full members of the political community. They are denied equal rights to express their collective identity. They do not feel themselves to be British and yet they are subject to the rule of the British state. For them it is as if they were subject to the state institutions of another community. Unionists, on the other hand, insofar as they think of themselves as British, consider the state institutions to be a legitimate political structure for their community. Does Walzer's contextualism deprive the minority of any plausible moral argument for equal rights to express their national identity and for this to be reflected in the political constitution and the institutions of the state? Can they make any claim to be unjustly denied those rights or are they dependent on the unlikely possibility of these political rights of national self-expression being granted willingly by the majority?[7]

Walzer does have some things to say about deeply divided societies in *Spheres of Justice*. He suggests that where political and historical communities do not coincide then decisions about distributive justice would have to be made in smaller more homogenous units rather than in the state as such.[8] Of course, a decision about what these smaller units should look like would have to be worked out politically, at the state level. This then is not very useful in a society where the legitimacy of the state itself is in question and where the majority would be in a strong position to secure advantages for themselves in any decentralization of power. Furthermore, there would be serious geopolitical difficulties involved in finding units of cultural homogeneity within Northern Ireland that would be of an appropriate size to offer a plausible forum for debate over issues of distributive justice. Walzer also asserts that in a community that "is so radically divided that a single citizenship is impossible then its territory must be divided."[9] Again we have already seen that this is not a very attractive proposition in this case.

In general, it seems that when Walzer deals with political problems arising from a plurality of historical communities he is thinking of American society. It seems reasonable that an American political theorist who is committed to a contextualist theory of justice would focus his attention on pluralism in a highly diverse political culture such as his own.[10] Walzer's vision is of a state that promotes pluralism by supporting intermediate associations such as labor unions, churches, neighbourhood groups, and so on. These groups foster communal ties in an otherwise atomized, fragmented society. They allow for a decentralized state to encourage participative citizens to take control of local affairs. The state acts as a "republic of republics."[11]

This might well be a thought provoking response to problems of pluralism in the United States but it could be argued that in Northern Ireland the problem is not one of individual atomization but rather that the two historical communities provide such strong communal ties that they make the division more difficult to bridge politically. Nor does this vision of a "republic of republics" have much chance of getting off the ground in a situation where the members of one community feel no loyalty to what they see as an illegitimate state. Perhaps we are expecting too much from Walzer here? We must recall however that there is, despite his emphasis on pluralism, an affirmation of a universalist code in his work. As we noted in chapter 4, the claim that all communities have their own norms of justice involves some minimal form of moral universalism. How might this relate to the very basic matter of justice that is at issue in Northern Ireland, the justness of the state boundary?

There is a hint of something more promising in Walzer's discussion about quota systems or the reservation of offices for members of particular groups within society. He claims that

> this sort of thing might be acceptable in a bi-national state, where the members of the two nations stand, in fact, as foreigners to one another. What is required between them is mutual accommodation, not justice in any positive sense; and accommodation may best be achieved in a federal system where both groups have some guaranteed representation.[12]

This would be a case of politics acting "as a substitute for justice."[13] It amounts to a proposal for a form of consociational democracy.[14] This system is based on the idea of an executive government formed as a grand coalition of political leaders from the different communities. It is supported by a number of other structural features such as a mutual veto, proportionality in key positions (perhaps even in all occupations throughout the society), and segmental autonomy for each community. These features combine to give an internal federalist system of government. Some of the features of consociational democracy have helped to provide a high degree of stable government in certain plural societies. Countries such as the Netherlands and Belgium or regions such as the Italian South Tyrol have all been successful in their efforts to find such political solutions to the problems of cultural pluralism. The idea of a

"balanced ticket" for elections in some of the more culturally heterogeneous states in the United States is a case where the general idea has also
been beneficial in more loosely pluralist societies.

Unfortunately, Northern Ireland does not enjoy many of the favorable conditions for such a political solution to its problem of cultural
plurality. The most crucial ingredient in working such a system is that
both communities are willing to take the reasonable claims of the other
into account when making claims of their own. It is the attitudes of the
members of the divided communities rather than the institutions themselves that make the system workable. The history of deep resistance to
the prospect of embarking on, or maintaining, power-sharing arrangements undermines any hope for a straightforward consociational solution.[15] Not only is there no tradition of accommodation among the leaders of the communities, but it is not all that clear, given for example the
excruciatingly slow progress of the peace process that was initiated by
the cease-fires of autumn 1994, that they are committed to the idea of a
plural democracy at all.[16] Furthermore, the relative absence of cross-cut-
ting cleavages or overarching loyalties exacerbate the divisions.

The consociational model does not offer much hope because of the
relative size and strength of the communities. An analysis of the history
of the origins of the Northern Ireland state and the way in which its politics were conducted in the first fifty years of its existence reveals that the
members of the Unionist community in general have not perceived it to
be in their interests to engage openly with the claims of Nationalists
regarding the question of the constitutional status.[17] The fact that they
are the majority community and their relative strength, based on the
guarantees of successive British governments, have acted as obstacles,
though not necessarily the only ones, to the emergence of any significant
degree of flexibility among political actors on the fundamental issue of
Northern Irish politics. The psychological scars of twenty-five years of
violent conflict have perpetuated entrenched attitudes characterized by
mutual suspicion, fear, resentment, and hostility between the communities. The threat of ongoing violence, and the continued resistance to dialogue about the future, tend to freeze these attitudes.[18]

It would appear then that what is needed in terms of a theory of justice adequate to the problems of a political entity like Northern Ireland
is some standard that will enable us to move beyond the pluralism that
is celebrated by Walzer. It is clear that the main weakness of Walzer's
theory of justice with respect to Northern Ireland is that it seems to
assume that each community has an equal and legitimate right to cultural and political self-expression. Is this assumption warranted? It

seems to me that it is not. It leaves us bereft of any universalist standard by which we might evaluate, in a critical manner, the claims of opposed traditions or conflicting identities. How are we otherwise to assess the extent to which the claims of either community are valid? Without some such standard we cannot even explain why it is that consociational democracy, or indeed any looser form of pluralism, does not seem to work in Northern Ireland.

Toward a Constitutional Patriotism

Since writing *Spheres of Justice*, Walzer has gone much further in clarifying how some such standard might be justified. In two lectures given under the title "Nation and Universe" he argues for a minimal universalist rank-ordering of nations.[19] He focuses on the nation as the paradigm example of a moral community since he maintains that "it is probably true that the greatest evils in human history have occurred and continue to occur between nations."[20] Although the evils of Northern Ireland may seem relatively insignificant in such a context, his choice of the nation is somewhat fortunate for our purposes here. What Walzer is seeking to do in these lectures is to justify a critical standard by which we can judge national communities morally in their relations with each other.

He begins by distinguishing between two kinds of moral universalism. These are first, what he calls "covering-law universalism" and second, "reiterative universalism." Covering-law universalism assumes that a certain substantive morality, which is at present only adhered to by the select few, is the true morality for all peoples. Most monotheistic religions, various forms of revolutionary Marxism and any supposedly liberal form of imperialism that takes as its mission the task of "civilizing" other cultures, fall into this category. Reiterative universalism is the kind that Walzer is interested in defending. This is characterized, not surprisingly, by "its particularist focus and its pluralizing tendency." It accepts that each community has its own morality and should enjoy the tolerance and respect of other communities. At the same time, it is rooted in particular historical experiences that lead to respect for the particularity of the experience of others and so is less likely to inspire confidence in any one substantive morality. This gives a positive foundation for tolerance of difference and respect for otherness.[21] Reiterative universalism demands that each nation respect the creativity and particularity of all other nations and with it their right to self-determination.[22] Some nations do well according to this standard, others not so well.

The nations that do badly are those that tend to disregard other nations' "spontaneous and natural forms of self-expression." This disregard may come naturally to them. Covering-law universalist doctrines are most often invoked as justifications for such an attitude.[23] This denies the reiterative rights to creative self-determination of other nations. Furthermore, such denial assumes a loss of agency on the part of the victim nationals and an implicit claim to inherent cultural superiority.[24] Walzer notes that for any nation that is under threat, or perhaps in the case of a newly independent nation, there is often a tendency for a new imperialism to emerge that forces a crude uniformity on the self-consciousness of the dominant community. This will often be premised on a claim to cultural superiority and it will often result in the corollary of such a claim, the oppression of minorities. In this sense "the test of every nationalism is the 'nation' that comes next."[25] Walzer's reiterative universalism can acknowledge the strength and meaning of nationalism while at the same time confronting this form of nationalist blindness. He also argues that it can help us to understand and to justify state boundaries, or intrastate boundaries (as in consociationalism). While admitting that there is no sure way of getting them right, his claim is that boundaries should be drawn in such a way as to prevent the disregard and repression of cultural creativity.[26]

Does this attempt by Walzer to transcend pluralism in this minimalist way get us any further in an understanding of what justice might demand in Northern Ireland? There are clearly some ideas worth pursuing in terms of an interpretation of the relationship between the two communities. We might suggest that Unionist disregard for some "spontaneous and natural forms" of (Irish nationalist) self-expression such as the Irish language, Gaelic sports, traditional Irish music and dancing, reveals an implicit sense of superiority in their own identity. Most importantly, of course, this disregard involves the oppression of the Nationalist minority by denying them, as human agents, their reiterative rights to creative political self-determination. This is often rationalized with a version of covering-law moral universalism that purports to be enlightened, progressive, and liberal.[27] We might be able to explain this denial of Nationalist rights in relation to Unionist insecurities. The Unionist community occupies a rather precarious position. They are of course dependent on British guarantees while at the same time they feel under threat from the territorial claims of the Irish Republic as well as the potential for an ongoing violent campaign by the IRA. These insecurities might help to explain why there has been an apparently crude uniformity forced on Unionist self-consciousness since the formation of the Northern Irish state.[28]

Walzer's reiterative universalist standard can give us some interpretive guide as to why the Northern Irish problem of plurality has been so difficult to resolve. However, it does not help us to move beyond this toward a view that could throw some normative light on the fundamental question of the constitutional status of Northern Ireland. The standard Walzer invokes appears to lead us fairly straightforwardly to the conclusion that the present boundary is unjustified since it permits the disregard and repression of (Irish nationalist) cultural creativity. This is all very well, but it does nothing to address Unionist reiterative claims, nor does it give us any indication as to how Unionists might accept that they have an inherent sense of cultural superiority and a tendency to dominate and disregard the self-expression of the Nationalist identity. I believe that a strong case can be made for the view that the main obstacle to progress toward a normatively justified solution to the Northern Ireland conflict is indeed a certain aspect of the Unionist identity that fails to respect the otherness of Irish Nationalists.[29] This would allow us to explain that the Unionist community's unwillingness to compromise is rooted in certain dominating tendencies that are partly constitutive of their very identity. As it stands, however, the analysis does not offer us any real hope for a just pluralism in Northern Ireland.

In order to overcome their blindness to Nationalist reiterative rights, Unionists would have to engage in a self-critical process of reinterpreting their own identity. A workable and justifiable solution will depend on any surviving vestiges of an imperialist attitude being overcome and discarded. Unionists, in so far as they think of themselves as inherently the cultural superiors of Nationalists, must be expected to reinterpret both their own identity and their understanding of the identity of the other. Indeed, the Unionist identity would itself have to be transformed if it were to achieve the required openness to otherness that justice demands. We need some idea as to why Unionists have good reason to engage in such a radical reinterpretation of their own identity. Walzer's pluralist approach to justice leaves us pretty much in the dark here. What is clear is that if a blindness to otherness in the Unionist identity is the main obstacle to progress toward a political solution to the Northern Ireland problem, then a simple appeal to the value of cultural pluralism is far from adequate.

What I am suggesting is that Walzer's hermeneutic approach to justice does not get us very far as a theoretical guide toward a normatively justified solution to the Northern Ireland conflict. What is missing is any grounds for the belief that Unionist blindness to otherness might be overcome. It seems to me that we might be able to address this problem more effectively by turning to the less ambiguous version of moral universalism that is defended by Habermas. Since moral discourse is concerned with the search for generalizable interests it might help us to discover what reasons Unionists would have to call the constitutional status quo into question. If they are genuinely to be open to alternative constitutional arrangements then Unionists must inevitably be drawn into the type of critical self-questioning that discourse requires. Engagement in this self-transformative process of identity reinterpretation is a necessary prerequisite to any political discourse that could possibly unearth a constitutional arrangement that would satisfy a generalizable interest in this case. Nothing short of this could, I suggest, provide a stable basis for social unity, harmony, and peace among all the people of Northern Ireland.

As we have already seen, Walzer does provide a general principle that protects pluralism. However this is simply too vague to yield any specific guidelines in a situation where two historical communities disagree about very basic norms, such as the dispute about the Irish border. The main problem with Walzer's account is that it cannot get beyond this disagreement, despite the fact that it can be critical of less tolerant, imperialist cultures. Specifically in this case it cannot reveal what legitimate rights of cultural expression Unionists do have, nor could it persuade them to overcome and discard the aspects of their identity that are at the root of the political stalemate. Habermas's procedural universalism endorses Walzer's rejection of substantive, determinate accounts of justice that claim universal scope. At the same time he offers us a way of conceiving how a discourse about disputes such as the one we are considering here might proceed in a normatively justified manner.

We will recall that the central claim of discourse ethics is that if we wish to come to a rational agreement with each other about the justness of a certain norm, then there are legitimate procedural constraints on the arguments that we can make.[30] These constraints constitute rules of discourse that are universally valid since they are grounded in the intuitive knowledge of all communicatively competent individuals in modern societies. When we are engaged in communicative action we presuppose a certain reciprocal accountability, that we can justify the claims we make if called upon to do so. If a certain validity claim is called into question, then in order to continue the quest for understanding we must engage in a process of argumentation that has as its goal a rationally motivated agreement.

Within a modern context, when we participate in a discourse we make certain necessary and unavoidable pragmatic presuppositions. As we have seen, Habermas expresses these in terms of rules of argumentation. Insofar as we seek a rational agreement over a disputed norm, we accept the following rules: that no subject capable of speech and action is excluded from the discourse; that all participants are allowed to question any assertion, to introduce any assertion, or to express their attitudes, desires, and needs; and that the exercise of these rights is not to be prevented by coercion, whether internal or external.[31] From these presuppositions Habermas grounds his universalist moral theory. What we must assess now is whether or not this particular defence of moral universalism throws more light on the problem of justice at hand, than our critical analysis of Walzer's work managed to do.

Before developing the argument in this direction it is important to stress once more some implications of the fact that Habermas's moral-theoretical claims are based on the universally valid presuppositions of argumentation rather than the particular context of a historical community. It would be wrong, for at least two reasons, to think of this theory as a version of covering-law universalism that fails to respect otherness. First, the principles of discourse ethics are formal and offer nothing more that a procedural test for substantive principles within concrete contexts. Second, it does not have any ongoing moral agenda as such itself but rather it only comes into play whenever a normative dispute arises in a particular context. Discourse ethics provides a procedure for normatively justified argumentation whenever that is needed. With regard to the case of Northern Ireland, discourse ethics does not claim to offer us the solution that has eluded everyone else. The point is that a moral theory cannot itself provide a substantive solution to a normative dispute. This is a matter for the relevant political actors. All a theory can do (and it should do it!) is to elaborate the procedural conditions under which a normatively justified solution could emerge.

Not surprisingly, Habermas brings a rather different perspective to bear on problems of national identity than that of Walzer's contextualism. Habermas argues that in Western societies an unquestioning and naive identification with the traditions of a particular nation has been shattered, by the experiences of the threat of nuclear war, the shrinking of the world through mass communication, mass immigration, but primarily through our collective experience of the horrors of Auschwitz.[32] A more abstract constitutional patriotism now sets limits to "the imperatives of the self-assertion of national forms of life."[33] This involves a shift in the balance between the two key elements of national consciousness, the universalist value orientations of democracy and the particularism of a nation that distinguishes itself from others.

> The abstract idea of the universalization of democracy and human rights forms the hard substance through which the rays of national tradition—the language, literature and history of one's own nation—are refracted.[34]

Becoming conscious of the ambivalence of our own tradition gives us a more critically reflexive stance. This allows us some distance to take a more flexible attitude in deciding which aspects of our traditions we want to carry forward and which we want to discard.

It is in this way that ethical discourses must be shaped by the demands of moral universalism. As we saw in the last chapter, ethical discourses, both at state level and intrastate level, play important roles in furthering reflection about the demands of justice. At state level ethical discourses must be open to the demand for recognition of the intrastate ethical discourses that constitute the variety of social groups in the particular context. At the same time, state-level ethical discourses are also important motivating sources for citizens' achievement of just institutions and the establishment, in concrete contexts, of a set of universally valid basic rights. Patriotic loyalty to a constitution is always a loyalty to a set of basic rights that does justice to all individuals and social groups within the state. It is always also a loyalty to the particular ethical pattern that constitutes the historical context in which these rights are established.

Constitutional patriotism can set its own limits by listening to and engaging with the claims of others. It is precisely this that characterizes for Habermas what moral universalism means today.

> Relativizing one's own form of existence to the legitimate claims of other forms of life, according equal rights to aliens and others . . . not sticking doggedly to the universalization of one's own identity, not marginalizing that which deviates from one's own identity.[35]

Each constitutional state will have its own ethical pattern, one that expresses its particular identity. Impartiality must however remain at the core of justice if the equal rights of all are to be guaranteed within the framework of any constitutional state. The ethical employment of practical reason will have an important role to play in the networks of communication around which a legitimate political discourse can be grounded. But it remains constrained and shaped by moral principles that are not justified in the context of a particular form of life but that rather claim to be valid universally.

DISCURSIVE LEGITIMATION AND
NORTHERN IRELAND'S CONSTITUTION

The notion of constitutional patriotism captures appropriately the way in which Habermas relates his moral theory to questions of national identity. Is it legitimate however to expect actors engaged in a discourse about a disputed norm to adopt the sort of flexible attitude toward tradition that constitutional patriotism demands? There is a necessary link for Habermas between this attitude and the rationality of the actors involved. This demand is not imposed externally but rather it is presupposed internally in the rules of discourse. A rational defense of a given norm must seek to show that a justification of the norm could meet with the approval of all those affected by it. It must be underpinned by a generalizable interest. It should be clear from our earlier discussion of discourse ethics that this quest for generalizable interests is only possible if the actors involved adopt a critically flexible attitude toward their need interpretations and toward their own identities.

If there is no agreement on any particular norm, as has clearly been the case up to now in the politics of Northern Ireland, then all participants are challenged to revise their own interpretations of their needs, interests, and identities until some form of agreement is made possible. We can distinguish between a legitimate agreement that is rationally motivated, and that could be justified according to discursive conditions, and an illegitimate compromise that is a function of a power relationship, and so is only acceptable to the participants on prudential grounds under conditions of unequal bargaining. It has been argued that an acceptable arrangement in Northern Ireland would be equal citizenship for all, integrated within a culturally heterogeneous British state.[36] It seems plausible that this argument does not transgress, in any obvious way, Walzer's principle of cultural tolerance. Unionism, it is claimed here, does not seek to be the dominant nation or culture, since this arrangement would be justified not in terms of national self-determination but rather in terms of the liberal principles underpinning the modern constitutional democratic (and culturally plural) state. However, despite initial appearances, this particular appeal to modern constitutional principles fails the legitimacy test that discourse ethics offers. This proposal can, I believe, be shown to be premised on an assumption of initially unequal bargaining positions.

The existence of the Irish border is itself a structure of inequality in the context of the dispute about the constitutional status of Northern Ireland. It privileges the Unionist majority politically and allows them to express their national identity through the institutions of the state. I think it is clear that the interests of the Nationalist community have not been and cannot be satisfied if the assumption is unquestioningly made that Northern Ireland is legitimately British. Offering equal British citizenship to Nationalists suppresses the vital issue of whether or not the border itself can be justified, leaving it off the liberal Unionist agenda entirely. This clearly cannot satisfy one of the rules of argumentation, that each participant can call any norm into question. Nor does it address the fact that the structures of power under present arrangements prevent Nationalists from expressing their own national identity in any meaningful way. The compromise advocated by liberal Unionists is therefore, according to this standard, illegitimate. They naively assume that a British state could act as a neutral arbiter between the conflicting parties in the dispute. This view incredibly presupposes that the real source of conflict, whether Northern Ireland should be British or not, is not at issue at all. Historically, of course, since they have failed to provide Nationalists with a moral justification for the border, they have had to rely on coercion to uphold their unequal status. The Union with Britain has been defended not with reasons but with power.

This leaves us with the question as to what grounds we might have for believing that Unionists have good, or even compelling, reasons for entering into an open discourse about the legitimacy of the constitutional status quo. As we have seen, it is at this stage that Walzer's reiterative universalism runs out of steam entirely. The attitude of critical flexibility that is required in any sincere quest for generalizable interests involves the type of self-transformative reinterpretation of Unionist identity that I have argued is required if blindness to the claims of Irish Nationalists is to be overcome. Naturally any identity resists such radical questioning. However, it must be kept in mind that discourse ethics does not bring the very identity of Unionism itself as a whole into question. It is only the aspects of the Unionist identity that act as an obstacle to the recognition of Nationalist rights that must be reinterpreted. This would be sufficient for the question of the constitutional status to become a subject of discourse.

It may well be argued that any political discourse on Northern Ireland would also require Nationalists to reinterpret aspects of their identity. This is certain to be the case should the question of the constitutional status actually become a subject of discourse. However, critical flexibility on the part of Unionists is of much greater immediate concern. This is because Nationalists are, as things stand, already predisposed to adopting a critical attitude toward the current constitutional arrangements. Their interests remain unsatisfied in very obvious ways. In contrast, given the structure of power at present, the reinterpretation of aspects of the Unionist identity is more problematic. For one thing, the Unionist community may not feel that it is necessary to engage in an open discourse in order to have what it takes to be its best interests satisfied. Furthermore, the reinterpretation of the Unionist identity is a necessary prerequisite to any possible discourse about the constitutional status getting under way at all.

This is certainly not to suggest, however, that the political responsibility for the creation of conditions under which a real discourse could take place lies entirely with the Unionist community. On the contrary, that responsibility must be shared by the British government, the government of the Irish Republic and all strands of the Nationalist community in Northern Ireland, along with all strands of the Unionist community. It might be shared even more widely to include European or UN institutions. The encouragement of other actors, not least the government of the United States, can also play a role. Every political actor must be judged according to the extent to which they contribute to the creation of favorable conditions for real discourse. This will presumably involve building up an atmosphere of trust that will assure the Unionist community that their identity as a whole is not in question. The critical reflection on identities involved in discourse can only be achieved cooperatively and never by one of the parties in isolation from the other relevant actors. A spirit of cooperation can be either fostered or undermined by any political action. But while the creation of favorable conditions for discourse is a task that all parties share, the actual reinterpretation of the Unionist identity that would allow them to enter such a discourse can only be achieved by Unionists themselves. They can be helped or hindered by others but ultimately it is how they act that will determine whether or not they adopt the critical attitude that would allow a discourse about the constitutional status to take place.

I believe that motivation for such reinterpretation of the Unionist identity exists in the concrete context of Northern Ireland at present. We have already alluded to the particular insecurities of Unionist identity. First, there is the relationship with Britain, which is at best uneasy. While Unionists depend on Britain to uphold their privileges they realize that public opinion in Britain (and beyond) does not look altogether favorably on their cause. For this reason alone the threat of a British withdrawal can never be discounted. Second, there is constant questioning of the status quo by Nationalists. This is supported by the claims of the Irish Republic and has been effectively publicized by the activities of the IRA. All of this uncertainty leads to self-questioning. These distressing circumstances might be described as disequilibrium-inducing phenomena for the Unionist identity.[37] They loosen the particularist strand of the identity that distinguishes Unionism from others and point toward the kind of moral universalism (implicit in constitutional patriotism) that is open to the legitimate claims of other identities. Insofar as the Unionist community seeks a normatively justified solution to the problem of pluralism in Northern Ireland, they must engage in a process of critically reinterpreting their needs, their interests and their own collective identity in ways that open them to the claims of Nationalists. Of course, I have already indicated that they can be assisted in this by assurances from the other relevant actors that neither their identity as such, nor their own legitimate reiterative rights, are under threat. Ultimately, however, they can only overcome their own insecurities when they can recognize the equal and legitimate rights of other forms of life.

As I have already argued discourse ethics offers us the basis for a critique of the liberal Unionist case for equal citizenship and full integration with the United Kingdom. It does not yield any alternative concrete norm as a solution to the problem. Rather it limits itself strictly to advocating a procedure that provides a test for competing norms. It might however allow us to project tentatively how a discourse might proceed. Such a projection would have no special claim to validity as norms can only be justified if they could be freely accepted by all those affected by them in a real (and not an idealized) discourse. At the same time it can make a contribution to a rethinking of the interests of the actors in relation to possible norms. I have suggested that the constitutional status quo is itself a structure of inequality that renders it normatively illegitimate under present conditions. Other possible solutions could be analyzed in the context of discourse theory with the hope of stimulating critical reflection on the part of the relevant actors. It might also be possible to assess the extent to which each projected solution could satisfy substantive generalizable interests. I cannot hope to offer such an analysis of the various possible constitutional arrangements that have been proposed with regard to Northern Ireland.[38] What I am proposing is that such assessments be made in the light of Habermas's discourse theory as this provides the most adequate normative basis for the critical task involved. It must be stressed however that concrete questions as to how such political discourse should actually be brought about, and as to how it should proceed, must be left up to the actors themselves.

One thing we can say is that the upshot of a real discourse should have certain clear advantages over the status quo. It should more adequately satisfy generalizable interests. The legitimate claims of both communities would be recognized and this would necessarily involve a gain for Irish Nationalists in terms of the self-expression of their national identity. Both communities would gain in the new pluralist context by being better able to relativize their own form of existence by "not sticking doggedly to the universalization of [their] own identity."[39] The emergence of this form of constitutional patriotism would bring further liberating gains. Nationalists would no longer suffer the indignity of oppression as a dominated minority. Unionists would overcome both their inability to come to terms with the disequilibrium-inducing phenomena that strain their identity under present circumstances and also their blindness to others, which deprives them of a rational justification for the status quo. No Unionist denies that it is in their interest to have normatively justified political institutions. This fact alone can provide some hope that the present stalemate in the politics of Northern Ireland will not be interminable.

How these features of an alternative framework for the politics of Northern Ireland are best to be institutionalized would become a pressing matter for participants in a real discourse.[40] I mention them here only briefly to elaborate some necessary features of any concrete norm that could emerge from the type of procedure that I have been advocating. Whether or not anything approaching a real discourse will take place depends very much on the actors involved. There are obviously no guarantees. If a theory of justice can help at all in this respect, then it should be made to do so. As I have suggested above, all political action should be evaluated according to the extent to which it encourages the form of critical reflection on identities that real discourse requires. I believe that cautious optimism can be justified as it is clear that many interests of the actors involved (including the Unionist community) remain unsatisfied at present. An alternative framework, based on the principles of constitutional patriotism, promises greater satisfaction of generalizable interests, not least of which would be a constitutional arrangement that is both rationally motivated and normatively justified. If we are to give an adequate account of what justice demands in a deeply divided society, such as Northern Ireland, then Walzer's concern with pluralism must be supplemented with the sharper normative bite that discourse ethics provides.

Finally, I think that this example can be used to illustrate the ways in which ethical and moral discourses can complement each other in a concrete dispute about justice. If a constitutional arrangement is to be found acceptable by all in Northern Ireland, then it will, I suggest, have to pass the test of a moral norm that could be the basis of a communicatively achieved agreement among all participants in a practical discourse. One such possible norm might be the principle that no citizen should suffer systematic political and social disadvantage because of a difference in national identity. Without prejudging the outcome of an actual discourse, I think there are grounds for believing that this principle could be acceptable to all. It protects each community from the status of second class nationals in a state that expresses itself as unambiguously British, or (in the case of the form of United Ireland sought by some Nationalists) unambiguously Irish. If this principle, or something like it, were to be found acceptable by all then it could guide the quest for a just constitutional arrangement. Should such an arrangement then be devised, we could be optimistic about the prospects for a constitutional settlement the legitimacy of which would be universally recognized.

This scenario of a future consensus on a moral principle that respects national differences, and that informs a stable and just constitutional settlement, must be taken to offer a long-term goal. It can only come about through political struggle and real effort from all concerned. A key element of the achievement of such a moral consensus on this norm of coexistence would be the way in which ethical discourses proceed within, and between, the two communities. We can think of the self-interpretive dialogue within each national community as an intrastate ethical discourse. These proceed historically and they involve for each a struggle to come to terms with many complex relations within the islands of Great Britain and Ireland. As I have stressed in relation to the Unionist community, it is only when each national community can interpret their own identity in a way which takes into account the legitimate claims of others, that they will be capable of endorsing a moral principle which could be a basis for justice in this context. This is a challenge for all national communities that share the two islands.

These intrastate ethical discourses, were they to achieve the required level of openness, would then feed into a state-level ethical discourse, or an ethical discourse between the communities. In that context a shared identity among all the people of Northern Ireland could emerge in parallel with a just constitutional framework. There are already many, more or less acknowledged, dimensions of shared culture between the two national communities. While they could certainly maintain their distinctive national identities, it is not inconceivable that they could build on their common history to achieve together loyalty to an ethical pattern that would bind them to a constitution that does justice to all. This ethical pattern would reflect not only a shared identity but also the divergent national identities that matter so much to the participants in this conflict. If peace and stability are to be achieved in Northern Ireland then they must be built on citizen loyalty not only to the basic rights of a just constitution, but also to the shared history, and the particular inclusive ethical pattern, that constitutes that state as an historically unique political society.

CONCLUSION

I have been advocating a liberal holist approach to the theory of justice. Liberals are right to defend the priority of right over good since there is no other way to do justice to the plurality of individual conceptions of the good in modern societies. In this sense the impartialist project that has been so crucial for many contemporary liberals, not least John Rawls, must be central to an adequate theoretical account of justice. On the other hand, there is an important truth in the holist claim that has been made by many communitarian critics of liberalism. The good of just institutions, which are always embedded in particular historical contexts, is constitutive of the identity of its citizens. If we fail to acknowledge this fact, then we have not taken seriously a second sense of pluralism that we must reckon with. This is the plurality of historically unique, modern, political societies. In this way the important insights of contemporary contextualists, not least Michael Walzer, must also be central to an adequate theoretical account of justice in modern societies. The liberal holist approach I advocate is a form of contextual impartialism. It builds on the framework of justice that is made available by Jürgen Habermas's project of discourse ethics.

Philosophers do not have any special qualification that would allow them to determine the content of a substantive account of justice for a modern society. They can, however, and indeed they should, seek to ground rationally a philosophical conception of an impartial point of view. An impartial procedure that is justified philosophically can then act as a test for the validity of substantive claims that are raised about justice in a modern political context. This test must be carried out, not by philosophers, but by all the members of the community who are to be affected by the norms and principles about which these claims are made. Habermas's procedure of impartiality is superior to that of Rawls because of its unambiguously dialogical nature. The rules of argumentation that characterize this impartial point of view represent the pragmatic presuppositions that no communicatively competent participant can avoid if a genuine attempt is being made to achieve a rationally justified consensus on a disputed moral norm. Anything and everything can be brought into question in a moral discourse that is regulated according to these procedural rules. Participants can even call into question Habermas's fallible reconstruction of the rules themselves. This procedure, unlike the view from the original position, is dynamic rather than static. It facilitates the generation of collective insights since, in the encounter, all participants adopt a hypothetical attitude toward their own initial moral intuitions as well as their interpretations of needs, interests, and identities.

Walzer is justified in maintaining that a substantive account of justice will reflect, to some degree, the historical context and the cultural traditions of particular communities. But Walzer's rejection of the impartialist project makes it impossible for him to show how his holism could allow for a defense of the priority of right. Without a philosophically justified conception of an impartial point of view, Walzer gives us an insufficient basis for an effective defense of reason from the operation of social power in processes of democratic deliberation about principles of justice. By providing us with a dialogical conception of an impartial point of view, Habermas shows us how such a philosophically justified procedure is necessary for, and not in any way a threat to, democracy. At the same time, his distinction between morality and ethical life allows him to affirm the priority of right in a way that is compatible with the holist view that the substance of justice is constitutive of the identities of citizens in particular modern contexts. Universalist moral norms and principles of justice are justified according to this discursive procedure that is not dependent on any one historical tradition. Under modern conditions these universalist principles penetrate into any form of ethical life that could claim to be just. In this way, Habermas overcomes the partiality of hermeneutics. But these universalist principles must be applied in particular contexts and so they will be ethically patterned. To this extent, Habermas approach to justice is a liberal holist one.

Liberal holism avoids the problems associated with a stronger communitarian ethos, one that ties the individual will too tightly to that of the community. This is one of the dangers involved in Walzer's rejection of the impartialist project. If we treat the community as a macro-subject in this way, then we do not allow the real differences between individuals and social groups of modern societies to be expressed in democratic deliberation. Indeed, the differences between us must be thought of as crucial dimensions of our shared identity. Neither atomistic liberalism nor a holism that is insufficiently liberal could account for a genuinely intersubjective basis for the generation of shared insights. Justice and solidarity, which facilitates these shared insights, are two sides of the one coin. The inextricable link between them is a necessary feature of the communicative reproduction of the lifeworld on which our identities depend.

While every modern community is ethically unique, the demands of the universalist moral code are the same for each of them. Justice demands that in modern societies this universalist code should become embedded in the political culture of each ethically unique community. It is the citizens' concern for the flourishing of their particular shared form of life that can motivate agreement on norms that can regulate justly their social relations. While much of the normative content of substantive accounts of justice in modern societies will be universal in scope, the principles involved will be ethically patterned in ways that are constitutive of the identities of citizens in particular political communities. While each set of just institutions will reflect a particular identity, they will also set in motion forms of discourse that reflect, at least in some approximate way, the philosophical conception of an impartial point of view that is reconstructed in discourse ethics. This achievement depends on the actual struggle that takes place in a variety of modern contexts.

The challenge that each modern political community now faces is to institutionalize discursive procedures that will allow for invigorated public spheres to engage in a critical analysis of substantive principles of justice. These institutions must facilitate a complex network of interaction where legal discourse is informed by both moral discourse and by ethical discourse, at state and intrastate levels. This network of interaction is the only guarantee we have that substantive principles of justice will be grounded both democratically and in an impartial manner. The content of a substantive account of justice must be the outcome of open and inclusive democratic encounters. Our hopes for a just future are best rooted in the institutionalization of some such discursive practices.

NOTES

INTRODUCTION

1. I will not have anything to say in this book about justice between political societies, or states, in the modern world. While this is of crucial importance, it raises issues that could only be dealt with in a very different book about justice.

2. John Rawls, *A Theory of Justice* (Oxford: Oxford University Press, 1972) and *Political Liberalism* (New York: Columbia University Press, 1993). Other representative liberals include: Bruce Ackerman, *Social Justice in the Liberal State* (New Haven: Yale University Press, 1980); Charles Larmore, *Patterns of Moral Complexity* (Cambridge: Cambridge University Press, 1987); and Brian Barry, *Justice as Impartiality* (Oxford: Oxford University Press, 1995).

3. While this is the dominant strand of contemporary liberalism, it is not the only one. Influential alternatives include those of Joseph Raz, *The Morality of Freedom* (Oxford: Clarendon Press, 1986); William Galston, *Liberal Purposes: Goods, Virtues and Diversity in the Liberal State* (Cambridge: Cambridge University Press, 1991); and Richard Rorty, *Contingency, Irony and Solidarity* (Cambridge: Cambridge University Press, 1989).

4. Recent examples here include Ackerman's "Political Liberalisms," *Journal of Philosophy* 91 (1994): 379–85, and Barry's most recent critique of Michael Walzer's work, "Spherical Justice and Global Injustice," in *Pluralism, Justice and Equality*, ed. David Miller and Michael Walzer (Oxford: Oxford University Press, 1995), 67–80.

5. See especially *Spheres of Justice: A Defence of Pluralism and Equality* (Oxford: Basil Blackwell, 1983) and *Interpretation and Social Criticism* (Cambridge, Mass.: Harvard University Press, 1987).

6. See especially *Moral Consciousness and Communicative Action* (Cambridge: Polity Press, 1990) and *Justification and Application: Remarks on Discourse Ethics* (Cambridge: Polity Press, 1993).

7. Note that Habermas wants his most recent criticisms of Rawls to "remain within the bounds of a family dispute." See "Reconciliation Through the Public Use of Reason: Remarks on John Rawls's Political Liberalism," *Journal of Philosophy* 92 (1995): 110. No such compliment is paid when he criticizes the work

of theorists who have been thought of as representative communitarians. See for example his remarks on Charles Taylor and Alasdair MacIntyre in *Justification and Application*, 69–76, 96–105.

8. This aspiration is expressed most directly in the essay "Morality and Ethical Life: Does Hegel's Critique of Kant Apply to Discourse Ethics," in *Moral Consciousness and Communicative Action*, 195–215.

9. Mark Kingwell also takes this basically Habermasian position, that justice must be conceived of dialogically, as his starting point in a recent illuminating book that defends the notion of justice as civility, *A Civil Tongue: Justice, Dialogue and the Politics of Pluralism* (University Park: Pennsylvania State University Press, 1995).

10. Although it is not the case in *A Theory of Justice*, it is clear in *Political Liberalism* that Rawls's procedure is justified with reference to the traditions of Western democratic societies. There is of course a significant difference between this type of justification and the strictly universalist one that Habermas offers for his conception of an impartial point of view. I will go on to argue that despite initial appearance, discourse ethics is more sensitive than justice as fairness to particular ethical contexts.

11. In his Amnesty Lecture of 1993 Rawls does indicate an appreciation of the plurality of just societies. The main focus of his work however, the account of justice as fairness and its justification, makes no clear provision for dealing with that plurality. See "The Law of Peoples," in *On Human Rights: The Oxford Amnesty Lectures 1993*, ed. Stephen Shute and Susan Hurley (New York: Basic Books, 1993), 41–82.

12. See chapter 1 of his *Thick and Thin: Moral Argument at Home and Abroad* (Notre Dame, Ind.: University of Notre Dame Press, 1994).

13. The possibility of ethical, as opposed to moral, discourse playing an important role in Habermas's approach is first put forward in the essay "On the Pragmatic, the Ethical and the Moral Employments of Practical Reason," in *Justification and Application*, 1–17.

1. THE ISOLATION OF THE POLITICAL

1. *A Theory of Justice*, 7.

2. *Anarchy, State and Utopia* (New York: Basic Books, 1974). For a clear and succinct case for egalitarian liberalism, see Ronald Dworkin, "Why Liberals Should Care about Equality," in *A Matter of Principle* (Cambridge, Mass.: Harvard University Press, 1985), 205–13.

3. Rawls presents his theory from the outset in two parts: the first concerns, in my terms, the attempt to outline a procedure of justification, the second, the attempt to defend substantive principles as justified. As I have already suggested I take the first task to be the philosophical one with which I will be concerned. The second task is to be thought of as an ongoing democratic project. See *A Theory of Justice*, 15.

4. Rawls maintains that justice as fairness rests on a notion of reciprocity that lies somewhere between the ideas of impartiality and mutual advantage. See *Political Liberalism*, 16–17. I think that the first part of Rawls's theory in which he describes the outline of the original position is to be thought of as a conception of impartiality. I will be concerned with this aspect of the theory since it represents a procedural test for principles of justice that will be equally good for all. The idea of mutual advantage enters into the Rawlsian framework in his characterization of the rationality of the parties to the original position. While there is no reason to question Rawls's view that the theory overall rests on the notion of reciprocity, it should be noted that the four-stage sequence which accounts for the application of the principles of justice presents a model of impartiality at each of the four stages, *A Theory of Justice*, 195–201. In any case I will focus on the impartialist aspects of Rawls's procedure of justification.

5. Two very useful overviews of Marxian critiques of Rawls's liberalism can be found in Allen Buchanan, *Marx and Justice* (London: Methuen, 1982), 103–61 and Rodney Peffer, *Marxism, Morality and Social Justice* (Princeton: Princeton University Press, 1990), 361–415.

6. *A Theory of Justice*, 31.

7. Rawls does of course assume that we will agree on a thin theory of the good that can account for his list of primary goods. These are introduced so that the parties in the original position are motivated to reach some agreement on the principles of justice. They are taken to be aspects of the good for each party regardless of what their various full conceptions of the good turn out to be. See *A Theory of Justice*, 90–95, 295–99.

8. *Political Liberalism*, 36–37. On the fact of reasonable pluralism, see also Joshua Cohen, "Moral Pluralism and Political Consensus," in *The Idea of Democracy*, ed. David Copp, Jean Hampton, and John E. Roemer (Cambridge: Cambridge University Press, 1993), 270–91.

9. The idea of an overlapping consensus is explained in *Political Liberalism*, 133–72.

10. See especially Michael Sandel, *Liberalism and the Limits of Justice* (Cambridge: Cambridge University Press, 1982). Other celebrated works of communitarian criticism include Roberto Mangabeira Unger, *Knowledge and Politics* (New York: Free Press, 1975); Alasdair MacIntyre, *After Virtue: A Study*

in Moral Theory (London: Duckworth, 1981); Charles Taylor, "Atomism," "What's Wrong with Negative Liberty?," "The Diversity of Goods," and "The Nature and Scope of Distributive Justice," all in his *Philosophical Papers, II: Philosophy and the Human Sciences* (Cambridge: Cambridge University Press, 1985).

11. Thomas Nagel, "Rawls on Justice," in *Reading Rawls*, ed. Norman Daniels (Oxford: Basil Blackwell, 1975), 1–15; Michael Teitelman, "The Limits of Individualism," *Journal of Philosophy* 69 (1972): 545–56; Adina Schwartz "Moral Neutrality and Primary Goods," *Ethics* 83 (1973): 294–307.

12. *A Theory of Justice*, 137.

13. Ibid., 151.

14. See especially "Kantian Constructivism in Moral Theory," *Journal of Philosophy* 77 (1980): 515–72 and "Social Unity and Primary Goods," in *Utilitarianism and Beyond*, ed. Amartya Sen and Bernard Williams (Cambridge: Cambridge University Press, 1982), 159–85. For Rawls's first response to these criticisms, see his "Fairness to Goodness," *Philosophical Review* 84 (1975): 536–54.

15. "Social Unity and Primary Goods," 164–65, but also *Political Liberalism*, 19.

16. *Political Liberalism*, 90–99. For an earlier account of the constructivist method, see "Kantian Constructivism in Moral Theory," 516–19.

17. *Political Liberalism*, 97.

18. Ibid., 116, also xx, 94, 243.

19. Ibid., 129.

20. This is what Rawls refers to as "the fact of oppression," ibid., 37.

21. We will see in chapter 3 that Rawls's political constructivism is to be clearly distinguished from Walzer's hermeneutics. One of the crucial differences is that Rawls recognizes the need for a theory of justice to present an abstract account of the procedural conditions of fairness. These are represented in the original position as an impartial point of view. Walzer does not theorize an impartial point of view at all and his stress on shared understandings leads him to reject the use of all abstract conceptions in political theory. See *Political Liberalism*, 43–46.

22. Ibid., 90.

23. See ibid., lecture III in general, especially 110–16.

24. Ibid., 119.

25. Ibid., 26.

26. On the distinction between the reasonable and the rational, see ibid., 48–54.

27. "Fairness to Goodness," 542–43.

28. "Kantian Constructivism in Moral Theory," 530–32.

29. "Social Unity and Primary Goods," 166, also *Political Liberalism*, 180.

30. See William A. Galston, "Moral Personality and Liberal Theory," *Political Theory* 10 (1982): 492–519.

31. For a critique of Kantian expressivism, see Charles E. Larmore, *Patterns of Moral Complexity* (Cambridge: Cambridge University Press, 1987). Although Larmore proposes liberal justice as a modus vivendi in his book, he has argued in a subsequent article that it was not his intention to imply any form of moral scepticism. Any difference he has with Rawls on this point is therefore to be thought of as a merely terminological one. See Larmore, "Political Liberalism," *Political Theory* 18 (1990): 358–59.

32. This was first clearly stated in "Justice as Fairness: Political not Metaphysical," *Philosophy and Public Affairs* 14 (1985): 223–51. See also: "The Idea of an Overlapping Consensus," *Oxford Journal of Legal Studies* 7 (1987): 1–25; "The Priority of Right and Ideas of the Good," *Philosophy and Public Affairs* 17 (1988): 251–76; and "The Domain of the Political and Overlapping Consensus," *New York University Law Review* 64 (1989): 233–55. All of these are incorporated in revised form into *Political Liberalism*.

33. *Political Liberalism*, 146–49.

34. Ibid., 10–11.

35. Ibid., 194–95.

36. Ibid., 173.

37. In ibid., 173–211, Rawls discusses five ideas of the good that play important roles in justice as fairness.

38. This is a key assumption throughout Rawls's recent work but see especially "The Domain of the Political and Overlapping Consensus," 249, and *Political Liberalism*, 38.

39. See Sandel, *Liberalism and the Limits of Justice*.

40. Charles Taylor, "Cross-Purposes: The Liberal-Communitarian Debate," in *Liberalism and the Moral Life*, ed. Nancy L. Rosenblum (Cambridge, Mass.:

Harvard University Press, 1989), 159–82. According to Taylor, this is an onto-logical issue in that it structures the field of possibilities for what we might advo-cate as a political policy.

41. Of contemporary communitarian theorists, Charles Taylor provides the most illuminating account of this holistic conception of the self in his *Sources of the Self: The Making of the Modern Identity* (Cambridge: Cambridge University Press, 1989) and *The Ethics of Authenticity* (Cambridge, Mass.: Harvard University Press, 1992).

42. In what follows I hope to show that Sandel's interpretation of Rawls is not plausible. For what remains one of the best defenses of Rawls on this point, see Amy Gutmann, "Communitarian Critics of Liberalism," *Philosophy and Public Affairs* 14 (1985): 308–22.

43. This rather naive assumption certainly leaves Rawls vulnerable to the criticism of feminists. I will be taking up the relevant issues in the next chapter.

44. *Political Liberalism*, 202, and, more generally, 35–43, 201–6.

45. Ibid., 204.

46. I am suggesting that Rawls's work is based on a holistic and not an atomistic ontology. There are many other versions of what I am calling liberal holism that differ in important respects from that of Rawls. See, for example, Ronald Dworkin, "Liberal Community," in *Communitarianism and Individualism*, ed. Shlomo Avineri and Avner de-Shalit (Oxford: Oxford University Press, 1992), 205–23, and his "Foundations of Liberal Equality," in *The Tanner Lectures on Human Values, XI*, ed. Grethe B. Peterson (Salt Lake City: University of Utah Press, 1990), 1–119. Charles Taylor also identifies with a tradition of holist individualism, "Cross-Purposes," 163. Taylor is influenced by Humboldt on this matter and it is interesting to note that Rawls too is influenced by Humboldt and so can be seen, at least in this respect, as part of the same tradition as Taylor; see *A Theory of Justice*, 520–29. It might be added that while both are holist individualists, Taylor's stress is more on the holism, Rawls's more on the individualism. We might also include as liberal holist theorists moderate liberal perfectionists such as Raz, *The Morality of Freedom* and Galston, *Liberal Purposes*. What distinguishes these others from Rawls is the fact that they offer an ethical foundation for liberalism, one that is comprehensive rather than political in Rawls's sense. See for example his comments on Dworkin, *Political Liberalism*, 211n.42. Ethical forms of liberal holism depend on particular traditions, while Rawls believes that political liberalism, which I maintain is still holist, can be affirmed by all reasonable traditions.

47. *Political Liberalism*, 27.

48. Ibid., 191. For his discussion of "neutrality," see 190–200.

49. This supports my interpretation of Rawls as a liberal holist.

50. *Political Liberalism*, 195.

51. This has been the case with some Irish and Basque Nationalists in the United Kingdom and Spain respectively. There are of course many other possible examples. In chapter 8, I will offer a detailed examination of the demands of justice in Northern Ireland.

52. This is a challenge not only for the state but also for the particular political culture within which the state institutions are embodied. As I have suggested above, some of those who do not identify with the historical constitution of the state, may themselves be committed to liberal principles of justice.

53. We will be returning to this in the discussion of ethical patterning in chapter 7.

54. "The Domain of the Political and Overlapping Consensus," 235.

55. "The Priority of Right and Ideas of the Good," 263.

56. *Political Liberalism*, 200.

57. Nothing in Rawls's more direct references to issues raised by religious fundamentalism solves this problem. See *Political Liberalism*, 60–61, 152–53.

58. For similar arguments, see William A. Galston, "Pluralism and Social Unity," *Ethics* 99 (1989): 711–26, and Patrick Neal, "Justice as Fairness: Political or Metaphysical?" *Political Theory* 18 (1990): 24–50.

59. *Political Liberalism*, 243n.32.

60. See also Thomas McCarthy, "Kantian Constructivism and Reconstructivism: Rawls and Habermas in Dialogue," *Ethics* 105 (1994): 53n.16.

61. A comprehensive liberal can still believe that abortion is wrong but the liberal belief that disagreement about this matter is reasonable will override their possible preference to have abortion banned in all circumstances. It seems to me to be impossible to hold this liberal belief and at the same time to consider abortion morally to be on a par with the murder of an independently existing human being.

62. See also Michael Sandel, "Review of *Political Liberalism*," *Harvard Law Review* 107 (1994): 1778.

63. Rawls himself seems to assume that the question of abortion should be included in this category, *Political Liberalism*, 244n.32.

64. For a trenchant account of the moral consequences of liberalism's strategy of avoiding public discussion of the good, see MacIntyre, *After Virtue*, especially chapter 17, and his *Whose Justice? Which Rationality?* (London: Duckworth, 1988), 342–48.

65. The work of Sandel, Taylor, and also Walzer is usually presented in this way. See Walzer, "The Communitarian Critique of Liberalism," *Political Theory* 18 (1990): 6–23.

66. I have in mind the strand of liberalism that is associated with the tradition of natural rights theory.

67. Taylor, "Cross-Purposes," 177–81, and Sandel, "The Procedural Republic and the Unencumbered Self," *Political Theory* 12 (1984): 81–96.

68. In this paragraph I am anticipating some of the ideas that Habermas has outlined in his major work on a discourse theory of law and democratic politics, *Faktizität und Geltung: Beiträge zur Diskurstheorie des Rechts und des demokratischen Rechtsstaats* (Frankfurt am Main: Suhrkamp Verlag, 1992), in English as *Between Facts and Norms*, trans. William Rehg (Cambridge, Mass.: MIT Press, 1996). See also Habermas, "Postscript to *Faktizität und Geltung*," *Philosophy and Social Criticism, Special Issue: Habermas, Modernity and Law* 20.4 (1994): 135–50. The most significant feature of Habermas's discourse theory is the fact that it presents us with a normatively justified procedure that is grounded thoroughly in intersubjectivist terms. As we will see in part three of the book, Habermas does not restrict the public agenda in the way that Rawls does by attempting to isolate the political. It is important to note, however, that Rawls agrees with the claim of this paragraph, that private and public rights presuppose one another. See his lengthy defense of justice as fairness on this point in his "Reply to Habermas," *Journal of Philosophy* 92 (1995): 150–70. This underlines once again that Rawls is offering a liberal holist account of justice. The problem is, however, that he is insufficiently vigilant in the way in which he conceives of rights to privacy as setting restrictions on the scope of democratic deliberation.

69. Rawls accepts that classical republicanism is not incompatible with justice as fairness, *Political Liberalism*, 205, but this is overshadowed by his failure the theorize adequately the role of a vibrant democratic public sphere.

70. Ibid., 161.

71. Rawls might deny this by claiming that the scope of the political must always be tested against our considered moral judgments, "Reply to Habermas," 153. But how can this happen except through democratic deliberation concerning controversial (and comprehensive) moral claims? Without such deliberation Rawls's procedure of justification could not get off the ground at all.

72. See also Patrick Neal, "Does He Mean What He Says? (Mis)Understanding Rawls's Practical Turn," *Polity* 27 (1994–95): 104–7. Also more generally, Seyla Benhabib, *Situating the Self: Gender, Community and Postmodernism in Contemporary Ethics* (Cambridge: Polity Press, 1992). We will be examining the claims of feminism in this regard in the next chapter.

73. The point is made at greater length by Chantal Mouffe, "Rawls: Political Philosophy without Politics," in *Universalism Vs. Communitarianism*, ed. David Rasmussen (Cambridge, Mass.: MIT Press, 1990), 217–36.

74. This must take place for Rawls in the background culture of society, "Reply to Habermas," 139–42, but of course it is within that context that the scope of the political is always in dispute.

75. Kenneth Baynes draws on the work of Habermas to give a convincing critique of Rawls's neglect of the need for widespread participation and a vibrant public sphere in a democratic society that could claim to be just. See Baynes, *The Normative Grounds of Social Criticism: Kant, Rawls, Habermas* (Albany: State University of New York Press, 1992), 161–81.

76. Benhabib, *Situating the Self*, 7.

2. The Feminist Challenge

1. *A Theory of Justice*, 11.

2. For a full account of the original position, see chapter 3 of *A Theory of Justice*, especially 118–50, and for a more recent account of its role as a device of representation, see *Political Liberalism*, 22–28.

3. *A Theory of Justice*, 12.

4. "Justice as Fairness: Political not Metaphysical," 237.

5. *A Theory of Justice*, 21–22, 48–51, and see Rawls's comments in "Justice as Fairness: Political not Metaphysical," 236–38.

6. *Political Liberalism*, 25.

7. *A Theory of Justice*, 140–42.

8. A detailed account of the justification of various features of the original position is given in lecture II of *Political Liberalism*. For earlier versions, see "Kantian Constructivism in Moral Theory"; "Justice as Fairness: Political not Metaphysical," especially section IV; and "A Kantian Conception of Equality," in *Post-Analytic Philosophy*, ed. John Rajchman and Cornel West (New York: Columbia University Press, 1985), 201–14.

9. *Political Liberalism*, 30.

10. See, for example, *Political Liberalism*, 125–29, also "Justice as Fairness: Political not Metaphysical," 230–31. See the discussion in the last chapter on the idea of an overlapping consensus.

11. The work of Iris Marion Young is perhaps most instructive in this regard, see *Justice and the Politics of Difference* (Princeton: Princeton University Press, 1990). Young's work is inspired, in part, by the French poststructuralism of, among others, Michel Foucault and Jacques Derrida. For clear accounts of their positions, see Foucault, *Power/Knowledge*, ed. Colin Gordon (New York: Pantheon Books, 1980), especially chapters 5 and 6, also Derrida, "Deconstruction and the Other," in Richard Kearney's *Dialogues with Contemporary Thinkers* (Manchester: Manchester University Press, 1984), 107–206. For a rare essay that confronts Rawls directly from a poststructuralist perspective, but drawing on the work of Jean-François Lyotard rather than Foucault or Derrida, see Anne Barron, "Lyotard and the Problem of Justice," in *Judging Lyotard*, ed. Andrew Benjamin (London: Routledge, 1992), 26–42. Other attempts to integrate the concerns of poststructuralism into recent debates about justice include Stephen K. White, *Political Theory and Postmodernism* (Cambridge: Cambridge University Press, 1991), and William E. Connolly, *Identity\Difference: Democratic Negotiations of Political Paradox* (Ithaca, N.Y.: Cornell University Press, 1991). For more critical perspectives, see the essays on Foucault and Derrida in Thomas McCarthy, *Ideals and Illusions* (Cambridge, Mass.: MIT Press, 1991) and Richard J. Bernstein, *The New Constellation* (Cambridge: Polity Press, 1991).

12. White, *Political Theory and Postmodernism*, 17–19.

13. *A Theory of Justice*, 64.

14. See Foucault, *Power/Knowledge*, 98, 142, 187–88, and also his essay "The Subject and Power," afterword to Hubert L. Dreyfus and Paul Rabinow, *Michel Foucault: Beyond Structuralism and Hermeneutics* (Chicago: University of Chicago Press, 1982).

15. Seyla Benhabib and Drucilla Cornell, "Introduction," to their *Feminism as Critique* (Cambridge: Polity Press, 1987), 11.

16. Seyla Benhabib, "The Generalized and the Concrete Other," in Benhabib and Cornell (eds.), *Feminism as Critique*, 93–94. Kenneth Baynes makes some telling points along similar lines in "The Liberal/Communitarian Controversy and Communicative Ethics," in Rasmussen (ed.), *Universalism Vs. Communitarianism*, 61–81.

17. See, for example, *Political Liberalism*, 13–15.

18. Michael Walzer, "A Critique of Philosophical Conversation," in *Hermeneutics and Critical Theory in Ethics and Politics,* ed. Michael Kelly (Cambridge, Mass.: MIT Press, 1990), 189. For evidence that the original position is a monological moral point of view, see *A Theory of Justice*, 19, 119, 139, 564, and "Kantian Constructivism in Moral Theory," 550. In "Reply to Habermas," 140n.14, Rawls denies that the "original position is monological in a way

that puts in doubt its soundness as a device of representation." This is because it is real citizens who judge over time the merits of the original position as a device of representation, or as I have described it, a conception of impartiality. As we will see later on the problem here, however, is that Rawls does not give any account of how that political discourse is itself to be conducted in an impartial manner.

19. *A Theory of Justice*, 7.

20. Ibid., 95.

21. Ibid., 303.

22. In his introduction to *Political Liberalism*, xxix, Rawls acknowledges the fact that he omits any discussion of justice "of and in the family" but he states immediately that he does assume that "in some form the family is just." In what form is the family just? How should a theory of justice address itself to the gender structure of the traditional family? These crucial questions are not tackled by Rawls.

23. *Political Liberalism*, 13, 195.

24. Ibid., 137.

25. In this section I will be drawing primarily on the work of Susan Moller Okin. See her "Humanist Liberalism," in Rosenblum (ed.), *Liberalism and the Moral Life*; "Gender, the Public and the Private," in *Political Theory Today*, ed. David Held (Cambridge: Polity Press, 1991), 67–90; and especially *Justice, Gender and the Family* (New York: Basic Books, 1989), where she gives numerous references to empirical evidence in support of her claims. For a comprehensive analysis of contemporary issues related to women's struggle for equality and the law, see Deborah L. Rhode, *Justice and Gender* (Cambridge, Mass.: Harvard University Press, 1989).

26. Okin, *Justice, Gender and the Family*, 160–69. Okin restricts herself to a discussion of divorce law in the United States, but I think that the general point clearly has a wider relevance.

27. In particular, *Justice, Gender and the Family*, 90–97.

28. Okin, *Women in Western Political Thought* (Princeton: Princeton University Press, 1979) and Jean Bekthe Elshtain, *Public Man, Private Woman: Women in Social and Political Thought* (Oxford: Martin Robertson, 1981). More specifically, since Rawls is usually identified within the tradition of Kantian moral theory, see Okin's critique of Kant, "Reason and Feeling in Thinking about Justice," *Ethics* 99 (1989): 231–35.

29. *A Theory of Justice*, 12.

30. It must be noted however that Rawls does place knowledge of one's sex behind the veil of ignorance in "Fairness to Goodness," 537. It should also be pointed out that while the parties to the original position know the "general facts about human society" they seem to have no knowledge of the gender structure. See *A Theory of Justice*, 137, and *Political Liberalism*, 66–67. Rawls might claim that knowledge of particular injustices, including gender-based ones, should be discounted from his account since it is a form of "ideal theory." Nonetheless, the failure to mention the gender structure in this context does raise the suspicion that Rawls's conception of impartiality might well be infected with a gender bias.

31. In *Justice, Gender and the Family*, Okin gives support to this suspicion by pointing out that in one article Rawls does not even mention the family as part of the basic structure. See "The Basic Structure as Subject," *American Philosophical Quarterly* 14 (1977): 159. However, this may be unfair to Rawls since in the longer, revised version of this paper, in *Values and Morals*, ed. Alvin I. Goldman and Jaegwon Kim (Dordrecht, The Netherlands: Reidel, 1978), 47, "the nature of the family" does remarkably reappear as part of the basic structure. This longer version of the essay is reproduced unchanged in *Political Liberalism*, 257–88, with the family reference at 258. Okin herself later acknowledges this change in her "*Political Liberalism*, Justice and Gender," *Ethics* 105 (1994): 24. What can certainly be said is that Rawls's indecisiveness does little to encourage feminist confidence in his work.

32. *A Theory of Justice*, 128.

33. Ibid., 284–95. Although Rawls later revises his account of motivation with regard to the savings principle, it is not because of the assumption that the parties are considered to be heads of families, *Political Liberalism*, 274n.12.

34. *A Theory of Justice*, 289.

35. Okin, *Justice, Gender and the Family*, 92.

36. Rawls mentions discrimination based on sex as a subject of justice in *A Theory of Justice*, 99, and he also notes that family members need protection from one another, *Political Liberalism*, 221. However, he cannot afford to consider in detail the fact that the institution of the family transcends the political/nonpolitical dichotomy. See also Okin's discussion in "*Political Liberalism*, Justice and Gender."

37. *A Theory of Justice*, 301, 511.

38. Ibid., 462–72.

39. Okin, *Justice, Gender and the Family*, 97–101; "Reason and Feeling in Thinking about Justice," 235–38; and "*Political Liberalism*, Justice and Gender," 32–37.

40. In *Political Liberalism*, xxix, Rawls defends his conception of justice by stating baldly that he believes "the alleged difficulties in discussing problems of gender and the family can be overcome." He also, rather unconvincingly, notes that he does not try to show this in the lectures included in the book. Nor does he show it elsewhere.

41. Okin herself fails to deal with many of these issues regarding the legal constitution of the family. She is therefore vulnerable to the charge that she takes far too many aspects of the traditional family for granted in her own work. The point is made by Will Kymlicka, "Rethinking the Family," *Philosophy and Public Affairs* 20 (1991): 77–97, and by Joshua Cohen, "Okin, Justice, Gender and the Family," *Canadian Journal of Philosophy* 22 (1992): 263–86.

42. The feminism I elaborate here is compatible with the type of liberal holism I defended in the last chapter. A commitment to a holist view does not preclude the questioning of any particular aspect of a tradition. Contemporary feminists tend to be critical, rightly in my view, of versions of communitarianism that stress the moral ties of tradition, as being insensitive to gender-based oppression. See, for example, Okin, *Justice, Gender and the Family*, chapter 3; Marilyn Friedman, "Feminism and Modern Friendship: Dislocating the Community," in Avineri and de-Shalit (eds.), *Communitarianism and Individualism*, 101–19; Iris Marion Young, "The Ideal of Community and the Politics of Difference," in *Feminism/Postmodernism*, ed. Linda Nicholson (London: Routledge, 1990), 300–23; Susan Heckman, "The Embodiment of the Subject: Feminism and the Communitarian Critique of Liberalism," *The Journal of Politics* 54 (1992): 1098–1119. Some feminists have turned to postmodern alternatives. Nancy Fraser and Linda Nicholson give a cogent account of the possibilities that such an alliance could open up in "Social Criticism without Philosophy: An Encounter between Feminism and Postmodernism," in Nicholson (ed.), *Feminism/Postmodernism*, 19–38. For the best account of why feminists should avoid such an alliance, see Benhabib, *Situating the Self*, especially her critique of postmodernism at 203–41.

43. Gilligan, *In A Different Voice: Psychological Theory and Women's Development* (Cambridge, Mass.: Harvard University Press, 1982) and "Do the Social Sciences Have an Adequate Theory of Moral Development," in *Social Science as Moral Inquiry*, ed. Norma Haan et al. (New York: Columbia University Press, 1983), 33–51.

44. "The Generalized and the Concrete Other: The Kohlberg-Gilligan Controversy and Feminist Theory," in Benhabib and Cornell (eds.), *Feminism as Critique*, 75–95. See also, in the same volume, Iris Marion Young, "Impartiality and the Civic Public: Some Implications of Feminist Critiques of Moral and Political Theory," 57–74.

45. Gilligan, "Do the Social Sciences Have an Adequate Theory of Moral Development," 35.

46. Young, *Justice and the Politics of Difference*, 99–107. See *A Theory of Justice*, 139, where Rawls's comments on the possible role of a referee in the original position make it clear that there would be no real dialogue between the parties.

47. Both Benhabib and Gilligan discuss the marginalization of moral feelings such as care, sympathy, and compassion from an overly rationalistic procedure. I do not consider rationality to be in tension with moral feeling and so I do not want to phrase the objection in terms of a rationalistic marginalization of moral feelings. It seems to me that a procedure that allows no place for our concern for concrete others is in fact insufficiently rational. This will be explained fully in later chapters when the centrality of intersubjectivity in Habermas's rational procedure will be discussed.

48. Benhabib, "The Generalized and the Concrete Other," 92.

49. "Toward a Discourse Ethic of Solidarity," *Praxis International* 5 (1986): 425–29.

50. This theme will be developed in our analysis of discourse ethics. The claim is based, in part, on the holistic conception of the self that I defended in the last chapter.

51. Fraser, "Toward a Discourse Ethic of Solidarity," 428.

52. *Justice, Gender and the Family*, 101–5, and "Reason and Feeling in Thinking about Justice," 238–49.

53. *Justice, Gender and the Family*, 108.

54. See Okin's comments in *Justice, Gender and the Family*, 107–8 on the revisions that might be made to Rawls's substantive account of justice were it to be reformulated under nongendered conditions.

55. "Reason and Feeling in Thinking about Justice" is an egalitarian, liberal, feminist response to Gilligan, Benhabib, Young, and other feminists who are highly sceptical about the use of the original position for feminist criticism.

56. *A Theory of Justice*, 148.

57. "Reason and Feeling in Thinking about Justice," 243–49. Rawls himself has clearly rejected a rational choice interpretation of the original position, see "Justice as Fairness: Political not Metaphysical," 237n.20.

58. "Reason and Feeling in Thinking about Justice," 246.

59. Benhabib gives a critical response to Okin in a revised version of "The Generalized and the Concrete Other," in *Situating the Self*, 165–68.

60. Benhabib, "Liberal Dialogue Versus a Critical Theory of Discursive Legitimation," in Rosenblum (ed.), *Liberalism and the Moral Life*, 154–55.

3. HERMENEUTICS AND JUSTICE

1. The main sources for Walzer's views in this regard are *Spheres of Justice, Interpretation and Social Criticism*, and *Thick and Thin*; but see also "Philosophy and Democracy," *Political Theory* 9 (1981): 379–99; *The Company of Critics: Social Criticism and Political Commitment in the Twentieth Century* (London: Peter Halban, 1989); and "A Critique of Philosophical Conversation."

2. *Spheres of Justice*, 314.

3. See the first chapter of *Spheres of Justice* and, for a recent defense, Walzer's "Response" in Miller and Walzer (eds.), *Pluralism, Justice and Equality*, 281–97.

4. For the most recent formulation of Rawls's two principles, see *Political Liberalism*, 5–6.

5. *A Theory of Justice*, 92.

6. Ibid., 433.

7. Ibid., 142.

8. *Spheres of Justice*, 8. Walzer's example here is bread, which he maintains can be given different "primary" meanings depending on the context ("the staff of life, the body of Christ, the symbol of the Sabbath, the means of hospitality and so on"). If this is a problem with bread as a social good then it will surely be even more so when we come to consider social goods such as liberties, powers, wealth, etc.

9. *Spheres of Justice*, 10.

10. I am not going to endorse fully the claim, implicit in the idea of complex equality, that there is a neat fit of spheres and principles in any given community. It seems to me that the demands of justice are even more complex than that. We will see why in the discussion of justification and application of norms from the perspective of Habermas's discourse ethics. At this point I am merely underlining the contextual appeal of complex equality.

11. *Spheres of Justice*, 231.

12. For a discussion of the pluralism of Walzer's view of citizenship, see Emily R. Gill, "Walzer's Complex Equality: Constraints and the Right to be Wrong," *Polity* 20 (1987): 37–43.

13. In a more recent article Walzer suggests that in *Spheres of Justice* he had underestimated the role of the state, the political sphere in a narrow sense, as an agent of just distribution, "Exclusion, Injustice and the Democratic State," *Dissent* (Winter 1993): 55–64. This does not alter the fact that Walzer's central idea

of the plurality of spheres of justice provides a more promising and contextually sensitive way of working out substantive principles of justice in concrete disputes than does Rawls's notion of primary goods. These substantive principles, each one from a different sphere of justice, can be taken together as a map of complex equality that are, I suggest, best understood as an elaboration of the requirements of equal citizenship.

14. For the contrast between dominance and monopoly, see *Spheres of Justice*, 14–17.

15. Ibid., 20.

16. Ibid., 86.

17. I cannot go into detail here about the full account of substantive justice that Walzer presents in *Spheres of Justice*. Throughout the book he draws on numerous historical illustrations to argue his case for an interpretation of a certain map of complex equality that best reflects the demands of justice in a Western pluralist society. See also "Liberalism and the Art of Separation," *Political Theory* 12 (1984): 315–30, and "Justice Here and Now," in *Justice and Equality Here and Now*, ed. Frank S. Lucash (Ithaca, N.Y.: Cornell University Press, 1986), 136–50.

18. *Spheres of Justice*, 321.

19. Ibid., 321.

20. For an early essay that points in the direction of this pluralist conception of citizenship, see "A Day in the Life of a Socialist Citizen," in Walzer, *Radical Principles: Reflections of an Unreconstructed Democrat* (New York: Basic Books, 1980), 128–38. See also Gill, "Walzer's Complex Equality," 43.

21. For a critique of Rousseau from a liberal holist perspective, see Charles Taylor's *Multiculturalism and "The Politics of Recognition,"* ed. Amy Gutmann (Princeton: Princeton University Press, 1992), 44–51, and note Walzer's general endorsement of Taylor's position in his "Comment" on Taylor's essay, 99–103.

22. See *A Theory of Justice*, 563–65.

23. Ibid., 101. This criticism is made by Nozick, *Anarchy, State and Utopia*, 189–97. See also Sandel, *Liberalism and the Limits of Justice*, 66–103.

24. Walzer argues against the idea that there might be a class of people without any talent in "Exclusion, Injustice and the Democratic State," 61–62.

25. See the final section of chapter 1, also Mouffe "Rawls: Political Philosophy without Politics," 230, and Baynes, *The Normative Grounds of Social Criticism*, 161–62.

26. "Exclusion, Injustice and the Democratic State," 59–61, and "The Communitarian Critique of Liberalism."

27. For a detailed look at the ways in which the theorization of civil society presents a challenge to traditional politics, see Jean Cohen and Andrew Arato, *Civil Society and Political Theory* (Cambridge, Mass.: MIT Press, 1992). Walzer himself relates his own concern for a pluralistic conception of citizenship to the theorization of civil society in "The Civil Society Argument," in *Dimensions of Radical Democracy: Pluralism, Citizenship, Community*, ed. Chantal Mouffe (London: Verso, 1992), 89–107.

28. On Walzer as a communitarian, see the chapter on him in Stephen Mulhall and Adam Swift, *Liberals and Communitarians* (Oxford: Basil Blackwell, 1992), 127–56.

29. See chapter 7 of White, *Political Theory and Postmodernism*.

30. *Spheres of Justice*, 227–42. Okin, *Justice, Gender and the Family*, 111–17, acknowledges Walzer's contribution on this point, although she does not agree fully with his interpretation of what justice in that sphere might require. My main point however is to show that complex equality facilitates very easily our consideration of the internal justice of the family.

31. We have already considered some of the manifestations of this trend. Later on we will assess Habermas's defense of universalism.

32. *Truth and Method*, 2nd ed. (London: Sheed and Ward, 1979) and also the collection of Gadamer's essays, *Philosophical Hermeneutics*, ed. David Linge (Berkeley: University of California Press, 1976).

33. *Interpretation and Social Criticism*, 61.

34. See "Philosophy and Democracy," which was published two years before *Spheres of Justice*.

35. "Philosophy and Democracy," 393.

36. "Philosophy and Democracy," 395. Walzer's characterization of philosophy is actually more of a caricature. It is both controversial and crude. To think of philosophy as a straightforward matter of articulating universal truth is to turn a blind eye to the current state of philosophy as a discipline. This raises many highly contentious issues about which there is no agreement among philosophers themselves. For samples of the work of some important voices in the conversation, see *After Philosophy: End or Transformation?*, ed. Kenneth Baynes et al. (Cambridge, Mass.: MIT Press, 1987). A brief consideration of the work of Gadamer, for example, should make it clear that philosophical hermeneutics gives a subtle and convincing critique of the quest for universal truth in a way that supports Walzer's argument much more effectively than he himself manages to do here.

37. See also Richard Rorty's essay on Rawls "The Priority of Democracy to Philosophy," in *Reading Rorty*, ed. Alan Malachowski (Oxford: Basil Blackwell, 1990), 279–302.

38. "Philosophy and Democracy," 395.

39. *Spheres of Justice*, 320, and Mulhall and Swift, *Liberals and Communitarians*, 134–39. Whether or not anybody theorizing about justice nowadays actually defends the strong Platonism that Walzer criticizes here is pretty dubious.

40. "A Critique of Philosophical Conversation." In "Philosophy and Democracy," 389, Walzer is implicitly critical of proceduralists, including both Rawls and Habermas. In the more recent essay he mentions Rawls and Habermas explicitly, as well as Bruce Ackerman, as theorists who are guilty of philosophizing in a way that is dangerous to democracy. I will show later that at least in the cases of Rawls and Habermas, Walzer is guilty of seriously misrepresenting both their understanding of proceduralism and their views on justice. These distorted readings are not excused by his acknowledgment early in the essay, 185, that his references "will not do justice to the complexity and sophistication of the theories involved." See also Georgia Warnke, "Rawls, Habermas and Real Talk: A Reply to Walzer," in Kelly (ed.), *Hermeneutics and Critical Theory in Ethics and Politics*, 197–203.

41. "A Critique of Philosophical Conversation," 184.

42. Ibid., 186.

43. Ibid., 184.

44. Ibid., especially 189 and 194.

45. Ibid., 194–95.

46. The importance of this theme is indicated by the first word of the title of Walzer's recent book, *Thick and Thin*. See the first three chapters of that work for a clear statement of his position.

47. *Thick and Thin*, 11.

48. The first chapter of *Interpretation and Social Criticism*, 3–32, is a defense of the path of interpretation over those of discovery and invention in moral philosophy.

49. *Interpretation and Social Criticism*, 21; *Thick and Thin*, 12.

50. These points are made by Georgia Warnke in *Justice and Interpretation* (Cambridge: Polity Press, 1992), 2–5. They reflect the most recent Hegelian response to Kantianism in ethics.

51. *Interpretation and Social Criticism*, 30.

52. Charles Taylor's account of the identity of the self offers important insights on this subject. "To know who you are is to be oriented in moral space, a space in which questions arise about what is good or bad, what is worth doing and what not, what has meaning and importance for you and what is trivial and secondary," *Sources of the Self*, 28. We might consider deliberation about substantive justice as an attempt to answer, in one important respect at least, the question of our common identity. The articulation of our principles of justice defines our identity to the extent that it provides orientation for us when we are confronted by certain inescapable questions. In any modern collective form of human life, the question of what justice demands is not one that just happens to be asked. On the contrary, it is a precondition of such a collective form of life.

53. "A Critique of Philosophical Conversation," 194.

54. I will be arguing later that Habermas's discursive proceduralism highlights very effectively the importance of this insight.

55. Walzer often takes the reading of a canonical text as an analogy for social criticism. Certain world religions often base their moral disputes on the interpretation of such texts, for example, Judaism, Christianity, Islam. The social critic reads in our social meanings the moral principles that give us orientation in matters of justice. For the clearest example of the analogy, see *Interpretation and Social Criticism*, 67–94.

56. See, for example, *Thick and Thin*, 45–47.

57. See especially *Interpretation and Social Criticism*, 43–44, and more generally, for Walzer's view of Gramsci as a critic, *Company of Critics*, 80–100.

58. At this point Walzer has to distance himself from Gramsci's own self-understanding. While his account of hegemonic struggle allows us to understand criticism democratically as a rearrangement of ideas that are already dominant, his own belief in objective and absolute knowledge leads him into contradiction as a "victim . . . of Marxist teleology," *Company of Critics*, 99. We might think of Walzer's Gramsci as offering not an objective, uniquely correct interpretation of the values of liberty and equality, but a reinterpretation that opens up the meaning of these values in new and liberating ways.

59. *Company of Critics*, 9–12. See his remarks on Herbert Marcuse at 184–87.

60. Ibid., 233–38.

61. Ibid., 229. It is according to criteria such as this that Walzer assesses the lives of the eleven twentieth century critics he considers in this work.

62. Ibid., 229–33.

63. Ibid., 229.

64. Walzer maintains that this is not inconsistent with a certain thin universalist moral code, *Thick and Thin*, chapter 1. I will discuss Walzer's universalism in the next chapter.

65. For a critique of metanarrative unity, see Jean-François Lyotard, *The Postmodern Condition: A Report on Knowledge* (Minneapolis: University of Minnesota Press, 1984). See also White, *Political Theory and Postmodernism*, 118 19.

66. Richard Bernstein gives a useful overview of the common concerns of Anglo-American and Continental philosophers with regard to the question of otherness, "Incommensurability and Otherness Revisited" in *The New Constellation*, 57–78.

67. In the final chapter I will discuss the extent to which Walzer's approach to issues of justice could serve any critical purpose in the context of a society where pluralism is a deeply divisive problem. I will take the example of Northern Ireland where it would appear that there are two historical communities uneasily coexisting in the territory of one political entity.

68. See Nancy Rosenblum, "Moral Membership in a Post-Liberal State," *World Politics* 36 (1984): 586–90.

69. This is Rawls's project, but for discussion of Walzer's views on this point see William Galston "Community, Democracy, Philosophy: The Political Thought of Michael Walzer," *Political Theory* 17 (1989): 120–22.

70. I have argued already, in the discussion of the feminist challenge to liberalism, that despite his intentions, Rawls's own procedure is vulnerable to the charge that it is insufficiently sensitive to difference.

71. "To Each His Own," *New York Review of Books* 30.6 (April 14, 1983): 4–6. A similar argument is made by Joshua Cohen, "Review of *Spheres of Justice*," *Journal of Philosophy* 83 (1986): 457–68. For the ensuing debate between Walzer and Dworkin, see "Spheres of Justice: An Exchange," *New York Review of Books* 30.12 (July 21, 1983): 44–46. Interestingly enough, while Dworkin's political philosophy contrasts with Walzer's because of its stress on abstract and general principles of equality, his legal theory is distinctively hermeneutic in orientation. See the three essays in "Law and Interpretation," part 2 of *A Matter of Principle*, 117–77. This collection also contains "To Each His Own" but under the title "What Justice Isn't," 214–20. More generally for Dworkin's view of legal theory, see *Law's Empire* (Cambridge, Mass.: Harvard University Press, 1986). The tension between the hermeneutic language of his approach to law and the appeal to abstract principles of justice is explored by Georgia Warnke, *Justice and Interpretation*, 77–80.

72. *Spheres of Justice*, 86–91.

73. For the best defense of Walzer in this debate, see Georgia Warnke, "Social Interpretation and Political Theory: Walzer and his Critics," in Kelly (ed.), *Hermeneutics and Critical Theory in Ethics and Politics*, 204–26. More generally, see Charles Taylor "Interpretation and the Sciences of Man," in his *Philosophical Papers, II*, 15–57.

74. Note Walzer's comments in "A Critique of Philosophical Conversation," 191–92.

75. Warnke, "Social Interpretation and Political Theory," 209.

76. "Spheres of Justice: An Exchange," 43.

77. *Political Liberalism*, 13–14.

78. Ibid., 25–26.

79. Ibid., 26. I think this supports the argument that Walzer's critique of Rawls is based, to some extent at least, on a misinterpretation of his project.

80. Ibid., 134. It is also for this reason that Rawls, unlike Walzer, believes it to be necessary to justify substantive principles of justice through an abstract conception of an impartial point of view. See ibid., 43–46. I agree with the view that we need a conception of impartiality but we should not accept one that depends on such a restrictive understanding of the political.

81. Ibid., 44.

82. Ibid., 90.

83. On the role of practical reason in Rawls's political constructivism, see Rainer Forst, "Review of *Political Liberalism*," *Constellations* 1 (1994): 162–71.

84. Warnke, "Walzer, Rawls and Gadamer: Hermeneutics and Political Theory," in *Festivals of Interpretation: Essays on Hans-Georg Gadamer's Work*, ed. Kathleen Wright (Albany: State University of New York Press, 1990), 136–60.

85. For an introduction to early hermeneutic theories, see Josef Bleicher, *Contemporary Hermeneutics: Hermeneutics as Method, Philosophy and Critique* (London: Routledge and Kegan Paul, 1980), especially 1–26.

86. These early theorists included F. D. E. Schleiermacher and Wilhelm Dilthey, but for an example of the work of a more recent exponent of objectivist hermeneutics see Emilio Betti "Hermeneutics as the General Methodology of the *Geisteswissenschaften*," reprinted in Bleicher's *Contemporary Hermeneutics*, 51–94.

87. The classical statement of Gadamer's position is *Truth and Method*. His development of philosophical hermeneutics in this direction away from the quest for

objectivity owes much to Heidegger's analysis of the forestructure of understanding in *Being and Time* (New York: Harper & Row, 1962). See *Truth and Method*, 265–71 and 291–300, and Bleicher, *Contemporary Hermeneutics*, 97–127. For a good introduction to Gadamer's hermeneutics, see Richard J. Bernstein, *Beyond Objectivism and Relativism* (Oxford: Basil Blackwell, 1983), 34–44 and 109–69, and for a recent collection of essays dealing with critical encounters between Gadamer's work and a variety of contemporary philosophical perspectives, see *Gadamer and Hermeneutics*, ed. Hugh Silverman (London: Routledge, 1991).

88. *Truth and Method*, 302–7.

89. For a discussion of Gadamer's critique of the idea that meaning is tied to authorial intention, see Georgia Warnke, *Gadamer: Hermeneutics, Tradition and Reason* (Cambridge: Polity Press, 1987), 42–72.

90. Gadamer, "The Universality of the Hermeneutical Problem," in his *Philosophical Hermeneutics*, 9. This essay is also reprinted in Bleicher, *Contemporary Hermeneutics*, 128–40.

91. This notion is closely related to the idea of a horizon of understanding. Gadamer introduces it in *Truth and Method*, 300–7, but goes on to develop an explanation of what is involved at length, 341–79. This includes a highly illuminating analysis of the priority of the question in human understanding where Gadamer takes the Platonic dialogues as his model.

92. See David Couzens Hoy, "Legal Hermeneutics: Recent Debates," in Wright (ed.), *Festivals of Interpretation*, 111–35. Hoy discusses the notion of historically effected consciousness in relation to debates surrounding Dworkin's legal hermeneutics. See also Gadamer on "The Exemplary Significance of Legal Hermeneutics" in *Truth and Method*, 324–41.

93. "Walzer, Rawls and Gadamer," 152–53. Warnke gives a hermeneutic reading of Rawls's contribution. Given the fact however that he understands his construction of a political conception of justice to derive from ideas of practical reason I do not think we can consider him to be a hermeneuticist. Bearing this in mind it is, I think, still legitimate from the perspective of hermeneutics to consider his two substantive principles to be a valuable interpretive account of justice in our tradition.

94. New circumstances present a challenge to a tradition's prejudices. When a community attempts to come to terms with new circumstances in an openly dialogical way then the prejudices of that community's tradition may have to be revised or even repudiated. I will return to this in the next chapter.

95. On the fusion of horizons as a self-transformative moment, see *Truth and Method*, 379. Gadamer thinks of this as an achievement of language, something which in part led to his debate with Habermas, as we will see in the next chapter.

96. Warnke's recent book *Justice and Interpretation* provides the clearest available account of how hermeneutics relates to matters of justice. I will have certain criticisms to make of her argument when I discuss contextualist critics of Habermas in chapter 7.

97. See Charles Taylor's comments on the Rushdie affair in *Multiculturalism and "The Politics of Recognition,"* 62–63. Taylor defends a version of liberal holism in this essay that, as he mentions here, avoids the distinction between political and comprehensive moralities that makes it so difficult for Rawls's proceduralism to deal with politicocultural controversies such as that sparked by the Rushdie affair. The hermeneutic account I am outlining here advocates a dialogue between the dominant liberal tradition and minority groups of citizens such as Moslem fundamentalist groups. While we must presume that these minorities can enrich our interpretive account of justice, there is no guarantee that this will lead to a significant shift in the moral standards that are constitutive of our self-understanding as a democratic community. What we can expect is that through the encounter we will have deepened our interpretive account of justice by clarifying what it is that we cannot accept in the demands such minorities might make.

98. Taylor, *Multiculturalism and "The Politics of Recognition,"* 65–73. He actually invokes Gadamer's idea of a "fusion of horizons," 67.

99. As well as the work of Gadamer and Taylor, Alasdair MacIntyre mounts a comprehensive defense of the centrality of tradition in moral reflection in *After Virtue*; in *Whose Justice? Which Rationality?*; and in *Three Rival Versions of Moral Inquiry* (London: Duckworth, 1990). On the other hand, Richard Rorty, unlike any of these hermeneuticists, does not allow for any significant degree of communal rational self-criticism since he tends to endorse whatever self-understanding a community just happens to have. This amounts to the conflation of the questions "Who are we?" and "Who do we aspire to be?" If Rorty were right, then our deliberations about justice would not only lack direction but they would also be devoid of any internal critical standards. Nor can Rorty's "neo-pragmatism" accommodate very easily differing interpretations of what our shared moral commitments require. For Rorty's view on matters of justice, see *Contingency, Irony and Solidarity* (Cambridge: Cambridge University Press, 1989); "The Priority of Democracy to Philosophy"; and also "Solidarity or Objectivity?" and "Postmodernist Bourgeois Liberalism," both included in his *Objectivity, Relativism and Truth: Philosophical Papers, vol. 1* (Cambridge: Cambridge University Press, 1991). For a contrast between Gadamer and Rorty, see Warnke, *Gadamer: Hermeneutics, Tradition and Reason*, 139–66, and for a sample of the numerous general criticisms of Rorty's political views, see Richard Bernstein, *The New Constellation*, 230–92, and Nancy Fraser, "Solidarity or Singularity?: Richard Rorty between Romanticism and Technocracy," in Malachowski (ed.), *Reading Rorty*, 303–21.

4. The Limits of Walzer's Immanent Critique

1. We will see precisely what aspect of our reflections on justice is involved here when I discuss the relation between moral and ethical employments of practical reason in the final part.

2. Thomas McCarthy gives a useful summary of the similarities and differences between the work of Foucault and the tradition of Marxian critical theory especially in relation to their reaction to hermeneutics. See "The Critique of Impure Reason: Foucault and the Frankfurt School," *Political Theory* 18 (1990): 439, 441–42. The essay is included in McCarthy's *Ideals and Illusions*, 43–75.

3. *Thick and Thin*, 1–6.

4. We will also see, in chapter 6, how Rawls and Habermas offer different perspectives on the relation between practical reason and tradition.

5. *Interpretation and Social Criticism*, 41–43. Here Walzer also mentions Ignazio Silone, like Gramsci, a one-time member of the Italian Communist Party. See also the chapter on Silone in *Company of Critics*, 101–16. Silone is one of Walzer's favored critics to a large extent because of his rejection of Communist Party orthodoxy. Walzer characterizes with approval Silone's later views (p. 115): "He is seized by a fear of abstractions; he is in retreat from world history; he is content to begin and end his narratives with the peasants of the Abruzzi. . . . Silone, we might say, is committed to his dialect, the party to its dialectics."

6. See also *Spheres of Justice*, 9n.

7. *Interpretation and Social Criticism*, 44.

8. Note Walzer's critique of Gramsci's Marxism which I mention in a note in the last chapter. In fact, Walzer's own interpretation of the demands of justice in modern complex societies suggests that workers would be wrong to believe that capitalism could realise "equality enough." He argues for a "decentralised democratic socialism," *Spheres of Justice*, 318, and he goes to some lengths to defend industrial democracy from the dangers of private government, *Spheres of Justice*, 291–303, and "Justice Here and Now," 146–48. In "Liberalism and the Art of Separation," 328, he notes that liberalism "passes definitively into democratic socialism when the map of society is socially determined." As we have seen, his interpretation is not presented as a uniquely correct one but rather as the one that best discloses to us the moral commitments that are constitutive of our common identity.

9. *Interpretation and Social Criticism*, 44.

10. Georgia Warnke notes that this rejection of Marxism implies that Walzer cannot but offer a subjectivist interpretation of principles of justice, *Jus-*

tice and Interpretation, 36. As noted in the last chapter, she sees Gadamer's stress on tradition as a means of defusing this problem of subjectivism, "Walzer, Rawls and Gadamer," 151–57, and *Justice and Interpretation*, especially 128–34.

11. Marxist-Leninism is clearly Walzer's main target here. There certainly would seem to be good grounds for believing Leninists to be guilty on this score but Walzer also finds non-Leninist Marxists, such as Gramsci and also Sartre and Marcuse, wanting here. Nor does he see this failing as one that is exclusive to Marxists, as is obvious from his discussion of Foucault. See *Interpretation and Social Criticism*, 62–64 on Lenin, 57–59 on Sartre, and *Company of Critics*, 170–90 on Marcuse and 191–209 on Foucault's "lonely politics."

12. This point is made by Kerry Whiteside in "Review of *The Company of Critics*," *Political Theory* 17 (1989): 689–92.

13. *Spheres of Justice*, 99.

14. Many of Walzer's critics make this point. For a fairly typical example see Alessandro Ferrara "Universalisms: Procedural, Contextualist and Prudential," in Rasmussen (ed.), *Universalism vs. Communitarianism*, 23.

15. See White, *Political Theory and Postmodernism*, 120–21, where Walzer's limitations in respect to the theorization of power are effectively exposed. White shows how Walzer's approach to matters of justice is undermined by his failure to grapple with specifically modern forms of power with anything like the sophistication of Foucault or Habermas. We will assess Habermas's own critique of hermeneutics later in this chapter. Walzer shows some awareness of this problem in "Exclusion, Injustice and the Democratic State," 56, where he acknowledges that "the convertibility of social goods and the dominance it makes possible take increasingly subtle and indirect forms in modern societies." His response is to argue that the state should play a more significant role in facilitating the "associations of civil society," 61, in trying to ensure that no social group is marginalized or excluded from social life as an underclass of second-class citizens. While this greater sensitivity to the real dangers of social marginalization is welcome, it does not seem to recognize the need to take theoretical steps beyond Walzer's preferred antiphilosophical, storytelling approach to social criticism. Furthermore, encouraging the state to greater intervention in civil society would seem to undermine some of the advantages of Walzer's pluralistic conception of citizenship through the variety of spheres of justice as against an overburdened welfare-state that Rawls's two principles might require.

16. See Steven Lukes, *Power: A Radical View* (London: Macmillan, 1974), especially 21–25.

17. While it seems that Walzer's antitheoretical stance would make it difficult for him to endorse this view, hermeneutic criticism is, as suggested in the last

chapter, generally concerned with deepening self-understanding. There is no reason why this should not be thought of in terms of overcoming illusions. See, for example, Taylor's essay "What's Wrong with Negative Liberty?" in *Philosophical Papers*, *II*, 211–29.

18. *Spheres of Justice*, 313–15.

19. Lukes, *Power: A Radical View*, 49–50. The work of John Gaventa offers a good example of an empirically based analysis of power in this respect; see Gaventa's *Power and Powerlessness: Quiescence and Rebellion in an Appalachian Valley* (Urbana: University of Illinois Press, 1980).

20. *Justice, Gender and the Family*, 65.

21. Ibid., 65.

22. For Habermas's initial response to *Truth and Method*, see his *On the Logic of the Social Sciences* (Cambridge: Polity Press, 1988), 151–70, especially 168–70. Some of the better commentaries on the controversy between Gadamer and Habermas include Bleicher's *Contemporary Hermeneutics*, 153–58; Paul Ricouer, "Hermeneutics and the Critique of Ideology," in his *Hermeneutics and the Human Sciences*, ed. John B. Thompson (Cambridge: Cambridge University Press, 1981), 63–100; Georgia Warnke, *Gadamer: Hermeneutics, Tradition and Reason*, 107–38; Thomas McCarthy, *The Critical Theory of Jürgen Habermas* (Cambridge: Polity Press, 1984), 169–93; Robert C. Holub, *Jürgen Habermas: Critic in the Public Sphere* (London: Routledge, 1991), 49–77; Graeme Nicholson, "Answers to Critical Theory," and Dieter Misgeld, "Modernity and Hermeneutics: A Critical-Theoretical Rejoinder," both in Silverman (ed.), *Gadamer and Hermeneutics*, 151–62 and 163–77; and for a special journal issue on the dispute and its relation to methods in the social sciences, including a contribution from Gadamer, see *Cultural Hermeneutics* 2.4 (February 1975), ed. David Rasmussen, 305–90. For an assessment of the implications of this dispute in relation to ethics, see Michael Kelly, "The Gadamer-Habermas Debate Revisited: The Question of Ethics," in Rasmussen (ed.), *Universalism vs. Communitarianism*, 139–59.

23. *Truth and Method*, 271–77. This phrase is used at 272.

24. This is the subject of part III of *Truth and Method*, 381–491. See, for example, page 474, where he maintains that "being that can be understood is language." See also "The Universality of the Hermeneutical Problem," 15–17, and "To What Extent Does Language Preform Thought?," included as "Supplement II" to *Truth and Method*, 542–49. This piece constitutes a partial response to Habermas's critique.

25. *On the Logic of the Social Sciences*, 172–74.

26. See also Habermas, "Technology and Science as Ideology," in *Toward a Rational Society: Student Protest, Science and Politics* (London: Heinemann, 1971), 81–122.

27. *On the Logic of the Social Sciences*, 172.

28. See Habermas, "The Hermeneutic Claim to Universality," in Bleicher, *Contemporary Hermeneutics*, 181–211.

29. In *Knowledge and Human Interests* (Cambridge: Polity Press, 1987), 214–300, Habermas discusses psychoanalysis in relation to a program of critical social science that is to serve a human interest in emancipation, but his attempt to use it as a means of transcending the limits of Gadamer's hermeneutics is more explicitly dealt with in "The Hermeneutic Claim to Universality" and also "On Systematically Distorted Communication," *Inquiry* 13 (1970): 205–18.

30. The intention is to offer a model for how we might explain the acquiescence of those whose real interests are systematically obscured and repressed while at the same time dispelling the ideological illusions that act as pseudo-justifications for the continued repression. We might think of examples such as those discussed in the previous section; patriarchy and the caste system.

31. "The Hermeneutic Claim to Universality," 192–95 and "On Systematically Distorted Communication," 207–9.

32. See Bleicher, *Contemporary Hermeneutics*, 167.

33. Habermas rejects certain scientistic assumptions in Freud's understanding of his own metapsychology, especially with regard to the relationship between causality and freedom, *Knowledge and Human Interests*, 246–73. See Jeffrey A. Abramson's comments on this issue in *Liberation and Its Limits* (Boston: Beacon Press, 1984), 114–19.

34. "On the Scope and Function of Hermeneutical Reflection," in his *Philosophical Hermeneutics*, 41–42.

35. Walzer explicitly rejects Freudian models of social criticism in *Interpretation and Social Criticism*, 65. He maintains there that criticism is "less the practical offspring of scientific knowledge than the educated cousin of common complaint."

36. *Knowledge and Human Interests*, 234.

37. McCarthy, *The Critical Theory of Jürgen Habermas*, 211–12.

38. Gadamer, "On the Scope and Function of Hermeneutical Reflection," 31, and "To What Extent Does Language Preform Thought?," 546.

39. See "On the Scope and Function of Hermeneutical Reflection," 32–35.

40. However, for a careful account of the possible uses of Habermas's psychoanalytic model, see Mark Warren, "The Self in Discursive Democracy," in *The Cambridge Companion to Habermas*, ed. Stephen K. White (Cambridge: Cambridge University Press, 1995), 167–200.

41. Dieter Misgeld gives a good summary of how the concerns of recent critical theory have been shaped by the encounter between Habermas and Gadamer. See "Modernity and Hermeneutics: A Critical-Theoretical Rejoinder," 175–77. We might suggest that while Gadamer would share many of Habermas's concerns, he is not primarily interested in the grounds of a critical social theory but rather in the ontological preconditions of all forms of human understanding.

42. The continuity between the notion of a critique of ideology and the theory of communicative action that is at the center of Habermas's later work is effectively established by James F. Bohman in "Formal Pragmatics and Social Criticism: The Philosophy of Language and the Critique of Ideology in Habermas's Theory of Communicative Action," *Philosophy and Social Criticism* 11 (1985): 331–53 and in his "Participating in Enlightenment: Habermas's Cognitivist Interpretation of Democracy," in *Knowledge and Politics*, ed. Marcelo Dascal and Ora Gruengard (Boulder, Colo.: Westview Press, 1989), 264–89, especially 281–87. For an interesting view of the way in which Habermas's views on communication and the public sphere correct and improve on Marx's critique of certain ideological tendencies within liberal discourses, see Mark Warren, "Liberal Constitutionalism as Ideology: Marx and Habermas," *Political Theory* 17 (1989): 511–34.

43. Habermas maintains that the traditional ideologies, such as religious ones, that were criticized by Marx, no longer even appear convincing. This may well also be the case for the bourgeois interpretations of the values of liberty and equality that were the object of Gramsci's critique. The effects of power now are to be thought of more in terms of a "fragmentation of consciousness" in the way that various aspects of everyday life are separated from each other and "colonized" by different expert cultures. This fragmentation is now the "functional equivalent" of an ideology and it must be exposed and criticized as a block to rational deliberation about the legitimacy of norms and principles that currently regulate the institutional life of modern societies. See Habermas, *The Theory of Communicative Action*, vol. 2 (Cambridge: Polity Press, 1987), 354–56, and Steven K. White, *The Recent Work of Jürgen Habermas: Reason, Justice and Modernity* (Cambridge: Cambridge University Press, 1988), 116–18. But see also the last note for references to work that stresses the fundamental continuity between the critique of ideology and Habermas's most recent social theory.

44. In the final chapter I will develop this criticism of Walzer by exposing the limits of his approach in the context of a deeply divided society. I will argue that Habermas's discourse ethics allows us more effectively to adopt a critical stance with regard to the effects of power in the political dispute at the centre of the Northern Ireland conflict.

45. *Thick and Thin*, 11.

46. Galston, *Liberal Purposes*, 46. See also *Spheres of Justice*, 312–16.

47. Walzer develops this rank-ordering in his two lectures given under the title "Nation and Universe," in *The Tanner Lectures on Human Values, XI*, ed. Grethe B. Peterson (Salt Lake City: University of Utah Press, 1990), 507–56. I will discuss this in more detail in the discussion of Northern Ireland in chapter 8.

48. As we will see, this is relevant in a case like that of Northern Ireland. It is also a common experience of immigrant cultures, especially in countries that were formerly colonial powers, where cultural imperialism almost always survives the end of colonial rule. Similar forms of cultural oppression occur in relation to minorities such as the disabled, lesbians and gays, the elderly, etc. See Young, *Justice and the Politics of Difference*, 58–61.

49. *Thick and Thin*, 17.

50. In *Spheres of Justice*, xv, Walzer argues that the (human) rights to life and liberty are central to a theory of just war but they do not get us very far in determining the substance of distributive justice for a particular society. See his *Just and Unjust Wars: A Moral Argument with Historical Illustrations*, 2nd ed. (New York: Basic Books, 1992). Apart from the first chapter of *Thick and Thin*, Walzer comments on the minimal code in *Interpretation and Social Criticism*, 24–25, 45, and on the prophet Jonah as a "minimalist critic," 76–78 and 89–90; see also *Company of Critics*, 226–27. It is rather odd to treat the question of human rights as an empirical matter since the rights that Walzer includes in his minimal code are clearly not respected universally.

51. *Spheres of Justice*, xiii.

52. Ibid., 314, and *Interpretation and Social Criticism*, 46–48, where he draws on Thomas Scanlon's important ideas on justification, as argued in "Contractualism and Utilitarianism," in Sen and Williams (eds.), *Utilitarianism and Beyond*, 103–28.

53. *Spheres of Justice*, 303.

54. Ibid., 303–11.

55. Ibid., 304.

56. *Interpretation and Social Criticism*, 22, also more generally *Thick and Thin*, chapter 3.

57. Walzer tends toward Rorty's position here in his apparent scepticism toward any substantive principles that could legitimately claim universal scope, except for a few empirical examples that just happen to be shared (almost?) universally. See Rorty's "Postmodernist Bourgeois Liberalism" and Walzer, *Interpretation and Social Criticism*, 24. See also Will Kymlicka's critique of Walzer and Rorty in "Liberalism and Communitarianism," *Canadian Journal of Philosophy* 18 (1988): 197–203.

58. Benhabib, *Situating the Self*, 228.

59. The following example is a version of one that is mentioned in Charles Taylor's discussion of this issue, "The Nature and Scope of Distributive Justice," in Lucash (ed.), *Justice and Equality Here and Now*, 49.

60. Of course, this is a case of justice in an international context conflicting with national arrangements. It might also be the case that some aspect of the universalist code clashes internally with the traditions of a particular community. In fact, this occurs whenever the traditions of a community fail to respect some or other human right that would be included as a structural feature of any valid account of justice. Again, Walzer's stress on local narratives, which obscures the extensiveness of the universalist code, explains the fact that he does not say enough to justify the claim that the human right should take precedence over the particular traditions of the community. We will see later how Habermas's moral theory deals much more directly with this problem.

61. See, however, *Interpretation and Social Criticism*, 45. The example used there relates to missionary activity and not to the kind of dilemma that most citizens of modern societies encounter with distressing regularity, as for example, whenever they are shocked by the fact that many human beings are in danger of starving to death.

62. Foucault, *Power/Knowledge*, 131–33.

63. It is important to note that the privilege of reason in politics has, for better or worse, become a hotly contested issue. For some indication as to why this is so, see Richard Bernstein's essay "The Rage against Reason," in *The New Constellation*, 31–56. My point here is simply that Walzer says very little about this, nor does he justify any procedural rules of rational argumentation.

64. For an account of the centrality of the notion of inclusivity to Walzer's social criticism, see Robert B. Thigpen and Lyle A. Downing, "Beyond Shared Understandings," *Political Theory* 14 (1986): 451–72.

65. Serious doubts are expressed on this score by William R. Lund in "Communitarian Politics, the Supreme Court and Privacy: The Continuing Need for Liberal Boundaries," *Social Theory and Practice* 16 (1990): 199–206. While Emily Gill shows how Walzer's defense of both nondiscrimination and participative rights defuses the dangers involved here, it is still the case that the dissenting individual is not that central to Walzer's concerns. See Gill's "Walzer's Complex Equality," 44–51.

66. Nancy Rosenblum, "Moral Membership in a Post-Liberal State," 593.

67. *Spheres of Justice*, 15n. See also his discussion of the blocked uses of political power in *Spheres of Justice*, 282–84.

68. Thomas Morawetz expresses some related concerns in "Tension in the 'Art of Separation,'" *Political Theory* 13 (1985): 599–606.

5. THE PRIORITY OF COMMUNICATIVE ACTION

1. *Knowledge and Human Interests* represented Habermas's first attempt at a systematic reformulation of a critical social theory. The project reaches its culmination with the two volumes of *The Theory of Communicative Action* (Cambridge: Polity Press, 1984 and 1987) and *The Philosophical Discourse of Modernity* (Cambridge: Polity Press, 1987). In his work since then Habermas has focused on the elaboration of discourse ethics, which can be thought of as an account of justice grounded in his critical understanding of modernity. More recently he has drawn out the implications of his discourse theory for an understanding of the law and the constitutional principles of a democratic state; see *Faktizität und Geltung*. I will be focusing on discourse ethics as a dialogical conception of an impartial point of view. Robert Holub's *Jürgen Habermas: Critic in the Public Sphere* gives an excellent overview of the debates, disputes, and controversies that have characterized Habermas's career. The best introduction to his thought remains Thomas McCarthy's *The Critical Theory of Jürgen Habermas*, but his work since the early eighties is considered in Stephen K. White's *The Recent Work of Jürgen Habermas* and in David M. Rasmussen's *Reading Habermas* (Cambridge, Mass.: Basil Blackwell, 1990).

2. See, for example, *Moral Consciousness and Communicative Action*, 67.

3. See his critical comments in relation to Rawls's attempt to justify his two principles in *Autonomy and Solidarity: Interviews with Jürgen Habermas*, rev. ed., ed. Peter Dews (London: Verso, 1992), 200–01.

4. On this paradigm shift, see especially *The Philosophical Discourse of Modernity*, 294–326.

5. The most detailed account of Habermas's theory of language as a basis for rational social criticism is Maeve Cooke's *Language and Reason: A Study of Habermas's Pragmatics* (Cambridge, Mass.: MIT Press, 1994).

6. *Autonomy and Solidarity*, 194.

7. The best account of this shift of emphasis in Habermas's work, from cognitive interests in *Knowledge and Human Interests* to communicative action, is given by Richard Bernstein in his "Introduction" to *Habermas and Modernity*, ed. Richard J. Bernstein (Cambridge: Polity Press, 1985), 1–32.

8. Gadamer's *Truth and Method*, in opposing "truth" to "method," offers the most thoroughgoing hermeneuticist critique of positivist social science. However, the implied relativism that Habermas is keen to avoid, from a social-theoretical perspective, is more clearly exemplified in the work of the neo-Wittgensteinian, Peter Winch, *The Idea of a Social Science*, 2nd ed. (London: Routledge, 1990), and the neo-pragmatist, Richard Rorty, *Philosophy and the Mirror of Nature* (Princeton: Princeton University Press, 1979).

9. Habermas, "Interpretive Social Science vs. Hermeneuticism," in Haan et al. (eds.), *Social Science as Moral Inquiry*, 251–69, especially 256–61. This article is reprinted as "Reconstruction and Interpretation in the Social Sciences," in *Moral Consciousness and Communicative Action*, 21–42.

10. Habermas, "What is Universal Pragmatics?" in *Communication and the Evolution of Society* (London: Heinemann, 1979), 9. The differences between reconstructive and empirical-analytical scientific methods are discussed in this essay, 15–20.

11. For a useful discussion of the idea of a reconstructive science, see McCarthy, *The Critical Theory of Jürgen Habermas*, 276–79. On Habermas's own views, see "What is Universal Pragmatics?," 8–25, and "Interpretive Social Science vs. Hermeneuticism," 258–61. For an exceptionally clear account of the relation between rational reconstruction and Habermas's critical social theory, see Kenneth Baynes "Rational Reconstruction and Social Criticism: Habermas's Model of Interpretive Social Science," in Kelly (ed.), *Hermeneutics and Critical Theory in Ethics and Politics*, 122–45.

12. "What is Universal Pragmatics?," 12.

13. "Interpretive Social Science vs. Hermeneuticism," 260. See also "A Reply to My Critics," in *Habermas: Critical Debates*, ed. John B. Thompson and David Held (London: Macmillan, 1982), 234.

14. "What is Universal Pragmatics?," 14.

15. "Interpretive Social Science vs. Hermeneuticism," 255.

16. While many broad philosophical currents, including hermeneutics and poststructuralism as well as recent approaches to the history of science, are engaged in the critique of philosophical foundationalism, Rorty's *Philosophy and the Mirror of Nature* constitutes one of the most trenchant attacks on the idea that there could be any ultimate grounds for a philosophical justification of reason, independent of the contingencies of history and culture. Antifoundationalism rejects in particular the autonomous rational subject that characterizes the philosophy of consciousness in the work of Descartes and Kant. Subjects do not so much constitute the world but rather they are embodied within the context of a particular linguistic world. Habermas also rejects foundationalism and

along with it any possibility of a pure conception of reason: "There is no pure reason that might don linguistic clothing only in the second place. Reason is by its very nature incarnated in contexts of communicative action and in structures of the lifeworld." *The Philosophical Discourse of Modernity*, 322. Habermas however, by defending a situated reason, does not endorse Rorty's outright rejection of the philosophical project.

17. "Philosophy as Stand-In and Interpreter," in *Moral Consciousness and Communicative Action*, 2.

18. This is, in part, why he moved away from the epistemological project of *Knowledge and Human Interests* that set about establishing critical theory in terms of cognitive interests. He now admits that this does not take sufficient account of historical change and the socially constituted nature of theoretical paradigms. See *Autonomy and Solidarity*, 192–93.

19. "Philosophy as Stand-In and Interpreter," 17.

20. Ibid., 3.

21. The whole argument of *The Philosophical Discourse of Modernity* can be thought of in these terms. For Habermas the paradigm of a philosophy of intersubjective understanding offers us a way out of this dilemma.

22. "Philosophy as Stand-In and Interpreter," 15. See also *Postmetaphysical Thinking: Philosophical Essays* (Cambridge: Polity Press, 1992), 38.

23. "Philosophy as Stand-In and Interpreter," 16.

24. We will see in the next chapter how Habermas sees Kohlberg's empirical work in the field of moral developmental psychology in this cooperative relationship with his own philosophical defense of discourse ethics as a cognitivist moral theory.

25. "Philosophy as Stand-In and Interpreter," 19.

26. Habermas is most concerned here with the ways in which the sphere of science and technology can encroach on the domains of morality and art. This has been a constant theme in his work from "Technology and Science as Ideology" in *Toward a Rational Society* through to the critique of functionalist reason in *The Theory of Communicative Action, vol. 2*.

27. While Habermas gives his most comprehensive account of this paradigm shift in *The Philosophical Discourse of Modernity*, the same theme is present in his early work, see "Labour and Interaction: Remarks on Hegel's Jena *Philosophy of Mind*," in *Theory and Practice* (London: Heinemann, 1974), 142–69.

28. "Questions and Counterquestions," in Bernstein (ed.), *Habermas and Modernity*, 197.

29. "Interpretive Social Science vs. Hermeneuticism," 260.

30. See, for example, "What is Universal Pragmatics?," 50–59; *Moral Consciousness and Communicative Action*, 59, 136–37; *The Theory of Communicative Action*, 1:305–19; and *Postmetaphysical Thinking*, 75–78. I cannot go into detail here about Habermas's argument in support of this separation of three, and only three validity claims. The most detailed critical analysis is provided by Cooke, *Language and Reason*, 51–94. Our main concern in this section is to lay the ground for an analysis of discourse ethics, which thematizes the claim to normative rightness. For an illuminating critical exchange on the question as to whether or not Habermas can defend a procedural unity of reason in his notion of communicative action, while also maintaining this three-way differentiation of validity claims and the corresponding separation of the specialist areas of science, morality, and art, see Martin Seel, "The Two Meanings of 'Communicative' Rationality: Remarks on Habermas's Critique of a Plural Concept of Reason," in *Communicative Action: Essays on Jürgen Habermas's "The Theory of Communicative Action,"* ed. Axel Honneth and Hans Joas (Cambridge: Polity Press, 1991), 36–48, and in the same collection Habermas's "A Reply," 214–64, especially 222–29, and his essay "The Unity of Reason in the Diversity of Its Voices," in *Postmetaphysical Thinking*, 115–48.

31. *Postmetaphysical Thinking*, 77.

32. *The Theory of Communicative Action*, 1:287–88. See also "A Reply to my Critics," 270.

33. This distinction is introduced in *The Theory of Communicative Action*, 1:287.

34. See ibid., 1:286–96; "A Reply to my Critics," 264–67; and for a more recent overview, *Postmetaphysical Thinking*, 78–84.

35. "A Reply," 241.

36. *Postmetaphysical Thinking*, 81.

37. "A Reply," 241. See also Habermas, "Remarks on the Discussion," *Theory, Culture and Society* 7 (1990): 131.

38. *Moral Consciousness and Communicative Action*, 94–95. This point will be developed below.

39. *The Theory of Communicative Action*, 1:293.

40. Ibid., 1:286.

41. See, for example, the collection of essays, Honneth and Joas (eds.), *Communicative Action*.

42. *The Theory of Communicative Action*, 1:288.

43. Ibid., 1:289.

44. Ibid.

45. Ibid., 1:291.

46. The case of imperatives adds a serious complication here, one which will be considered below.

47. Ibid., 1:293.

48. Ibid., 1:305.

49. See, for example, Jonathan Culler, "Communicative Competence and Normative Force," *New German Critique* 35 (1985): 133–44.

50. "A Reply," 239; *Postmetaphysical Thinking*, 83–84.

51. "A Reply," 240.

52. Ibid., 242.

53. *The Theory of Communicative Action*, 2:22. See also *On the Logic of the Social Sciences*, 134–35, where Habermas discusses this point in the context of a critical analysis of Winch's linguistic approach to social studies. If communicative action were not the original mode of language use this would raise important questions about the possibility of learning a new language or translating from one language into another.

54. See chapter 5 of Nicholas H. Smith, *Strong Hermeneutics* (London: Routledge, 1997), and the discussion of related matters in Cooke, *Language and Reason*, 19–27.

55. *The Theory of Communicative Action*, 2:124. Habermas's most complete account of the lifeworld is given here at 119–52.

56. "A Reply," 244–45, and *The Theory of Communicative Action*, 2:130–35.

57. *The Philosophical Discourse of Modernity*, 342; *The Theory of Communicative Action*, 2:145; and Baynes, "Rational Reconstruction and Social Criticism," 135. This makes it clear that we are not simply products of the lifeworld, but rather the lifeworld is reproduced by the interactive achievements of concrete individuals and groups.

58. *The Philosophical Discourse of Modernity*, 316.

59. *The Theory of Communicative Action*, 2:137.

60. This is a suggestion of Agnes Heller, "Habermas and Marxism," in Thompson and Held (eds.), *Habermas: Critical Debates*, 21–41.

61. Habermas's thinking on personal identity is very much shaped by his reading of the work of Mead. See *The Theory of Communicative Action*, 2:96–106, and especially the essay "Individuation through Socialization: On George Herbert Mead's Theory of Subjectivity," in *Postmetaphysical Thinking*, 149–204. The conception of the self implicit in Habermas's work has much in common with the holist view I defended earlier.

62. *Moral Consciousness and Communicative Action*, 199.

63. "A Reply to My Critics," 227.

64. *Moral Consciousness and Communicative Action*, 101–2.

65. For a similar argument, see Tony Smith, *The Role of Ethics in Social Theory: Essays from a Habermasian Perspective* (Albany: State University of New York Press, 1991), 190–92. For an interesting attempt to show how an examination of rational choice theory can strengthen the claim that strategic action cannot adequately sustain political interaction, see James Johnson, "Is Talk Really Cheap? Prompting Conversation between Critical Theory and Rational Choice," *American Political Science Review* 87 (1993): 74–86.

66. *Autonomy and Solidarity*, 112–13. For a fuller account of this aspect of modernization and for his use of the systems theory of Talcott Parsons in this respect, see *The Theory of Communicative Action*, 2:153–97 and 199–299. Sympathetic commentators have criticized Habermas on the grounds that his appropriation of Parsonian systems theory undermines the emancipatory potential of his critical theory. See Thomas McCarthy, "Complexity and Democracy, or the Seducements of Systems Theory," and Dieter Misgeld, "Critical Hermeneutics versus Neoparsonianism?," *New German Critique* 35 (1985): 27–53 and 55–82 respectively; see also Rasmussen, *Reading Habermas*, 37–55.

67. Habermas draws heavily on Max Weber in his understanding of modernity and processes of rationalization. Unlike Weber, Habermas sees the "iron cage" as a product, not of rationalization as such, but of one-sided (instrumental) rationalization. The idea of a communicatively rationalized lifeworld is offered as a corrective to the pessimism of Weber and the early critical theorists. See *The Theory of Communicative Action*, 1:143–271 and 339–99. Some of Habermas's own work reveals signs of increasing pessimism, for example, "The New Obscurity: The Crisis of the Welfare State and the Exhaustion of Utopian Energies," *Philosophy and Social Criticism* 11 (1986): 1–18.

68. *Autonomy and Solidarity*, 227.

69. *The Philosophical Discourse of Modernity*, 363.

70. For an earlier formulation of Habermas's conception of crisis, see *Legitimation Crisis* (London: Heinemann, 1976). The colonization thesis is developed in *The Theory of Communicative Action,* 2:301–403. For a highly instructive critique of the distinction between system and lifeworld from a feminist perspective, see Nancy Fraser, "What's Critical about Critical Theory? The Case of Habermas and Gender," *New German Critique* 35 (1985): 97–131, but see James Bohman's defense of Habermas's distinction in "'System' and 'Lifeworld': Habermas and the Problem of Holism," *Philosophy and Social Criticism* 15 (1989): 381–401. The potential usefulness of Habermas's theoretical work for feminist theory and practice is the subject of the collection *Feminists Read Habermas: Gendering the Subject of Discourse,* ed. Johanna Meehan (London: Routledge, 1995). See especially Jean Cohen's "Critical Theory and Feminist Critiques: The Debate with Jürgen Habermas," 57–90.

71. Concern about the public sphere has been constant in Habermas's work. Although it has only recently been translated into English, his first major book was written on this subject, in 1962, *Structural Transformation of the Public Sphere* (Cambridge: Polity Press, 1989). See the collection of essays on this theme, *Habermas and the Public Sphere,* ed. Craig Calhoun (Cambridge, Mass.: MIT Press, 1992). Habermas updates his own views here in "Further Reflections on the Public Sphere," 421–61. Habermas has been an important influence on recent theorists of civil society and the role of new social movements in protest politics, Jean Cohen, "Discourse Ethics and Civil Society," in Rasmussen (ed.), *Universalism vs. Communitarianism,* 83–105, and Cohen and Arato, *Civil Society and Political Theory.* On new potentials for protest, see *The Theory of Communicative Action,* 2:391–96; Baynes, *The Normative Grounds of Social Criticism,* 172–81; and White, *The Recent Work of Jürgen Habermas,* 107–27. On feminist uses of Habermas's conception of the public sphere, Joan B. Landes, "The Public and Private Sphere: A Feminist Reconsideration"; and Marie Fleming "Women and the 'Public Use of Reason'" both in Meehan (ed.), *Feminists Read Habermas,* 91–116 and 117–37.

72. We might note that neither Rawls nor Walzer develops a critical social theory in conjunction with their normative theories. The fact that Habermas's work on justice forms a coherent whole with such a comprehensive critical social theory strengthens the claim that discourse ethics overcomes the inadequacies of these alternative approaches to the theory of justice.

6. DISCURSIVE IMPARTIALITY

1. See, for example, *Moral Consciousness and Communicative Action,* 88–89.

2. See especially the essay "Morality and Ethical Life: Does Hegel's Critique of Kant Apply to Discourse Ethics?," in *Moral Consciousness and Communicative Action,* 195–215.

3. *Moral Consciousness and Communicative Action*, 201.

4. Ibid., 108.

5. For criticisms of the view that discourse ethics can serve not merely as a test of democratic legitimacy, or political justice, but also as a procedure that could guide an individual's moral judgment and action, see Albrecht Wellmer "Ethics and Dialogue: Elements of Moral Judgement in Kant and Discourse Ethics," in *The Persistence of Modernity* (Cambridge: Polity Press, 1991); Jean Cohen, "Discourse Ethics and Civil Society," 86–91; and Grace Clement, "Is the Moral Point of View Monological or Dialogical? The Kantian Background of Habermas' Discourse Ethics," *Philosophy Today* 34 (1989): 169–72. Seyla Benhabib rejects the view that discourse ethics should be limited to a model of political legitimacy, although her interpretation of discourse ethics differs in important ways from Habermas's, as we will see in chapter 7. See the first chapter of Benhabib's *Situating the Self*. My only concern is with discourse ethics as a test of principles of political and social justice, so when I speak of a morally valid norm, this can be taken to indicate a rationally justifiable principle of justice. See also David Ingram, "The Limits and Possibilities of Communicative Ethics for Democratic Theory," *Political Theory* 21 (1993): 298–300, and for a sympathetic but critical account of discourse ethics as a project of democratic legitimation, see Simone Chambers, "Discourse and Democratic Practices," in White (ed.), *The Cambridge Companion to Habermas*, 233–59.

6. For what follows, see *Moral Consciousness and Communicative Action*, 196–98. The most comprehensive account of discourse ethics is William Rehg's *Insight and Solidarity: The Discourse Ethics of Jürgen Habermas* (Berkeley: University of California Press, 1994).

7. *Moral Consciousness and Communicative Action*, 134.

8. Ibid., 59, 136–38. More generally see *The Theory of Communicative Action*, 1:233–42, 305–19. According to Habermas we can further differentiate between three basic attitudes, each of which entails a different perspective on the world: an objectivating attitude (that concentrates on claims to truth), a norm-conformative attitude (that concentrates on claims to normative rightness, or justice), and an expressive attitude (that concentrates on claims to truthfulness, or personal taste). We can confront any of the three worlds with any of these three basic attitudes. Since our focus is on claims to normative rightness that relate to the regulation of interpersonal relations in the social world, we need not concern ourselves with the complex interplay between these differentiated relations to the world, claims to validity and basic attitudes. It is however important to note that this differentiation, according to Habermas, is itself characteristic of the process of rationalization in a modern lifeworld.

9. *Moral Consciousness and Communicative Action*, 138.

10. Ibid., 107.

11. Ibid., 156.

12. The claim to truthfulness is not redeemed discursively, that is by giving reasons in support of the claim, but rather through consistent behaviour on the part of the speaker who raises the claim, ibid., 59.

13. *The Theory of Communicative Action*, 1:17–18.

14. *Moral Consciousness and Communicative Action*, 67.

15. Ibid., 59–62; *Autonomy and Solidarity*, 256; and McCarthy, *Ideals and Illusions*, 187–88. For an earlier formulation of the sense in which practical questions admit of truth, see *Legitimation Crisis*, 102–10.

16. *Moral Consciousness and Communicative Action*, 61.

17. *Justification and Application*, 39.

18. We will return to this point in the next chapter when we discuss the relation between the justification of norms and their application.

19. See especially Habermas's critique of Ernst Tugendhat in *Moral Consciousness and Communicative Action*, 68–76.

20. See Habermas's comments on Mead in *The Theory of Communicative Action*, 2:94–96.

21. *Moral Consciousness and Communicative Action*, 68.

22. Seyla Benhabib, *Critique, Norm and Utopia: A Study of the Foundations of Critical Theory* (New York: Columbia University Press, 1986), 313–16. For an interesting analysis of the political significance of need interpretation, see Nancy Fraser, "Women, Welfare and the Politics of Need Interpretation" and "Struggle over Needs: Outline of a Socialist-Feminist Critical Theory of Late Capitalist Political Culture," chapters 7 and 8 of her *Unruly Practices* (Cambridge: Polity Press, 1989).

23. For a more comprehensive account of the justification of discourse ethics, see Rehg, *Insight and Solidarity*, 19–83.

24. This aspect of rational accountability is to be understood as an obligation that is immanent to speech acts. It is a distinguishing feature of communicative action. See "What is Universal Pragmatics?," especially 59–65, and for useful comments, see McCarthy, *The Critical Theory of Jürgen Habermas*, 282–91, and White, *The Recent Work of Jürgen Habermas*, 50–55. We have already discussed the structure of communicative action in the last chapter.

25. "A Reply to my Critics," 254–58; *Moral Consciousness and Communicative Action*, 76–98; White, *The Recent Work of Jürgen Habermas*, 55–58; and for a distinctive interpretation of these rules, Benhabib, *Situating the Self*, 29.

26. *Moral Consciousness and Communicative Action*, 89.

27. For a good discussion of this much misunderstood idea, see McCarthy, *The Critical Theory of Jürgen Habermas*, 306–10. Habermas now believes that the term "ideal speech situation" is misleading in that it seems to imply an ideal that we must realize in all discourses that are actually carried out. In fact, the term was intended to describe the conditions under which claims to truth and normative rightness can be discursively redeemed, that is the general, unavoidable, idealizing, communicative presuppositions that all participants must make if they are to engage in argumentation at all. See "A Reply to my Critics," 235–36; *The Philosophical Discourse of Modernity*, 322–23; *Moral Consciousness and Communicative Action*, 201–3; *Autonomy and Solidarity*, 160–61, 171, and note especially the tone of regret here at 260. For recent comments that provide a clear and detailed account of the role of these idealizing presuppositions, *Justification and Application*, 54–60. For a typical misreading of Habermas on this issue, see Walzer "A Critique of Philosophical Conversation." Steven Lukes gives an incisive critical analysis in "Of Gods and Demons: Habermas and Practical Reason," in Thompson and Held (eds.), *Habermas: Critical Debates*, 134–48, but for Habermas's response, see "A Reply to my Critics," 250–63, and *Justification and Application*, 57–58.

28. Habermas had earlier discussed some of the implications of this approach for social criticism in terms of the suppression of generalizable interests; see *Legitimation Crisis*, 111–17.

29. *Justification and Application*, 56. See also the discussion in *Moral Consciousness and Communicative Action*, 89–92.

30. Habermas makes the point eloquently: "As little as we can do without the supposition of a purified discourse, we have equally to make do with 'unpurified' discourse" (*The Philosophical Discourse of Modernity*, 323). On this tension between the actual and the ideal, see also "A Reply to my Critics," 221; "Questions and Counterquestions," 197; and *Moral Consciousness and Communicative Action*, 203, where Habermas argues that the "factual force of counterfactual presuppositions" offers a bridge that Kant could not provide, between the realms of the intelligible and the empirical. In *Faktizität und Geltung*, Habermas presents a discourse theory of law that theorizes the centrality of this tension between the actual and the ideal in terms of the facticity of the legal and the validity of rationally justifiable norms.

31. *Justification and Application*, 31.

32. For a fairly recent example of this disturbingly common misreading of Habermas, see Nicholas Rescher, *Pluralism: Against the Demand for Consensus* (Oxford: Clarendon Press, 1993). The most infamous version of this familiar charge against Habermas is to be found in Jean-François Lyotard *The Postmodern Condition.*

33. *Autonomy and Solidarity*, 171, also *Postmetaphysical Thinking*, 140. We will discuss the implications of this increasing generality in the next chapter. See also McCarthy, *Ideals and Illusions*, 188–90, and for an interesting discussion of this point, Brian Walker, "Habermas and Pluralist Political Theory," *Philosophy and Social Criticism* 18 (1992): 81–102. Habermas is, as I have indicated, keen to point out here that idealization itself "leaves the identity of the participants and sources of conflict originating in the lifeworld untouched." This does not, however, preclude the possibility of moral transformation, discussed above, taking place in the course of a procedure of argumentation. The acceptance of the moral demands of justice will sometimes lead to ethical reflection that could transform identities. Both individual and collective identities can, and sometimes do, change in the face of the reasonable demands of other forms of life. This point will be developed in the last chapter when we will examine the case of Northern Ireland.

34. *Justification and Application*, 56, also "A Reply to My Critics," 235.

35. *Justification and Application*, 57. This is a matter for a discourse theory of law and politics, which has been the subject of Habermas's recent work. See especially *Faktizität und Geltung*, but for a brief statement of some of the themes of that major work "Three Normative Models of Democracy," *Constellations* 1 (1994): 1–10. An earlier work on this theme is "Law and Morality," in *The Tanner Lectures on Human Values, VIII*, ed. Sterling M. McMurrin (Salt Lake City: University of Utah Press, 1988), 217–79. For a useful account of Habermas's work on law prior to *Faktizität und Geltung*, see Robert Shelly, "Habermas and the Normative Foundations of a Radical Politics," *Thesis Eleven* 35 (1993): 62–83.

36. *Justification and Application*, 16.

37. For a detailed account of the derivation of (U), see Rehg, *Insight and Solidarity*, 65–75.

38. *Moral Consciousness and Communicative Action*, 93.

39. Ibid., 93.

40. In *Faktizität und Geltung*, 135–51, Habermas also introduces a principle of democracy that is to act as a test for the legitimacy of legal norms. The principle of discourse (D) is a general principle that informs procedures of justification for both moral and legal norms. It is (D), the discursive test for general

principles of justice that is our concern in this work. It should, however, be noted that Habermas himself thinks that the introduction of the principle of democracy addresses certain problems of indeterminacy that were associated with discourse ethics as an account of moral argumentation. See Kenneth Baynes, "Democracy and the *Rechtsstaat*: Habermas's *Faktizität und Geltung*," in White (ed.), *The Cambridge Companion to Habermas*, 208.

41. For a useful discussion, see Maeve Cooke, "Habermas and Consensus," *European Journal of Philosophy* 1 (1993): 247–67, also McCarthy, *Ideals and Illusions*, 189–90. One implication of this point is that Habermas's concept of a generalizable (or shared) interest is more fluid and flexible than Rawls's notion of primary goods. For brief but suggestive comments on how these two concepts might be related, see Baynes, *The Normative Grounds of Social Criticism*, 151, and for a more extensive discussion, see Carol C. Gould, "On the Conception of the Common Interest: Between Procedure and Substance," in Kelly (ed.), *Hermeneutics and Critical Theory in Ethics and Politics*, 253–73.

42. *Moral Consciousness and Communicative Action*, 178; *Autonomy and Solidarity*, 248–49.

43. See especially the essay "On the Pragmatic, the Ethical and the Moral Employments of Practical Reason," in *Justification and Application*, 1–18.

44. *Moral Consciousness and Communicative Action*, 79–82, 89–91.

45. The argument about performative contradiction runs through Habermas's critique of contemporary critics of reason, especially in *The Philosophical Discourse of Modernity*. See Martin Jay, "The Debate over Performative Contradiction: Habermas versus the Poststructuralists," in *Philosophical Interventions in the Unfinished Project of Enlightenment*, ed. Axel Honneth et al. (Cambridge, Mass.: MIT Press, 1992), 261–79.

46. *Moral Consciousness and Communicative Action*, 95–98. For a more extended discussion of his differences with Apel, see *Justification and Application*, 76–88.

47. *Justification and Application*, 83–84.

48. *Moral Consciousness and Communicative Action*, 15–16, 39, 116–19.

49. See "Moral Development and Ego Identity," in *Communication and the Evolution of Society*, 69–94; *Moral Consciousness and Communicative Action*, 33–41, 119–33, 171–88. Habermas outlines the differences between Kohlberg's moral-philosophical theory and discourse ethics in "Justice and Solidarity: On the Discussion Concerning 'Stage 6,'" in Kelly (ed.), *Hermeneutics and Critical Theory in Ethics and Politics*, 32–52.

50. What follows, in this and the next paragraph, is an exceptionally brief sketch. A somewhat more detailed summary of the stage sequence is provided by Stephen White in *The Recent Work of Jürgen Habermas*, 66–68.

51. *Moral Consciousness and Communicative Action*, 37–39, 116–19.

52. Ibid., 168.

53. See *Autonomy and Solidarity*, 254. Habermas's arguments in relation to social evolution are developed in detail in *Communication and the Evolution of Society* and especially in *The Theory of Communicative Action*, vol. 1.

54. This point was made in the discussion of the lifeworld toward the end of the last chapter. See especially *Moral Consciousness and Communicative Action*, 99–102.

55. An interesting exchange on this matter took place within the context of a symposium on Charles Taylor's *Sources of the Self* in *Inquiry* 34 (1991). See Martin Löw-Beer, "Living a Life and the Problem of Existential Impossibility," 217–36 and Taylor's response, "Comments and Replies," 251–53. Löw-Beer argues that since a principle of equal respect is a presupposition of communication, discourse ethics can explain why it is impossible to avoid a moral, or an impartial, point of view. Taylor, on the other hand, maintains that it is not the presuppositions of communicative action but rather the acknowledgment of a crucial human good ("the way in which human identity is formed through dialogue and recognition," 252) that makes the moral point of view inescapable. It seems to me that these arguments collapse into each other (as Taylor seems to suggest, 253) if we bear in mind that the socialization of the individual depends on the reproduction of the lifeworld through the communicative achievements of its participants. The procedure for testing norms that discourse ethics justifies can also, as we will see, affirm certain structural features of any good life. The good that Taylor sees as crucial in this context would, I suggest, have to be included as one of these structural features. On the dispute between Taylor and Habermas, see also Rehg, *Insight and Solidarity*, 134–49, and chapter 6 of Smith, *Strong Hermeneutics*.

56. See Benhabib's similar point, that inegalitarianism is either irrational or unjust, *Situating the Self*, 33.

57. The most extensive discussion available comparing the work of Habermas and Rawls is Baynes, *The Normative Grounds of Social Criticism*, but see also Thomas McCarthy, "Kantian Constructivism and Reconstructivism: Rawls and Habermas in Dialogue," *Ethics* 105 (1984): 44–63, and J. Donald Moon, "Practical Discourse and Communicative Ethics," in White (ed.), *The Cambridge Companion to Habermas*, 143–64. A number of points of difference between their positions are clarified in their recent exchange in the *Journal of Philosophy*; see Habermas, "Reconciliation through the Public Use of Reason," and Rawls, "Reply to Habermas."

58. Apart from "Reconciliation through the Public Use of Reason," Habermas makes the case for the superiority of discourse ethics as against Rawls's theory most explicitly in "Justice and Solidarity" but see also *Moral Consciousness and Communicative Action*, 66–67, 198; *Autonomy and Solidarity*, 158, 199–202, 271; *Justification and Application*, 25–30, 48–54, 92–96. In contrast with Habermas's encounter with scepticism, the contest between competing postconventional moral theories cannot be based on arguments about a logic of development, but rather it must be decided on the basis of philosophical argument, "Justice and Solidarity," 32–35.

59. *Moral Consciousness and Communicative Action*, 201.

60. It is for this reason that the arguments of Taylor and Löw-Beer, as noted above, collapse into each other.

61. *Moral Consciousness and Communicative Action*, 207. On the role of morality in protecting the vulnerable individual through the protection of the web of intersubjective recognition on which the individual's identity depends, see also *Justification and Application*, 109. This should make clear the superiority of discourse ethics on this point as against Walzer's hermeneutics. Walzer's weakness in this regard was discussed at the end of chapter 4 above. An incisive discussion of Habermas's notion of autonomy is given by Maeve Cooke, "Habermas, Autonomy and the Identity of the Self," *Philosophy and Social Criticism* 18 (1992): 269–92.

62. Habermas's discussion of ideal role-taking draws on the work of Mead, although "practical discourse transforms what Mead viewed as *individual, privately enacted* role-taking into a *public* affair, practiced intersubjectively by all involved," *Moral Consciousness and Communicative Action*, 198. See also "Justice and Solidarity," 38–41.

63. "Justice and Solidarity," 40.

64. "Contractualism and Utilitarianism," 116.

65. Ibid., 122.

66. See "Justice and Solidarity," 37–41, and Warnke, *Justice and Interpretation*, 92–94. Kenneth Baynes points out that, unlike Habermas, Scanlon fails to distinguish adequately between social norms that regulate behavior from the general rules for reaching agreement, or, in the terms that I have been using, substantive principles from procedures of justification, *The Normative Grounds of Social Criticism*, 117–18. Again Habermas takes us beyond contractualism by differentiating clearly between substantive norms that are generated within the context of a particular form of life, and the rationally reconstructed rules of discourse that constitute necessary conditions for the communicative reproduction of any, and every, modern, pluralist lifeworld.

67. *Justification and Application*, 28. See also Ingram, "The Limits and Possibilities of Communicative Ethics for Democratic Theory," 305–6.

68. See McCarthy, "Kantian Constructivism and Reconstructivism," 61.

69. See Rawls, "Reply to Habermas," 132.

70. On the interplay between these "weak" and "strong" publics, see Baynes, "Democracy and the *Rechtsstaat*," 216–18.

71. Baynes, "The Liberal/Communitarian Controversy and Communicative Ethics," 74.

72. Walker, "Habermas and Pluralist Political Theory," 84–86.

7. MORALITY AND ETHICAL LIFE

1. *Moral Consciousness and Communicative Action*, 178, also *Autonomy and Solidarity*, 266–68, and especially "On the Pragmatic, the Ethical and the Moral Employments of Practical Reason," in *Justification and Application*, 1–17. I will leave aside the pragmatic employment of practical reason. While this, along with fairly regulated bargaining processes, is certainly of some significance in the network of communicative processes that constitute the type of deliberative politics that Habermas advocates, it is not of direct relevance to our concerns here. For some of Habermas's recent reflections on that communicative network, see "Three Normative Models of Democracy," 1–10, especially 5–6.

2. Habermas does not make this distinction explicit himself. By exploring the implications of such a distinction, I am hoping to make clear the ways in which the plurality of historically unique modern societies can be taken into account in a discursive theory of justice. It should be noted that there are also interstate ethical discourses. We might think of the contributions of the citizens of each member state of the European Union to the formation of a European identity in terms of an interstate ethical discourse.

3. Habermas, *Faktizität und Geltung*, 134.

4. The most impressive recent alternatives to deontological moral theory have come from contemporary neo-Hegelian and neo-Aristotelian critics of proceduralism such as Charles Taylor, *Sources of the Self* and *The Ethics of Authenticity*; Alasdair MacIntyre, *After Virtue, Whose Justice? Which Rationality?*, and *Three Rival Versions of Moral Inquiry*; and Bernard Williams, *Ethics and the Limits of Philosophy* (London: Fontana, 1985). Habermas provides excellent critical commentary on these three alternatives in *Justification and Application*, on Williams, 21–25, on Taylor, 69–76, and on MacIntyre, 96–105. I will discuss an aspect of Taylor's work below, but I have chosen to focus, in the earlier parts

of this chapter, on the work of two theorists who do not claim to present strongly contextualist alternatives to Habermas's approach, but who rather make explicit attempts to mediate between the universalist and contextualist positions.

5. See *Situating the Self* generally. The reference to a "postconventional *Sittlichkeit*" is on page 11. Benhabib seeks to incorporate contextualist insights into a universalist position.

6. See *Justice and Interpretation* generally. On the inevitability of interpretive pluralism, see 11–12. Warnke, in contrast to Benhabib, can be thought of as a contextualist who seeks to incorporate universalist insights into that position.

7. See *Multiculturalism and "The Politics of Recognition,"* 25–73, especially 60–61. This essay represents an attempt by Taylor to draw out the implications of his own philosophical hermeneutics for political questions of cultural difference. That philosophical position is developed in *Philosophical Papers, I: Human Agency and Language* (Cambridge: Cambridge University Press, 1985); *Philosophical Papers, II: Philosophy and the Human Sciences*; *Sources of the Self*; and *The Ethics of Authenticity*. For a more direct challenge to Kantian proceduralism, see his "The Motivation behind a Procedural Ethics," in *Kant and Political Philosophy: The Contemporary Legacy*, ed. Ronald Beiner and William James Booth (New Haven: Yale University Press, 1993), 337–59. Two other essays in which Taylor explicitly distinguishes his philosophical position from that of Habermas are "Language and Society," in Honneth and Joas (eds.), *Communicative Action*, 23–35, and "Inwardness and the Culture of Modernity," in Honneth et al. (eds.), *Philosophical Interventions in the Unfinished Project of Enlightenment*, 88–110.

8. *Situating the Self*, 2.

9. Ibid., 34.

10. *Moral Consciousness and Communicative Action*, 204.

11. *Situating the Self*, 75.

12. On ethical cognitivism, see ibid., 49–50.

13. See also Maeve Cooke's critique of Benhabib in her "Habermas and Consensus."

14. *Situating the Self*, 74.

15. Ibid., 30.

16. Habermas's reconstruction is elaborated in the two volumes of *The Theory of Communicative Action*. For evidence of Benhabib's dependence on, what we might call this critical Weberian account of modernity, see *Situating the Self*, 32–33, 40–42, 80–82, 86–87, 225–28.

17. *Moral Consciousness and Communicative Action*, 175.

18. "Justice and Solidarity"; *Moral Consciousness and Communicative Action*, 200; and *Justification and Application*, 67–69.

19. *Situating the Self*, 8.

20. See the revised version of the essay "The Generalized and the Concrete Other," in ibid., 148–77.

21. Ibid., 183.

22. Ibid., 189.

23. Ibid., 184–85.

24. *Moral Consciousness and Communicative Action*, 199–203. Habermas insists that this is simply a requirement of rational justification itself. It is not therefore to be thought of as a task of working out a proper balance for the roles of reason and emotion in moral discourse, "Justice and Solidarity," 40–41.

25. *Situating the Self*, 189–90. Benhabib's criticisms of Rawls's monological proceduralism, which I upheld in chapter 2, remain valid. The criticism cannot however be pressed, even in a diluted form, against Habermas's dialogical conception of impartiality.

26. See especially *Justification and Application*, 4–8.

27. Habermas, *Justification and Application*, 59–60.

28. We might note that this requires the kind of open public debate that Rawls's strategy of avoidance seemed to preclude. Through argumentation we can work out whether a dispute admits of a moral or an ethical solution without deciding what is and what is not a matter of political morality in advance.

29. On the issues involved in such a shift, see the interesting proposals of Thomas McCarthy in chapter 7 of his *Ideals and Illusions*, 196–99. See also McCarthy's "A Reply to Georgia Warnke and David Couzens Hoy," *Philosophy and Social Criticism* 22 (1996): 99–108, especially 99–103. McCarthy is concerned with an exploration of the possibilities of achieving agreement at some level so as to ground the democratic legitimacy of a decision regarding conflicts that raise important moral questions for some citizens. This issue is also considered by James Bohman, "Public Reason and Cultural Pluralism: Political Liberalism and the Problem of Moral Conflict," *Political Theory* 23 (1995): 253–79, and by William Rehg and James Bohman, "Discourse and Democracy: The Formal and Informal Bases of Legitimacy in Habermas' *Faktizität und Geltung*," *Journal of Political Philosophy* 4 (1996): 79–99. The most significant attempt to show how agreement could emerge from a diversity of ethical perspectives on

abortion (and euthanasia) has been made by Ronald Dworkin, *Life's Dominion: An Argument about Abortion, Euthanasia and Individual Freedom* (New York: Knopf, 1993).

30. *Situating the Self*, 187.

31. See also Warnke's "Communicative Rationality and Cultural Values," in White (ed.), *The Cambridge Companion to Habermas*, 120–42, and "Legitimacy and Consensus: Comments on Part of the Work of Thomas McCarthy," *Philosophy and Social Criticism* 22 (1996): 67–81.

32. *Justice and Interpretation*, 3–4.

33. Ibid., 157.

34. Ibid., 5.

35. In the first half of the book Warnke works through a careful analysis of the contributions of Walzer, Rawls, and Dworkin without managing to relieve herself of worries about conventionalism and subjectivism. As we have already seen, Walzer believes that hermeneutic interpretations of the shared understandings of a particular community can allow for an immanent critique of practices that deviate from that understanding. Warnke rightly points out that it is not clear how one critic's interpretation can guarantee agreement and so Walzer's account of the substance of justice for his own society remains a subjectivist one, *Justice and Interpretation*, 30. She also points out that Rawls's appeal to an overlapping consensus fails to resolve this problem since the model conceptions of moral personality and a well-ordered society on which it depends build on what Rawls's critics, rightly or wrongly, take to be a selective reading of our public political culture, *Justice and Interpretation*, 54–58. Dworkin's account of legal interpretation, see especially *A Matter of Principle* and *Law's Empire*, tends to deviate from its own hermeneutic implications, *Justice and Interpretation*, 78–80. Despite this however, it allows us to think of constrained legal judgment as an educational process of self-development where we learn something about ourselves in trying to understand the law in the context of a test case. But the value of such an education might be put in question if the constraints involved cannot in principle rule out even sexist or racist interpretations of the law, *Justice and Interpretation*, 88.

36. Ibid., 96–97.

37. See for example, *Moral Consciousness and Communicative Action*, 205, and *Justification and Application*, 91.

38. See for example "Lawrence Kohlberg and Neo-Aristotelianism," in *Justification and Application*, 113–32, especially 127–28.

39. *Moral Consciousness and Communicative Action*, 181–82; *Justification and Application*, 36–39. See also Klaus Günther, "Impartial Application of

Moral and Legal Norms: A Contribution to Discourse Ethics," in Rasmussen (ed.), *Universalism vs. Communitarianism*, 199–206. For more complete discussions, see Günther's *The Sense of Appropriateness: Application Discourses in Morality and Law* (Albany: State University of New York Press, 1993) and Rehg, *Insight and Solidarity*, 184–210.

40. *Justification and Application*, 37.

41. *Moral Consciousness and Communicative Action*, 205.

42. *Justification and Application*, 62.

43. Ibid., 97.

44. I think that this relationship between the justification and the application of moral norms allows for greater flexibility and complexity than does Walzer's approach to substantive principles of justice. The assumption that is fundamental to complex equality is that there will be a neat fit between spheres of justice and the principles that are intrinsic to each particular sphere. This does not appear to be complex enough.

45. Ibid., 39.

46. Ibid., 12–17, 33–35, 127–28.

47. Ibid., 74–76.

48. Ibid., 33.

49. *Moral Consciousness and Communicative Action*, 207–8. It is this theme that has occupied Habermas in his most recent writings, especially in *Faktizität und Geltung*. This point may give us some idea as to how discourse ethics might guide us with regard to the possible clash between certain human rights and local arrangements regarding principles of distributive justice. In chapter 4, I mentioned the example of a controversy that might arise among citizens of a relatively wealthy country who realize that they will have to change their own patterns of distribution if they are to take sufficiently seriously the rights of people who are starving as a result of famine. If such a basic human right as the right not to die of starvation is to be taken seriously, we must seek to create global institutions that would have some legal right to draw on the resources of countries that can afford to make a contribution to the setting up of a long-term project that could overcome effectively the causes of the suffering that people caught in such disastrous circumstances have to endure. The creation of such institutions will depend very much on the outcome of a political struggle that is barely under way.

50. It is only with the essays collected in *Justification and Application* that Habermas began to turn his attention toward the ethical employment of practical reason in relation to questions of public discourse. His concern with ethicopolitical discourses feeds into some of the central arguments of *Faktizität und Geltung*.

51. *Justice and Interpretation*, 155.

52. Ibid., 148.

53. Ibid., 36–39.

54. *Faktizität und Geltung*, 515 (emphasis in the original text).

55. See Anna Elisabetta Galeotti, "Citizenship and Equality: The Place for Toleration," *Political Theory* 21 (1993): 585–605, and Norma Claire Moruzzi, "A Problem with Headscarves: Contemporary Complexities of Political and Social Identity," *Political Theory* 22 (1994): 653–72, also Galeotti, "A Problem with Theory: A Reply to Moruzzi," and Moruzzi, "A Response to Galeotti," *Political Theory* 22 (1994): 673–77 and 678–79.

56. Will Kymlicka and Wayne Norman, "Return of the Citizen: A Survey of Recent Work on Citizenship Theory," *Ethics* 104 (1994): 374.

57. See also Seyla Benhabib, "Deliberative Rationality and Models of Democratic Legitimacy," *Constellations* 1 (1994): 48–49n.22.

58. The regions of the Basque Country and Catalonia in Spain might be good examples here.

59. I think that Galeotti's argument for toleration in the case of the Muslim girls wearing headscarves in class is one that should and probably would be endorsed as the outcome of a fully inclusive public discourse on the matter. See Galeotti, "Citizenship and Equality: The Case for Toleration." My primary intention of course is not to advocate any particular outcome to these controversies but rather to clarify philosophically what the political requirements (and preconditions) of state impartiality would be in such cases.

60. *Multiculturalism and "The Politics of Recognition,"* 32. It is this kind of account that I defended in chapter 1. It should be clear by now that Habermas also considers the identity of the self to be dialogically constituted.

61. *Multiculturalism and "The Politics of Recognition,"* 42–43.

62. Ibid., 60.

63. In ibid., 51–61, Taylor reaches his conclusion, that this alternative to Kantianism is necessary, from an examination of the argument made by some Quebeckers, that the state's legislation should reflect the fact that it is a "distinct society." He is keen to point out however that so long as diversity is respected and fundamental rights protected, this is still a liberal model of politics. It is, however, a model that is organized not around a procedure of impartiality, but rather a definition of the good life. On Taylor's hopes for a future Quebec, see his "Shared and Divergent Values," in *Options for a New Canada*, ed. Ronald L. Watts and Douglas G. Brown (Toronto: University of Toronto Press, 1991),

53–76. The work of Axel Honneth presents an interesting alternative attempt to ground morality on the concept of recognition, "Integrity and Disrespect: Principles of a Conception of Morality Based on a Theory of Recognition," *Political Theory* 20 (1992): 187–201, and for a much more extensive discussion, *The Struggle for Recognition: The Moral Grammar of Social Conflicts* (Cambridge: Polity Press, 1994).

64. *Multiculturalism and "The Politics of Recognition,"* 70.

65. Ibid., 66–73.

66. Ibid., 71.

67. These are the kinds of example that Taylor mentions in relation to the Quebec case; see ibid., 55.

68. "Struggles for Recognition in Constitutional States," *European Journal of Philosophy* 1 (1993): 131.

69. Ibid., 132.

70. Ibid., 132–34, and for a detailed discussion, *Faktizität und Geltung*, 493–515.

71. Habermas, "Struggles for Recognition in Constitutional States," 136–37, but see also Will Kymlicka, *Liberalism, Community and Culture* (Oxford: Clarendon Press, 1991) and *Multicultural Citizenship: A Liberal Theory of Minority Rights* (Oxford: Clarendon Press, 1995).

72. *Multiculturalism and "The Politics of Recognition,"* 59.

73. Note Taylor's criticism of Kymlicka, *Multiculturalism and "The Politics of Recognition,"* 40–41n.16.

74. Habermas, "Struggles for Recognition in Constitutional States," 142.

75. *Multiculturalism and "The Politics of Recognition,"* 66.

76. Habermas, "Struggles for Recognition in Constitutional States," 141–42, and Susan Wolf, "Comment," in Taylor's *Multiculturalism and "The Politics of Recognition,"* 78–81.

77. This protection is of course subject to the particular culture's capacity to affirm the demands of justice, a matter of historical struggle.

78. "Struggles for Recognition in Constitutional States," 138.

79. Ibid. See also Habermas's "Citizenship and National Identity: Some Reflections on the Future of Europe," *Praxis International* 12 (1992): 1–19, especially 12.

80. Habermas has discussed at length the implications of immigration in this regard, especially in the particularly volatile context that is of special interest to him, in postunification Germany, "Struggles for Recognition in Constitutional States," 145–53; "Citizenship and National Identity," 13–18; and see also his biting critique of contemporary right-wing German nationalism in "The Second Life-Fiction of the Federal Republic: We Have Become 'Normal' Again," *New Left Review* 197 (1993): 58–66.

81. We will examine the case of Northern Ireland in detail in the next chapter.

82. "Struggles for Recognition in Constitutional States," 144.

83. Ibid.

84. This allows us to deflect the charge that constitutional patriotism can only be on founded on shared abstract principles of justice and democracy. According to my reading it can be founded on something more thickly constitutive of particular identities than this criticism would suggest. See, for example, Will Kymlicka and Wayne Norman, "Return of the Citizen," 377n.34.

85. In contrast, see Taylor's "Reply and Re-articulation," in *Philosophy in an Age of Pluralism: The Work of Charles Taylor in Focus*, ed. James Tully (Cambridge: Cambridge University Press, 1994), 250–52.

86. This discussion should also justify the claim that I made earlier, that hermeneutics is at best an important aspect of, but never an adequate substitute for, a philosophical conception of an impartial point of view. Hermeneutic self-clarification in the form of ethicopolitical discourse comes into play once moral norms are institutionalized in historical contexts.

8. THE CASE OF NORTHERN IRELAND

1. See, for example, "Philosophy and Democracy" and "A Critique of Philosophical Conversation."

2. *Spheres of Justice*, 314.

3. Ibid., 313.

4. Ibid., 28.

5. See John Whyte, *Interpreting Northern Ireland* (Oxford: Clarendon Press, 1991). Whyte gives a comprehensive survey of the intensive social scientific research on Northern Ireland.

6. This claim is a matter of some dispute. While I have crudely simplified the issue here, I do wish to defend the view that the conflict is primarily one

between two separate historical communities. See Whyte, *Interpreting Northern Ireland*, 14–18, 101–10, 194–201. It does not follow that the roles of either Britain or the Irish Republic should be excluded from an analysis of the conflict. See Joseph Ruane and Jennifer Todd, "Diversity, Division and the Middle Ground in Northern Ireland," *Irish Political Studies* 7 (1992): 73–98.

7. For an argument that Walzer's communitarian sensitivities ironically weaken the case for minority cultural rights, see Kymlicka, *Liberalism, Community and Culture*, 220–36.

8. *Spheres of Justice*, 29.

9. Ibid., 62. It is worth noting that Walzer's views on partition are most probably influenced by his liberal Jewish perspective on the Israel/Palestine question. See his *Exodus and Revolution* (New York: Basic Books, 1985), and for a sharp review from a Palestinian perspective, see Edward W. Said, "Michael Walzer's *Exodus and Revolution*: A Canaanite Reading," in *Blaming the Victims: Spurious Scholarship and the Palestinian Question*, ed. Edward Said and Christopher Hitchens (London: Verso, 1988), 161–78.

10. See, for example, "Pluralism in Political Perspective," in Michael Walzer et al., *The Politics of Ethnicity* (Cambridge, Mass.: Belknap Press, 1982), 1–28.

11. See "The Communitarian Critique of Liberalism" and also Walzer's "Comment" in Taylor, *Multiculturalism and "The Politics of Recognition,"* 99–103, where he argues that, given the peculiarity of its political culture, citizens of an immigrant society, like the United States, might well choose to have a liberal neutral state, not for its own sake, but as the best political expression of its own distinctive collective goals.

12. *Spheres of Justice*, 149.

13. He uses this formulation in his encounter with Dworkin, "Spheres of Justice: An Exchange," 44.

14. See Arend Lijphart, *Democracy in Plural Societies: A Comparative Exploration* (New Haven: Yale University Press, 1977).

15. See Whyte, *Interpreting Northern Ireland*, 224–25.

16. On more recent developments, see Brendan O'Leary and John McGarry, *The Politics of Antagonism: Understanding Northern Ireland*, 2nd ed. (London: Athlone Press, 1996).

17. Whyte, *Interpreting Northern Ireland*, 163–69, and Jennifer Todd, "Unionist Political Thought," in *Political Thought in Ireland Since the Seventeenth Century*, ed. D. George Boyce, Robert Eccleshall, and Vincent Geoghegan (London: Routledge, 1993), 190–211.

18. It is impossible to predict at this stage the extent to which the abrupt end of the IRA cease-fire on February 9, 1996, or the street violence of July 1996, will damage the prospects of a real dialogue taking place between the relevant parties. Certainly, at the time of writing, there is less cause for optimism than at any stage since the 1994 cease-fires were called.

19. "Nation and Universe," in *The Tanner Lectures on Human Values, XI,* ed. Grethe B. Peterson (Salt Lake City: University of Utah Press, 1990), 507–56.

20. Ibid., 536.

21. All of the brief quotations in this paragraph are from ibid., 510–15.

22. Presumably Walzer would maintain that this differs from conventional liberalism in at least three ways. First, it rejects substantive universalist principles of justice. Second, the emphasis here is on cultural pluralism and not just a plurality of individual plans of life. Third, this approach involves a much more positive view of the enriching effects of being open to cultural, and not just individual, otherness.

23. "Nation and Universe," 546–47.

24. Ibid., 543.

25. Ibid., 544.

26. Ibid., 554–55.

27. I will suggest below that arguments for Unionism that invoke liberal principles are often blind to the real grievances of the Nationalist community. For two pertinent examples, see Arthur Aughey, *Under Siege: Ulster Unionism and the Anglo-Irish Agreement* (Belfast: Blackstaff Press, 1989) and R. L. McCartney, *Liberty and Authority in Ireland* (Derry: Field Day Pamphlets, 1985).

28. See Terence Brown, *The Whole Protestant Community: The Making of a Historical Myth* (Derry: Field Day Pamphlets, 1985).

29. Jennifer Todd, "Unionist Political Thought" and also "The Limits of Britishness," *The Irish Review* 5 (1989): 11–16. For further references that support this interpretation, see Whyte, *Interpreting Northern Ireland,* 162–69.

30. We assessed the details of Habermas's justification for this claim in chapter 6.

31. Habermas, *Moral Consciousness and Communicative Action,* 89.

32. Habermas developed his thinking in this regard in the context of the recent German *Historikerstreit* (Historian's Controversy) about the legacy of the Third Reich. See "A Kind of Settling of Damages" and "Historical Consciousness and Post-Traditional Identity: The Federal Republic's Orientation to the

West" in the collection of Habermas's writing on this and related themes, *The New Conservatism* (Cambridge, Mass.: MIT Press, 1989), 207–48 and 249–67. Some of Habermas's more recent reflections on these issues are gathered in his *The Past as Future*, ed. Max Pensky (Cambridge: Polity Press, 1994).

33. *The New Conservatism*, 256. The notion of constitutional patriotism was introduced briefly in the last chapter. Habermas has developed this idea at much greater length in *Faktizität und Geltung*, but see also "Citizenship and National Identity" and "Struggles for Recognition in Constitutional States."

34. *The New Conservatism*, 262.

35. "Jürgen Habermas: An Interview on Ethics, Politics and History by Jean-Marc Ferry," in Rasmussen (ed.), *Universalism vs. Communitarianism*, 210.

36. See the first chapter of Aughey, *Under Siege*.

37. See White, *The Recent Work of Jürgen Habermas*, 77–83, for a relevant discussion.

38. See Whyte, *Interpreting Northern Ireland*, 209–43.

39. See note 35 above.

40. While I have alluded to alternative arrangements, solutions and frameworks, I am not assuming that the entity of Northern Ireland would continue in some form or other after a real discourse. There are many other possibilities (repartition, a United Ireland, fuller integration with the United Kingdom, new European arrangements) that would alter the geopolitical structure of the territory under consideration. Nothing is ruled out nor is anything guaranteed, least of all the boundaries, or indeed the existence, of the political entity of Northern Ireland.

BIBLIOGRAPHY

Abramson, Jeffrey A. *Liberation and Its Limits*. Boston: Beacon Press, 1984.

Ackerman, Bruce. *Social Justice in the Liberal State*. New Haven: Yale University Press, 1980.

——. "Political Liberalisms." *Journal of Philosophy* 91 (1994): 364–86.

Aughey, Arthur. *Under Siege: Ulster Unionism and the Anglo-Irish Agreement*. Belfast: Blackstaff Press, 1989.

Avineri, Shlomo, and Avner de-Shalit (eds.). *Communitarianism and Individualism*. Oxford: Oxford University Press, 1992.

Barron, Anne. "Lyotard and the Problem of Justice." In Andrew Benjamin (ed.), *Judging Lyotard*, 26–42. London: Routledge, 1992.

Barry, Brian. *Justice as Impartiality*. Oxford: Oxford University Press, 1995.

——. "Spherical Justice and Global Injustice." In David Miller and Michael Walzer (eds.), *Pluralism, Justice and Equality*, 67–80.

Baynes, Kenneth. "The Liberal/Communitarian Controversy and Communicative Ethics." In David Rasmussen (ed.), *Universalism vs. Communitarianism*, 61–81.

——. "Rational Reconstruction and Social Criticism." In Michael Kelly (ed.), *Hermeneutics and Critical Theory in Ethics and Politics*, 122–45.

——. *The Normative Grounds of Social Criticism: Kant, Rawls, Habermas*. Albany: State University of New York Press, 1992.

——. "Democracy and the *Rechtsstaat*: Habermas's *Faktizität und Geltung*." In Stephen K. White (ed.), *The Cambridge Companion to Habermas*, 201–32.

Baynes, Kenneth, James Bohman, and Thomas McCarthy (eds.). *After Philosophy: End or Transformation?* Cambridge, Mass.: MIT Press, 1987.

Benhabib, Seyla. *Critique, Norm and Utopia: A Study of the Foundations of Critical Theory*. New York: Columbia University Press, 1986.

261

——. "The Generalized and the Concrete Other: The Kohlberg-Gilligan Controversy and Feminist Theory." In Seyla Benhabib and Drucilla Cornell (eds.), *Feminism as Critique*, 75–95.

——. "Liberal Dialogue versus a Critical Theory of Discursive Legitimation." In Nancy L. Rosenblum (ed.), *Liberalism and the Moral Life*, 143–56.

——. *Situating the Self: Gender, Community and Postmodernism in Contemporary Ethics*. Cambridge: Polity Press, 1992.

——. "Deliberative Rationality and Models of Democratic Legitimacy." *Constellations* 1 (1994): 26–52.

Benhabib, Seyla, and Drucilla Cornell (eds.). *Feminism as Critique*. Cambridge: Polity Press, 1987.

Bernstein, Richard J. *Beyond Objectivism and Relativism*. Oxford: Basil Blackwell, 1983.

——. "Introduction." In Richard J. Bernstein (ed.), *Habermas and Modernity*, 1–32.

——. *The New Constellation*. Cambridge: Polity Press, 1991.

Bernstein, Richard J. (ed.). *Habermas and Modernity*. Cambridge: Polity Press, 1985.

Betti, Emilio. "Hermeneutics as the General Methodology of the *Geisteswissenschaften*." In Josef Bleicher, *Contemporary Hermeneutics*, 51–94.

Bleicher, Josef. *Contemporary Hermeneutics: Hermeneutics as Method, Philosophy and Critique*. London: Routledge and Kegan Paul, 1980.

Bohman, James F. "Formal Pragmatics and Social Criticism: The Philosophy of Language and the Critique of Ideology in Habermas's Theory of Communicative Action." *Philosophy and Social Criticism* 11 (1985): 331–53.

——. "'System' and 'Lifeworld': Habermas and the Problem of Holism." *Philosophy and Social Criticism* 15 (1989): 381–401.

——. "Participating in Enlightenment: Habermas's Cognitivist Interpretation of Democracy." In Marcelo Dascal and Ora Gruengard (eds.), *Knowledge and Politics*, 264–89. Boulder: Westview Press, 1989.

——. "Public Reason and Cultural Pluralism: Political Liberalism and the Problem of Moral Conflict." *Political Theory* 23 (1995): 253–79.

Brown, Terence. *The Whole Protestant Community: The Making of a Historical Myth*. Derry: Field Day Pamphlets, 1985.

Buchanan, Allen E. *Marx and Justice*. London: Methuen, 1982.

Calhoun, Craig (ed.). *Habermas and the Public Sphere*. Cambridge, Mass.: MIT Press, 1992.

Chambers, Simone. "Discourse and Democratic Practices." In Stephen K. White (ed.), *The Cambridge Companion to Habermas*, 233–59.

Clement, Grace. "Is the Moral Point of View Monological or Dialogical? The Kantian Background of Habermas' Discourse Ethics." *Philosophy Today* 34 (1989): 159–73.

Cohen, Jean. "Discourse Ethics and Civil Society." In David Rasmussen (ed.), *Universalism vs. Communitarianism*, 83–105.

——— . "Critical Theory and Feminist Critiques: The Debate with Jürgen Habermas." In Johanna Meehan (ed.), *Feminists Read Habermas: Gendering the Subject of Discourse*, 57–90.

Cohen, Jean, and Andrew Arato. *Civil Society and Political Theory*. Cambridge, Mass.: MIT Press, 1992.

Cohen, Joshua. "Review of *Spheres of Justice*." *Journal of Philosophy* 83 (1986): 457–68.

——— . "Okin, Justice, Gender and the Family." *Canadian Journal of Philosophy* 22 (1992): 263–86.

——— . "Moral Pluralism and Political Consensus." In David Copp, Jean Hampton, and John E. Roemer (eds.), *The Idea of Democracy*, 270–91. Cambridge: Cambridge University Press, 1993.

Connolly, William E. *Identity\Difference: Democratic Negotiations of Political Paradox*. Ithaca, N.Y.: Cornell University Press, 1991.

Cooke, Maeve. "Habermas, Autonomy and the Identity of the Self." *Philosophy and Social Criticism* 18 (1992): 269–92.

——— . "Habermas and Consensus." *European Journal of Philosophy* 1 (1993): 247–67.

——— . *Language and Reason: A Study of Habermas's Pragmatics*. Cambridge, Mass.: MIT Press, 1994.

Culler, Jonathan. "Communicative Competence and Normative Force." *New German Critique* 35 (1985): 133–44.

Cultural Hermeneutics 2.4 (February 1975). David Rasmussen (ed.).

Daniels, Norman (ed.). *Reading Rawls*. Oxford: Basil Blackwell, 1975.

Derrida, Jacques. "Deconstruction and the Other." An interview in Richard Kearney, *Dialogues with Contemporary Thinkers*, 107–26. Manchester: Manchester University Press, 1984.

Dworkin, Ronald. "To Each His Own." *New York Review of Books* 30.6 (April 14, 1983): 4–6.

———. *A Matter of Principle.* Cambridge, Mass.: Harvard University Press, 1985.

———. *Law's Empire.* Cambridge, Mass.: Harvard University Press, 1986.

———. "Foundations of Liberal Equality." In Grethe B. Peterson (ed.), *The Tanner Lectures on Human Values*, XI, 1–119.

———. "Liberal Community." In Shlomo Avineri and Avner de-Shalit (eds.), *Communitarianism and Individualism*, 205–23.

———. *Life's Dominion: An Argument about Abortion, Euthanasia and Individual Freedom.* New York: Knopf, 1993.

Dworkin, Ronald, and Michael Walzer. "Spheres of Justice: An Exchange." *New York Review of Books* 30.12 (July 21, 1983): 44–46.

Elshtain, Jean Bekthe. *Public Man, Private Woman: Women in Social and Political Thought.* Oxford: Martin Robertson, 1981.

Ferrara, Alessandro. "Universalisms: Procedural, Contextualist and Prudential." In David Rasmussen (ed.), *Universalism vs. Communitarianism*, 11–37.

Fleming, Marie. "Women and the 'Public Use of Reason.'" In Johanna Meehan (ed.), *Feminists Read Habermas: Gendering the Subject of Discourse*, 117–37.

Forst, Rainer. "Review of *Political Liberalism*." *Constellations* 1 (1994): 162–71.

Foucault, Michel. *Power\Knowledge*, ed. Colin Gordon. New York: Pantheon Books, 1980.

———. "The Subject and Power." An afterword to Hubert L. Dreyfus and Paul Rabinow, *Michel Foucault: Beyond Structuralism and Hermeneutics*, 208–26. Chicago: University of Chicago Press, 1982.

Fraser, Nancy. "What's Critical about Critical Theory? The Case of Habermas and Gender." *New German Critique* 35 (1985): 97–131.

———. "Toward a Discourse Ethic of Solidarity." *Praxis International* 5 (1986): 425–29.

———. *Unruly Practices.* Cambridge: Polity Press, 1989.

———. "Solidarity or Singularity? Richard Rorty between Romanticism and Technocracy." In Alan Malachowski (ed.), *Reading Rorty*, 303–21.

Fraser, Nancy, and Linda Nicholson. "Social Criticism without Philosophy: An Encounter between Feminism and Postmodernism." In Linda Nicholson (ed.), *Feminism/Postmodernism*, 19–38.

Friedman, Marilyn. "Feminism and Modern Friendship: Dislocating the Community." In Shlomo Avineri and Avner de-Shalit (eds.), *Communitarianism and Individualism*, 101–19.

Gadamer, Hans-Georg. *Philosophical Hermeneutics*, ed. David Linge. Berkeley: University of California Press, 1976.

———. *Truth and Method*. 2nd ed. London: Sheed and Ward, 1979.

Galeotti, Anna Elisabetta. "Citizenship and Equality: The Place for Toleration." *Political Theory* 21 (1993): 585–605.

———. "A Problem with Theory: A Reply to Moruzzi." *Political Theory* 22 (1994): 673–77.

Galston, William. "Moral Personality and Liberal Theory." *Political Theory* 10 (1982): 492–519.

———. "Pluralism and Social Unity." *Ethics* 99 (1989): 711–26.

———. "Community, Democracy, Philosophy: The Political Thought of Michael Walzer." *Political Theory* 17 (1989): 119–30.

———. *Liberal Purposes: Goods, Virtues and Diversity in the Liberal State*. Cambridge: Cambridge University Press, 1991.

Gaventa, John. *Power and Powerlessness: Quiescence and Rebellion in an Appalachian Valley*. Urbana: University of Illinois Press, 1980.

Gill, Emily R. "Walzer's Complex Equality: Constraints and the Right to be Wrong." *Polity* 20 (1987): 32–56.

Gilligan, Carol. *In a Different Voice: Psychological Theory and Women's Development*. Cambridge, Mass.: Harvard University Press, 1982.

———. "Do the Social Sciences Have an Adequate Theory of Moral Development?" In Norma Haan et al. (eds.), *Social Science as Moral Inquiry*, 33–51.

Gould, Carol C. "On the Conception of the Common Interest: Between Procedure and Substance." In Michael Kelly (ed.), *Hermeneutics and Critical Theory in Ethics and Politics*, 253–73.

Günther, Klaus. "Impartial Application of Moral and Legal Norms: A Contribution to Discourse Ethics." In David Rasmussen (ed.), *Universalism vs. Communitarianism*, 199–206.

———. *The Sense of Appropriateness: Application Discourses in Morality and Law*. Albany: State University of New York Press, 1993.

Gutmann, Amy. "Communitarian Critics of Liberalism." *Philosophy and Public Affairs* 14 (1985): 308–22.

Gutmann, Amy (ed.). *Multiculturalism and "The Politics of Recognition."* An essay by Charles Taylor with commentary by Steven C. Rockefeller, Michael Walzer, and Susan Wolf. Princeton: Princeton University Press, 1992.

Haan, Norma, Robert N. Bellah, Paul Rabinow, and William M. Sullivan (eds.). *Social Science as Moral Inquiry*. New York: Columbia University Press, 1983.

Habermas, Jürgen. "On Systematically Distorted Communication." *Inquiry* 13 (1970): 205–18.

———. *Toward a Rational Society: Student Protest, Science and Politics*. London: Heinemann, 1971.

———. *Theory and Practice*. London: Heinemann, 1974.

———. *Legitimation Crisis*. London: Heinemann, 1976.

———. *Communication and the Evolution of Society*. London: Heinemann, 1979.

———. "The Hermeneutic Claim to Universality." In Josef Bleicher, *Contemporary Hermeneutics*, 181–211.

———. "A Reply to My Critics." In John B. Thompson and David Held (eds.), *Habermas: Critical Debates*, 219–83.

———. "Interpretive Social Science vs. Hermeneuticism." In Norma Haan et al. (eds.), *Social Science as Moral Inquiry*, 251–69.

———. *The Theory of Communicative Action. Volume 1: Reason and the Rationalization of Society*. Cambridge: Polity Press, 1984.

———. "Questions and Counterquestions." In Richard J. Bernstein (ed.), *Habermas and Modernity*, 192–216.

———. "The New Obscurity: The Crisis of the Welfare State and the Exhaustion of Utopian Energies." *Philosophy and Social Criticism* 11 (1986): 1–18.

——— . *Knowledge and Human Interests.* Cambridge: Polity Press, 1987.

——— . *The Theory of Communicative Action. Volume 2: The Critique of Functionalist Reason.* Cambridge: Polity Press, 1987.

——— . *The Philosophical Discourse of Modernity.* Cambridge: Polity Press, 1987.

——— . *On the Logic of the Social Sciences.* Cambridge: Polity Press, 1988.

——— . "Law and Morality." In Sterling M. McMurrin (ed.), *The Tanner Lectures on Human Values, VIII*, 217–279. Salt Lake City: University of Utah Press, 1988.

——— . *The Structural Transformation of the Public Sphere.* Cambridge: Polity Press, 1989.

——— . *The New Conservatism*, Cambridge, Mass.: MIT Press, 1989.

——— . *Moral Consciousness and Communicative Action.* Cambridge: Polity Press, 1990.

——— . "Justice and Solidarity: On the Discussion Concerning 'Stage 6.'" In Michael Kelly (ed.), *Hermeneutics and Critical Theory in Ethics and Politics*, 32–52.

——— . "Jürgen Habermas: An Interview on Ethics, Politics and History by Jean-Marc Ferry." In David Rasmussen (ed.), *Universalism vs. Communitarianism*, 207–13.

——— . "Remarks on the Discussion." *Theory, Culture and Society* 7 (1990): 127–32.

——— . "A Reply." In Axel Honneth and Hans Joas (eds.), *Communicative Action*, 214–64.

——— . *Postmetaphysical Thinking: Philosophical Essays.* Cambridge: Polity Press, 1992.

——— . *Autonomy and Solidarity: Interviews with Jürgen Habermas*, rev. ed., ed. Peter Dews. London: Verso, 1992.

——— . *Faktizität und Geltung: Beitrage zur Diskurstheorie des Rechts und des demokratischen Rechtstaats.* Frankfurt am Main: Suhrkamp Verlag, 1992; in English as *Between Facts and Norms*, trans. William Rehg. Cambridge, Mass.: MIT Press, 1996.

——— . "Further Reflections on the Public Sphere." In Craig Calhoun (ed.), *Habermas and the Public Sphere*, 421–61.

——— . "Citizenship and National Identity: Some Reflections on the Future of Europe." *Praxis International* 12 (1992): 1–19.

——— . *Justification and Application: Remarks on Discourse Ethics.* Cambridge: Polity Press, 1993.

——— . "The Second Life-Fiction of the Federal Republic: We Have Become 'Normal' Again." *New Left Review* 197 (1993): 58–66.

——— . "Struggles for Recognition in Constitutional States." *European Journal of Philosophy* 1 (1993): 128–55.

——— . "Three Normative Models of Democracy." *Constellations* 1 (1994).

——— . *The Past as Future,* ed. Max Pensky. Cambridge: Polity Press, 1994.

——— . "Postscript to *Faktizität und Geltung.*" *Philosophy and Social Criticism, Special Issue: Habermas, Modernity and Law,* Mathieu Duflem (Guest ed.), 20.4 (October 1994): 132–50.

——— . "Reconciliation through the Public Use of Reason: Remarks on John Rawls's Political Liberalism." *Journal of Philosophy* 92 (1995): 109–31.

Heckman, Susan. "The Embodiment of the Subject: Feminism and the Communitarian Critique of Liberalism." *The Journal of Politics* 54 (1992): 1098–1119.

Heidegger, Martin. *Being and Time.* New York: Harper & Row, 1962.

Heller, Agnes. "Habermas and Marxism." In John B. Thompson and David Held (eds.), *Habermas: Critical Debates,* 21–41.

Holub, Robert C. *Jürgen Habermas: Critic in the Public Sphere.* London: Routledge, 1991.

Honneth, Axel. "Integrity and Disrespect: Principles of a Conception of Morality Based on a Theory of Recognition." *Political Theory* 20 (1992): 187–201.

——— . *The Struggle for Recognition: The Moral Grammar of Social Conflicts.* Cambridge: Polity Press, 1994.

Honneth, Axel, and Hans Joas (eds.). *Communicative Action: Essays on Jürgen Habermas's "The Theory of Communicative Action."* Cambridge: Polity Press, 1991.

Honneth, Axel, Thomas McCarthy, Claus Offe, and Albrecht Wellmer (eds.). *Philosophical Interventions in the Unfinished Project of Enlightenment.* Cambridge, Mass.: MIT Press, 1992.

Hoy, David Couzens. "Legal Hermeneutics: Recent Debates." In Kathleen Wright (ed.), *Festivals of Interpretation*, 111–35.

Ingram, David. "The Limits and Possibilities of Communicative Ethics for Democratic Theory." *Political Theory* 21 (1993): 294–321.

Jay, Martin. "The Debate over Performative Contradiction: Habermas versus the Poststructuralists." In Axel Honneth et al. (eds.), *Philosophical Interventions in the Unfinished Project of Enlightenment*, 261–79.

Johnson, James. "Is Talk Really Cheap? Prompting Conversation between Critical Theory and Rational Choice." *American Political Science Review* 87 (1993): 74–86.

Kelly, Michael. "The Gadamer-Habermas Debate Revisited: The Question of Ethics." In David Rasmussen (ed.), *Universalism vs. Communitarianism*, 139–59.

Kelly, Michael (ed.). *Hermeneutics and Critical Theory in Ethics and Politics*. Cambridge, Mass.: MIT Press, 1990.

Kingwell, Mark. *A Civil Tongue: Justice, Dialogue and the Politics of Pluralism*. University Park: Pennsylvania State University Press, 1995.

Kymlicka, Will. "Liberalism and Communitarianism." *Canadian Journal of Philosophy* 18 (1988): 181–203.

——— . *Liberalism, Community and Culture*. Oxford: Clarendon Press, 1991.

——— . "Rethinking the Family." *Philosophy and Public Affairs* 20 (1991): 77–97.

——— . *Multicultural Citizenship: A Liberal Theory of Minority Rights*. Oxford: Clarendon Press, 1995.

Kymlicka, Will, and Wayne Norman. "Return of the Citizen: A Survey of Recent Work on Citizenship Theory." *Ethics* 104 (1994): 352–81.

Landes, Joan B. "The Public and Private Sphere: A Feminist Reconsideration." In Johanna Meehan (ed.), *Feminists Read Habermas: Gendering the Subject of Discourse*, 91–116.

Larmore, Charles. *Patterns of Moral Complexity*. Cambridge: Cambridge University Press, 1987.

——— . "Political Liberalism." *Political Theory* 18 (1990): 339–60.

Lijphart, Arend. *Democracy in Plural Societies: A Comparative Exploration*. New Haven: Yale University Press, 1977.

Löw-Beer, Martin. "Living a Life and the Problem of Existential Impossibility." *Inquiry* 34 (1991): 217–36.

Lucash, Frank S. (ed.). *Justice and Equality Here and Now*. Ithaca, N.Y.: Cornell University Press, 1986.

Lukes, Steven. *Power: A Radical View*. London: Macmillan, 1974.

———. "Of Gods and Demons: Habermas and Practical Reason." In John B. Thompson and David Held (eds.), *Habermas: Critical Debates*, 134–48.

Lund, William R. "Communitarian Politics, the Supreme Court and Privacy: The Continuing Need for Liberal Boundaries." *Social Theory and Practice* 16 (1990): 191–215.

Lyotard, Jean-François. *The Postmodern Condition: A Report on Knowledge*. Minneapolis: University of Minnesota Press, 1984.

McCarthy, Thomas. *The Critical Theory of Jürgen Habermas*. Cambridge: Polity Press, 1984.

———. "Complexity and Democracy, or the Seducements of Systems Theory." *New German Critique* 35 (1985): 27–53.

———. "The Critique of Impure Reason: Foucault and the Frankfurt School." *Political Theory* 18 (1990): 437–69.

———. *Ideals and Illusions: On Reconstruction and Deconstruction in Contemporary Critical Theory*. Cambridge, Mass.: MIT Press, 1991.

———. "Kantian Constructivism and Reconstructivism: Rawls and Habermas in Dialogue." *Ethics* 105 (1994): 44–63.

———. "A Reply to Georgia Warnke and David Couzens Hoy." *Philosophy and Social Criticism* 22 (1996): 99–108.

McCartney, R. L. *Liberty and Authority in Ireland*. Derry: Field Day Pamphlets, 1985.

MacIntyre, Alasdair. *After Virtue*. London, Duckworth, 1981.

———. *Whose Justice? Which Rationality?* London: Duckworth, 1988.

———. *Three Rival Versions of Moral Inquiry*. London: Duckworth, 1990.

Malachowski, Alan (ed.). *Reading Rorty*. Oxford: Basil Blackwell, 1990.

Meehan, Johanna (ed.). *Feminists Read Habermas: Gendering the Subject of Discourse*. London: Routledge, 1995.

Miller, David, and Michael Walzer (eds.). *Pluralism, Justice and Equality*. Oxford: Oxford University Press, 1995.

Misgeld, Dieter. "Critical Hermeneutics versus Neoparsonianism?" *New German Critique* 35 (1985): 55–82.

——— . "Modernity and Hermeneutics: A Critical-Theoretical Rejoinder." In Hugh Silverman (ed.), *Gadamer and Hermeneutics*, 163–77.

Moon, J. Donald. "Practical Discourse and Communicative Ethics." In Stephen K. White (ed.), *The Cambridge Companion to Habermas*, 143–64.

Morawetz, Thomas. "Tension in the 'Art of Separation.'" *Political Theory* 13 (1985): 599–606.

Moruzzi, Norma Claire. "A Problem with Headscarves: Contemporary Complexities of Political and Social Identity" and "A Response to Galeotti." *Political Theory* 22 (1994): 653–72 and 678–79.

Mouffe, Chantal. "Rawls: Political Philosophy without Politics." In David Rasmussen (ed.), *Universalism vs. Communitarianism*, 217–36.

Mulhall, Stephen, and Adam Swift. *Liberals and Communitarians*. Oxford: Basil Blackwell, 1992.

Nagel, Thomas. "Rawls on Justice." In Norman Daniels (ed.), *Reading Rawls*, 1–15.

Neal, Patrick. "Justice as Fairness: Political or Metaphysical?" *Political Theory* 18 (1990): 24–50.

——— . "Does He Mean What He Says? (Mis)undereestanding Rawls's Practical Turn." *Polity* 27 (1994–95): 77–111.

Nicholson, Graeme. "Answers to Critical Theory." In Hugh Silverman (ed.), *Gadamer and Hermeneutics*, 151–62.

Nicholson, Linda (ed.). *Feminism/Postmodernism*. London: Routledge, 1990.

Nozick, Robert. *Anarchy, State and Utopia*. New York: Basic Books, 1974.

Okin, Susan Moller. *Women in Western Political Thought*. Princeton: Princeton University Press, 1979.

——— . *Justice, Gender and the Family*. New York: Basic Books, 1989.

——— . "Humanist Liberalism." In Nancy L. Rosenblum (ed.), *Liberalism and the Moral Life*, 39–53.

——— . "Reason and Feeling in Thinking about Justice." *Ethics* 99 (1989): 229–49.

——— . "Gender, the Public and the Private." In David Held (ed.), *Political Theory Today*, 67–90. Cambridge: Polity Press, 1991.

————. "*Political Liberalism*. Justice and Gender." *Ethics* 105 (1994): 23–43.

O'Leary, Brendan, and John McGarry. *The Politics of Antagonism: Understanding Northern Ireland*, 2nd ed. London: Athlone Press, 1996.

Peffer, Rodney G. *Marxism, Morality and Social Justice*. Princeton: Princeton University Press, 1990.

Peterson, Grethe B. (ed.). *The Tanner Lectures on Human Values, XI*. Salt Lake City: University of Utah Press, 1990.

Philosophy and Social Criticism. Special Issue: Habermas, Modernity and Law, Mathieu Duflem (Guest ed.), 20.4 (October 1994).

Rasmussen, David. *Reading Habermas*. Cambridge, Mass.: Basil Blackwell, 1990.

Rasmussen, David (ed.). *Universalism vs. Communitarianism*. Cambridge, Mass.: MIT Press, 1990.

Rawls, John. *A Theory of Justice*. Oxford: Oxford University Press, 1972.

————. "Fairness to Goodness." *Philosophical Review* 84 (1975): 536–54.

————. "The Basic Structure as Subject." *American Philosophical Quarterly* 14 (1977): 159–65, and the extended version in Alvin I. Goldman and Jaegwon Kim (eds.), *Values and Morals*, 47–71. Dordrecht, The Netherlands: Reidel, 1978.

————. "Kantian Constructivism in Moral Theory." *Journal of Philosophy* 77 (1980): 515–72.

————. "Social Unity and Primary Goods." In Amartya Sen and Bernard Williams (eds.), *Utilitarianism and Beyond*, 159–85.

————. "A Kantian Conception of Equality." In John Rajchman and Cornel West (eds.), *Post-Analytic Philosophy*, 201–14. New York: Columbia University Press, 1985.

————. "Justice as Fairness: Political not Metaphysical." *Philosophy and Public Affairs* 14 (1985): 223–51.

————. "The Idea of an Overlapping Consensus." *Oxford Journal of Legal Studies* 7 (1987): 1–25.

————. "The Priority of Right and Ideas of the Good." *Philosophy and Public Affairs* 17 (1988): 251–76.

————. "The Domain of the Political and Overlapping Consensus." *New York University Law Review* 64 (1989): 233–55.

———. *Political Liberalism.* New York: Columbia University Press, 1993.

———. "The Law of Peoples." In Stephen Shute and Susan Hurley (eds.), *On Human Rights: The Oxford Amnesty Lectures 1993,* 41–82. New York: Basic Books, 1993.

———. "Reply to Habermas." *Journal of Philosophy* 92 (1995): 132–80.

Raz, Joseph. *The Morality of Freedom.* Oxford: Clarendon Press, 1986.

Rehg, William. *Insight and Solidarity: The Discourse Ethics of Jürgen Habermas.* Berkeley: University of California Press, 1994.

Rehg, William, and James Bohman. "Discourse and Democracy: The Formal and Informal Bases of Legitimacy in Habermas' *Faktizität und Geltung.*" *Journal of Political Philosophy* 4 (1996): 79–99.

Rescher, Nicholas. *Pluralism: Against the Demand for Consensus.* Oxford: Clarendon Press, 1993.

Rhode, Deborah L. *Justice and Gender.* Cambridge, Mass.: Harvard University Press, 1989.

Ricoeur, Paul. *Hermeneutics and the Human Sciences,* ed. John B. Thompson. Cambridge: Cambridge University Press, 1981.

Rorty, Richard. *Philosophy and the Mirror of Nature.* Princeton: Princeton University Press, 1979.

———. *Contingency, Irony and Solidarity.* Cambridge: Cambridge University Press, 1989.

———. "The Priority of Democracy to Philosophy." In Alan Malachowski (ed.), *Reading Rorty,* 279–302.

———. *Objectivity, Relativism and Truth: Philosophical Papers, volume 1.* Cambridge: Cambridge University Press, 1991.

Rosenblum, Nancy L. "Moral Membership in a Post-Liberal State." *World Politics* 36 (1984): 581–96.

Rosenblum, Nancy L. (ed.). *Liberalism and the Moral Life.* Cambridge, Mass.: Harvard University Press, 1989.

Ruane, Joseph, and Jennifer Todd. "Diversity, Division and the Middle Ground in Northern Ireland." *Irish Political Studies* 7 (1992): 73–98.

Said, Edward W. "Michael Walzer's *Exodus and Revolution*: A Canaanite Reading." In Edward W. Said and Christopher Hitchens (eds.), *Blaming the Victims: Spurious Scholarship and the Palestinian Question,* 161–78. London: Verso, 1988.

Sandel, Michael. *Liberalism and the Limits of Justice*. Cambridge: Cambridge University Press, 1982.

——— . "The Procedural Republic and the Unencumbered Self." *Political Theory* 12 (1984): 81–96.

——— . "Review of *Political Liberalism*." *Harvard Law Review* 107 (1994): 1765–94.

Scanlon, Thomas. "Contractualism and Utilitarianism." In Amartya Sen and Bernard Williams (eds.), *Utilitarianism and Beyond*, 103–28.

Schwartz, Adina. "Moral Neutrality and Primary Goods." *Ethics* 83 (1973): 294–307.

Seel, Martin. "The Two Meanings of 'Communicative' Rationality: Remarks on Habermas's Critique of a Plural Concept of Reason." In Axel Honneth and Hans Joas (eds.), *Communicative Action*, 36–48.

Sen, Amartya, and Bernard Williams (eds.). *Utilitarianism and Beyond*. Cambridge: Cambridge University Press, 1982.

Shelly, Robert. "Habermas and the Normative Foundations of a Radical Politics." *Thesis Eleven* 35 (1993): 62–83.

Silverman, Hugh (ed.). *Gadamer and Hermeneutics*. London: Routledge, 1991.

Smith, Nicholas H. *Strong Hermeneutics*. London: Routledge, 1997.

Smith, Tony. *The Role of Ethics in Social Theory: Essays from a Habermasian Perspective*. Albany: State University of New York Press, 1991.

Taylor, Charles. *Philosophical Papers, I: Human Agency and Language*. Cambridge: Cambridge University Press, 1985.

——— . *Philosophical Papers, II: Philosophy and the Human Sciences*. Cambridge: Cambridge University Press, 1985.

——— . "The Nature and Scope of Distributive Justice." In Frank S. Lucash (ed.), *Justice and Equality Here and Now*, 34–67.

——— . *Sources of the Self: The Making of the Modern Identity*. Cambridge: Cambridge University Press, 1989.

——— . "Cross-Purposes: The Liberal-Communitarian Debate." In Nancy L. Rosenblum (ed.), *Liberalism and the Moral Life*, 159–82.

——— . "Comments and Replies." *Inquiry* 34 (1991): 237–54.

———. "Language and Society." In Axel Honneth and Hans Joas (eds.), *Communicative Action*, 23–35.

———. "Shared and Divergent Values." In Ronald L. Watts and Douglas G. Brown (eds.), *Options for a New Canada*, 53–76. Toronto: University of Toronto Press, 1991.

———. *The Ethics of Authenticity.* Cambridge, Mass.: Harvard University Press, 1992.

———. "The Politics of Recognition." In his *Multiculturalism and "The Politics of Recognition,"* ed. Amy Gutmann, 25–73.

———. "Inwardness and the Culture of Modernity." In Axel Honneth et al. (eds.), *Philosophical Interventions in the Unfinished Project of Enlightenment*, 88–110.

———. "The Motivation behind a Procedural Ethics." In Ronald Beiner and William James Booth (eds.), *Kant and Political Philosophy: The Contemporary Legacy*, 337–59. New Haven: Yale University Press, 1993.

———. "Reply and Re-articulation." In James Tully (ed.), *Philosophy in an Age of Pluralism: The Work of Charles Taylor in Focus*, 213–57. Cambridge: Cambridge University Press, 1994.

Teitelman, Michael. "The Limits of Individualism." *Journal of Philosophy* 69 (1972): 545–56.

Thigpen, Robert B., and Lyle Downing. "Beyond Shared Understandings." *Political Theory* 14 (1986): 451–72.

Thompson, John B., and David Held (eds.). *Habermas: Critical Debates.* London: Macmillan, 1982.

Todd, Jennifer. "The Limits of Britishness." *The Irish Review* 5 (1989): 11–16.

———. "Unionist Political Thought." In D. George Boyce, Robert Eccleshall, and Vincent Geoghegan (eds.), *Political Thought in Ireland Since the Seventeenth Century*, 190–211. London: Routledge, 1993.

Unger, Roberto Mangabeira. *Knowledge and Politics.* New York: Free Press, 1975.

Walzer, Michael. *Radical Principles: Reflections of an Unreconstructed Democrat.* New York: Basic Books, 1980.

———. "Philosophy and Democracy." *Political Theory* 9 (1981): 379–99.

———. "Pluralism in Political Perspective." In Michael Walzer et al., *The Politics of Ethnicity*, 1–28. Cambridge, Mass.: Belknap Press, 1982.

————. *Spheres of Justice: A Defence of Pluralism and Equality*. Oxford: Basil Blackwell, 1983.

————. "Liberalism and the Art of Separation." *Political Theory* 12 (1984): 315–30.

————. *Exodus and Revolution*. New York: Basic Books, 1985.

————. "Justice Here and Now." In Frank S. Lucash (ed.), *Justice and Equality Here and Now*, 136–50.

————. *Interpretation and Social Criticism*. Cambridge, Mass.: Harvard University Press, 1987.

————. *The Company of Critics: Social Criticism and Political Commitment in the Twentieth Century*. London: Peter Halban, 1989.

————. "Nation and Universe." In *The Tanner Lectures on Human Values, XI*, ed. Grethe B. Peterson, 507–56.

————. "A Critique of Philosophical Conversation." In Michael Kelly (ed.), *Hermeneutics and Critical Theory in Ethics and Politics*, 182–96.

————. "The Communitarian Critique of Liberalism." *Political Theory* 18 (1990): 6–23.

————. *Just and Unjust Wars: A Moral Argument with Historical Illustrations*, 2nd ed. New York: Basic Books, 1992.

————. "The Civil Society Argument." In Chantal Mouffe (ed.), *Dimensions of Radical Democracy*, 89–107. London: Verso, 1992.

————. "Comment." In Charles Taylor, *Multiculturalism and "The Politics of Recognition,"* ed. Amy Gutmann, 99–103.

————. "Exclusion, Injustice and the Democratic State." *Dissent*, Winter 1993, 55–64.

————. *Thick and Thin: Moral Argument at Home and Abroad*. Notre Dame, Ind.: University of Notre Dame Press, 1994.

————. "Response." In David Miller and Michael Walzer (eds.), *Pluralism, Justice and Equality*, 281–97.

Walker, Brian. "Habermas and Pluralist Political Theory." *Philosophy and Social Criticism* 18 (1992): 81–102.

Warnke, Georgia. *Gadamer: Hermeneutics, Tradition and Reason*. Cambridge: Polity Press, 1987.

———. "Rawls, Habermas and Real Talk: A Reply to Walzer" and "Social Interpretation and Political Theory." In Michael Kelly (ed.), *Hermeneutics and Critical Theory in Ethics and Politics*, 197–203 and 204–26.

———. "Walzer, Rawls and Gadamer: Hermeneutics and Political Theory." In Kathleen Wright (ed.), *Festivals of Interpretation*, 136–60

———. *Justice and Interpretation*. Cambridge: Polity Press, 1992.

———. "Communicative Rationality and Cultural Values." In Stephen K. White (ed.), *The Cambridge Companion to Habermas*, 120–42.

———. "Legitimacy and Consensus: Comments on Part of the Work of Thomas McCarthy." *Philosophy and Social Criticism* 22 (1996): 67–81.

Warren, Mark. "Liberal Constitutionalism as Ideology: Marx and Habermas." *Political Theory* 17 (1989): 511–34.

———. "The Self in Discursive Democracy." In Stephen K. White (ed.), *The Cambridge Companion to Habermas*, 167–200.

Wellmer, Albrecht. *The Persistence of Modernity*. Cambridge: Polity Press, 1991.

White, Stephen K. *The Recent Work of Jürgen Habermas: Reason, Justice and Modernity*. Cambridge: Cambridge University Press, 1988.

———. *Political Theory and Postmodernism*. Cambridge: Cambridge University Press, 1991.

White, Stephen K. (ed.). *The Cambridge Companion to Habermas*. Cambridge: Cambridge University Press, 1995.

Whiteside, Kerry. "Review of *The Company of Critics*." *Political Theory* 17 (1989): 689–92.

Whyte, John H. *Interpreting Northern Ireland*. Oxford: Clarendon Press, 1991.

Williams, Bernard. *Ethics and the Limits of Philosophy*. London: Fontana, 1985.

Winch, Peter. *The Idea of a Social Science and its Relation to Philosophy*. 2nd ed. London: Routledge, 1990.

Wolf, Susan. "Comment." In Charles Taylor, *Multiculturalism and "The Politics of Recognition,"* ed. Amy Gutmann, 75–85.

Wright, Kathleen (ed.). *Festivals of Interpretation: Essays on Hans-Georg Gadamer's Work*. Albany: State University of New York Press, 1990.

Young, Iris Marion. "Impartiality and the Civic Public: Some Implications of Feminist Critiques of Moral and Political Theory." In Seyla Benhabib and Drucilla Cornell (eds.), *Feminism as Critique*, 57–74.

——— . *Justice and the Politics of Difference*. Princeton: Princeton University Press, 1990.

——— , "The Ideal of Community and the Politics of Difference." In Linda Nicholson (ed.), *Feminism/Postmodernism*, 300–23.

INDEX

abortion, 27–29, 32, 211n.61; and
discourse ethics, 162–63, 165,
166; Rawls on, 27, 163,
211n.63
Ackerman, Bruce, 222n.40
adoption law, 41, 45
Apel, Karl-Otto, 139–40, 160
application of norms: and cultural
difference, 169–71, 177; and
impartiality, 166–67, 169–70,
253n.44
atomism, 17, 22–24, 30, 182
Austin, J. L., 119–22
autonomy: and intersubjectivity, 143;
private and civic, 170, 172, 175

basic structure of society, 13–14; and
the family, 40–42; and gender
structure, 43–45, 216n.31; and
original position, 35, 38–39
Baynes, Kenneth, 248n.66
Benhabib, Seyla, 165, 167–68,
218n.47; on concrete others,
46–48, 51–52; and Habermas,
157–64
bureaucracies, state, 98, 125

care, ethic of, 46–48; and discourse
ethics, 161; and original position,
51–52; and solidarity, 48–49, 52
caste society, 88
citizenship: and equality, 61–64, 193,
196; and ethical discourse,
170–73; as membership of a political community, 23–24, 184; rights
of, 29–32, 54

cognitivism: in Benhabib, 159–60; in
discourse ethics, 109, 130–33,
139, 141, 166
colonization of the lifeworld, 126,
241n.70
communicative action, 8, 116–18,
181; and discourse, 129, 131–33,
142, 146; and emancipation, 111;
and idealization, 135–36; and the
lifeworld, 118, 123–26; and moral
development, 141–42; its priority
as a use of language, 107, 119–26,
139; and rational reconstruction,
112–16; as opposed to strategic
action, 108, 118–19
communitarianism: as critique of liberalism, 3–5, 15, 201; and
Habermas, 109, 147; and Rawls,
17–33, 45–46, 54–55, 147, 179;
and recognition of difference,
153–54
complex equality, 7, 60–63, 101,
219n.8, 253n.44; blocked
exchanges, 62; as open-ended distributive principle, 61
compromise, fair, 165
concrete others, 46–49, 166; collective as opposed to individualized,
48–49, 51–52, 145; as opposed to
generalized others, 47
connected criticism, 67–71, 81–82,
92; as an alternative to impartial
justice, 65; and loyalty, 70, 87, 98;
and partiality, 85
consensus, rationally motivated: and
Benhabib's critique of Habermas,

279

monological conception, 49–56, 107–9, 115, 119, 130–34, 142–49, 160, 179; and ethical discourse, 154, 156, 173, 176–78, 192; and particular contexts, 3, 110, 129–30, 146–49, 169–73, 181, 201–3; and pluralism, 2, 64, 81, 83, 123; and postconventional morality, 141–42; and practical reason, 84–85; and public discourse, 6, 15, 39, 51; and power, 83–85, 87; Rawls's conception, 13–16, 35–37, 49–56, 74–75; and social criticism, 59, 81–85, 99–103; and social group differences, 4, 40, 48–49, 54–55, 84, 136, 138, 177–79; and Walzer's hermeneutics, 79–80, 81–85, 225n.80; and Warnke, 164, 168–69. *See also* discourse ethics; original position; procedures of normative justification

imperatives: and the priority of communicative action, 121

individual rights: and the democratic will, 83, 100–1; and discourse ethics, 143, 161, 175; Rawls's conception of, 29–30

interpretation: conflict of, 72–72, 86; of law, 76–77; and social meaning, 68–70. *See also* hermeneutics

justice: as a basis of social unity, 17, 20, 190; and care, 46–49, 51–52, 161; and dialogue, 75–80; in the family, 6, 40–46, 50, 215n.22; and the good, 1–2, 55; and health care, 62, 72–73; and impartiality, 2–3, 13–16; and liberal holism, 30–33, 79–80, 201–3; and moral universalism, 82–83, 96–99; in Northern Ireland, 181–99; and pluralism, 4, 127, 129, 156, 164; and practical reason, 84–85; and social meaning, 59–62, 66; and

shared understandings, 3; and solidarity, 48–52, 143–44, 148, 161, 170–71, 202; and state boundaries, 185; its structural requirements, 96, 98, 101; substantive principles of, 1, 4, 9, 81; and tradition, 77–79, 102, 164–65

justice as fairness: political not metaphysical, 21–24. *See also* Rawls

justification: and application of norms, 166–67, 169, 171, 253n.44; and contextualism, 158–79; and dialogue, 3, 9, 48, 115, 130, 170; and hermeneutics, 7; and impartiality, 2–3, 81–85, 101; rational grounds of, 82–85, 132, 146–48, 159–60, 193; and social criticism, 107; and subjectivism, 165, 169. *See also* procedures of normative justification

Kant, Immanuel, 156: categorical imperative, 129; foundationalism of, 113; and moral universalism, 131, 143; the priority of right over good, 2, 15–16

Kantian moral theory: and contextualism, 157–58, 160, 164, 169, 173–76, 254n.63

Kohlberg, Lawrence, 140–41

language: and ideology, 90–91, 93; and reconstructive science, 112–13, 115; and rule-consciousness, 122

language use. *See* communicative action; strategic action

Larmore, Charles E., 209n.31

law: and hermeneutics, 76–77

Leninism: and elitism, 87, 94, 229n.11

liberalism: its critics, 15; and impartiality; 2–3 and the public and private, 6, 13, 39, 41, 101; as a tradition, 78. *See also* atomism; holism

public discourse: as hermeneutic self-
clarification, 69, 75, 78; and
impartiality, 32–33, 54–56, 148,
175; and social power, 81–84
public sphere: and civil society, 63;
and the colonization of the lifeworld, 126; and democratic deliberation, 29–33, 203, 241n.71; and
ethical discourses, 173; and impartial justice, 6, 148

rank-ordering: of political communities in Walzer, 95–96, 187–88
rational discourse, 135–36. *See also*
discourse ethics; practical reason
rational reconstruction. *See* reconstructive scientific theory
rationalization processes: one-sided-
ness of, 126
Rawls, John: and communitarianism,
5, 16–33, 45–46, 54–55, 147,
179, 201; and ethic of care,
47–48, 161; gender blindness in,
43–46, 50; and Habermas, 8–10,
107, 115–16, 143–49, 160,
212n.68; and feminism, 5, 16,
35–56, 144, 147, 179; as liberal
holist, 23–24, 210n.46; and Marx,
14; on impartiality 2–6, 13–24,
35–37, 46–49, 103, 129; and
Nozick, 13–12; on neutrality, 25;
between perfectionism and scepticism, 21; and Sandel, 22–24; two
substantive principles of justice, 5;
and utilitarianism, 16; and Walzer,
7, 60–64, 74–75, 77–80, 84, 101,
208n.21, 219n.13. *See also* basic
structure of society; difference
principle; fair equality of opportunity; moral personality; neutrality;
original position; overlapping consensus; political constructivism;
political morality; political virtues;
primary goods; reflective equilibrium; veil of ignorance

Raz, Joseph, 210n.46
reasons, rule of: in political sphere,
97, 100
recognition, politics of. *See* differences; ethical discourse; Taylor
reconstructive scientific theory,
110–15, 119, 126, 140–41, 146
reflective equilibrium, 36
regime of truth, 82
relativism, 64, 112, 129, 164,
236n.8; and universalism in
Walzer, 95
rights: and liberal holism, 30–33. *See
also* citizenship; human rights;
individual rights; minority cultures; political rights
Rorty, Richard, 227n.99, 233n.57,
236n.16
rules of argumentation, 108, 131,
135–37, 139, 191
Rushdie affair, 227n.97

sadomasochism, 157, 167
Sandel, Michael, 22–23
Scanlon, Thomas, 145, 160, 248n.66
scepticism, moral: and Habermas,
129, 139–40, 142; and Rawls, 21
self-transformation: and discourse,
78, 108, 134, 148, 162–63,
245n.33; and the conflict in
Northern Ireland, 182, 189–90,
193–97
scenic understanding, 91
shared understandings, 3, 59, 72–74,
95, 182
Silone, Ignazio, 228n.5
social integration: and the reproduction of the lifeworld, 124–25
social systems; and the colonization
of the lifeworld, 125–26
socialization of the individual,
124–25
solidarity: and justice, 48–51,
143–44, 148, 170–71, 202; and
social integration, 125